STEPHAN HILGE / ROMAN PFEFFER / NITA TANDON (eds.)

TransArts

AMBRA | V

edition: 'ʌngewʌndte

Book Series of the
University of Applied Arts Vienna

Edited by Gerald Bast, Rector

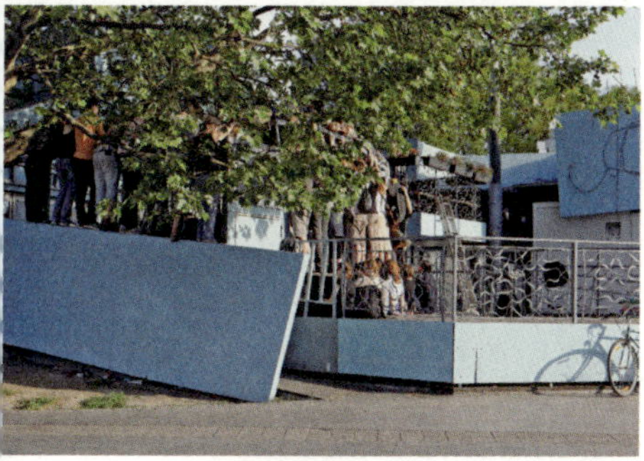

1

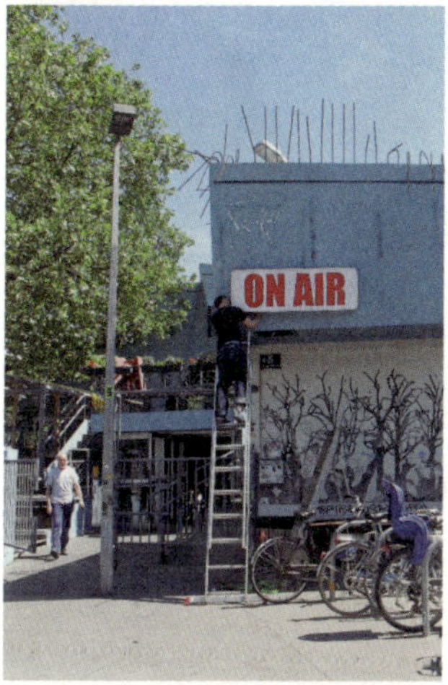

2

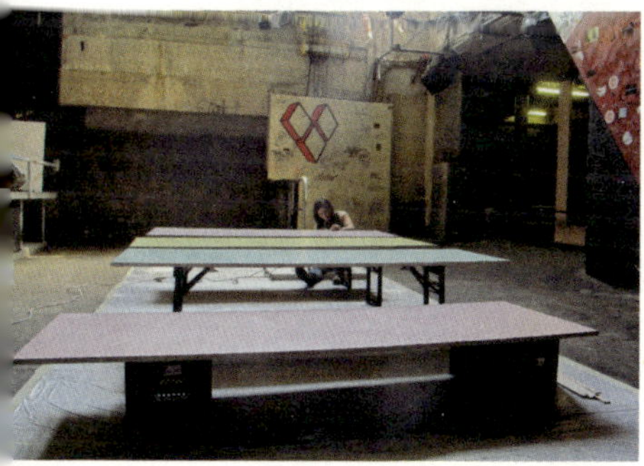

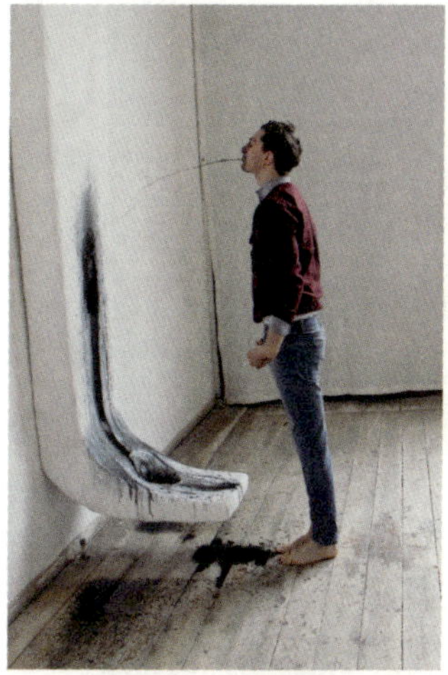

4

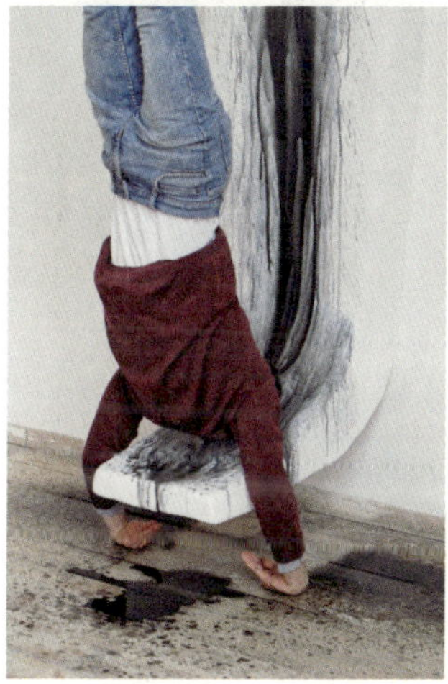

5

1–3 Exhibition: VON AUSSEN NACH INNEN NACH AUSSEN, Fluc, Vienna, 2012

4/5 Performance: semester presentation, 2013

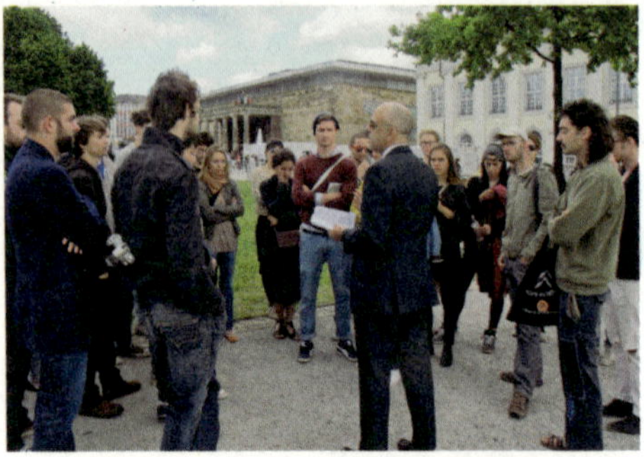

1

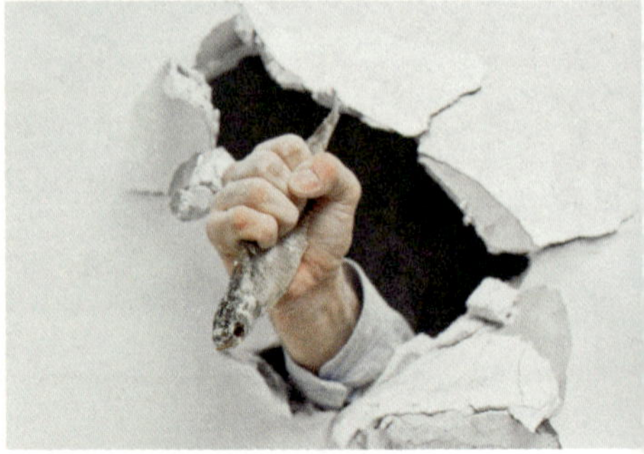

3

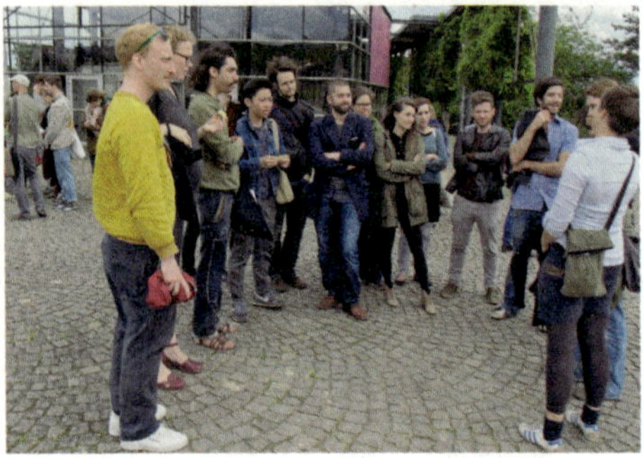

2

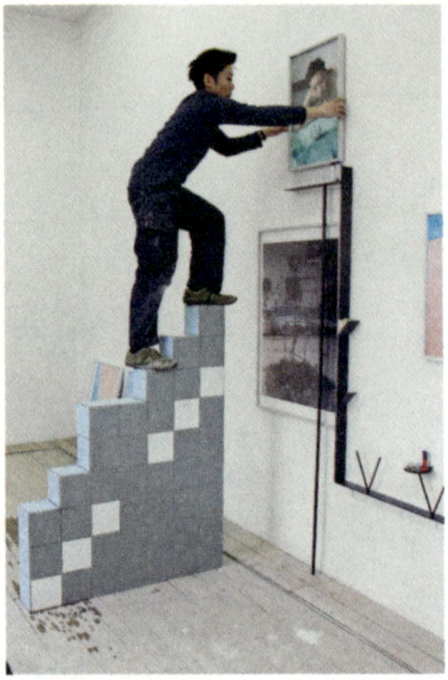

4

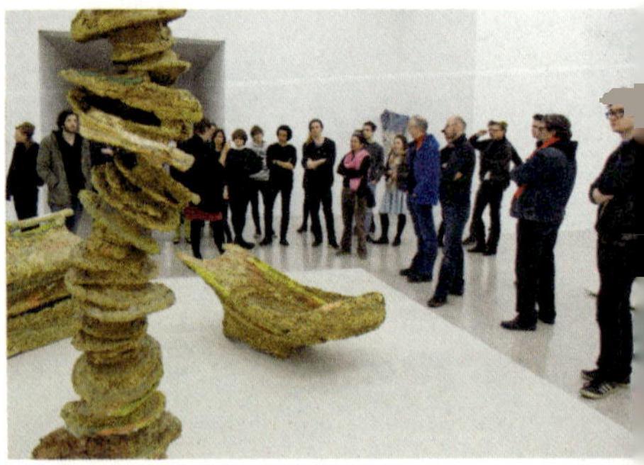

1/2	Excursion: Dokumenta 13, Kassel, 2012
3	Exhibition: SITUAKTION, Krinzinger Projekte, Vienna, 2012
4	Performance: semester presentation, 2013
5	Excursion: MUMOK, 2013

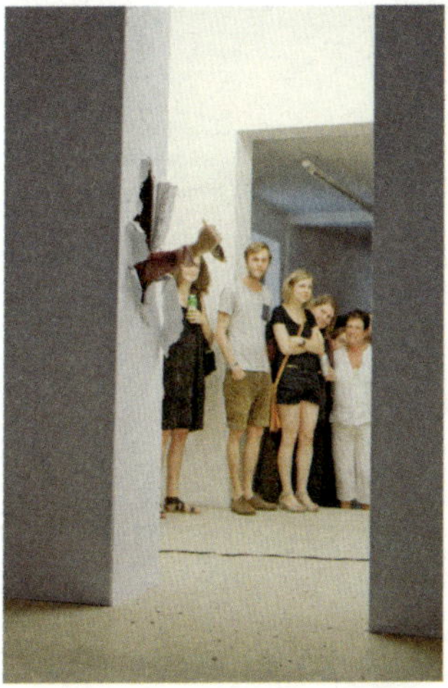

1

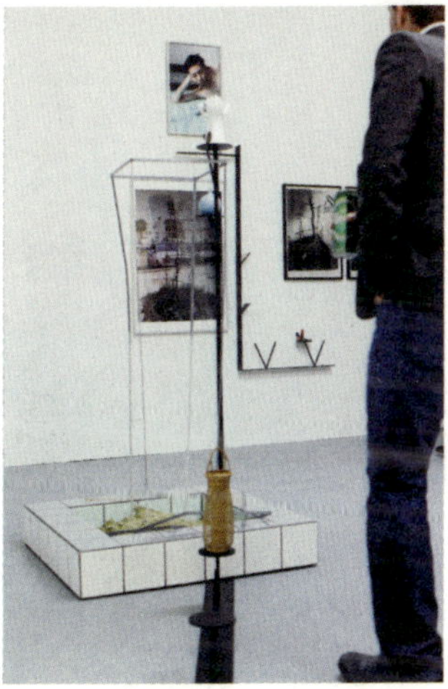

2

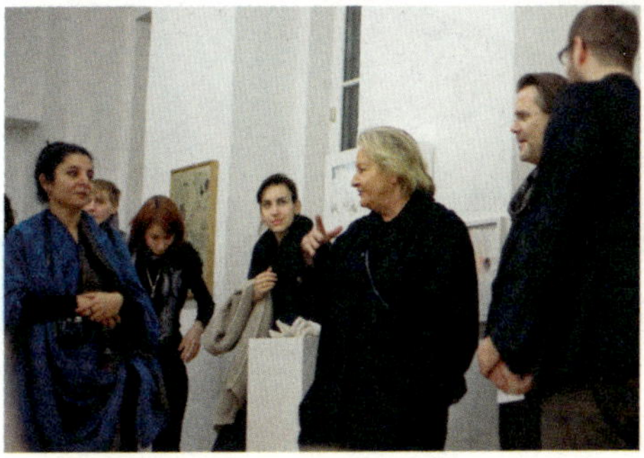

3

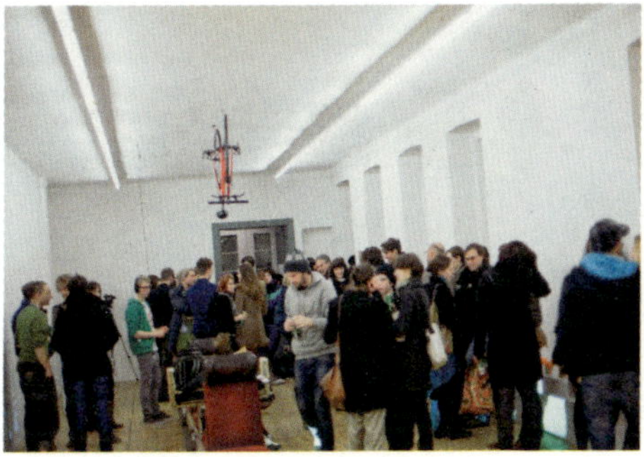

4

1 Exhibition: SITUAKTION, Krinzinger Projekte, Vienna, 2012

2 Exhibition: EPHEMERAL, Kunstraum am Schauplatz, Vienna, 2013

3/4 Exhibition: DON'T HAVE SEX WITH YOUR EX, Krinzinger Projekte, Vienna, 2010

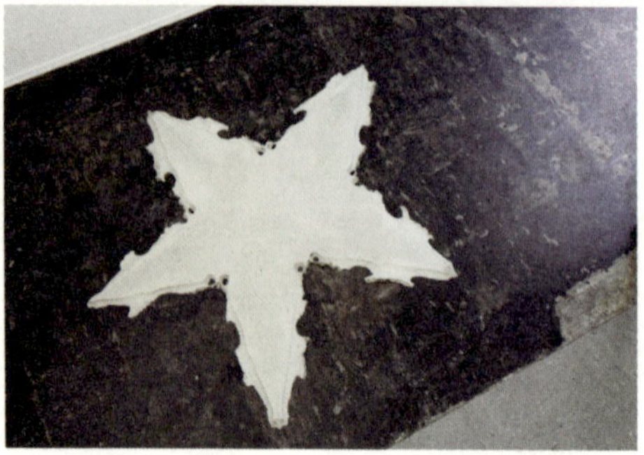

1

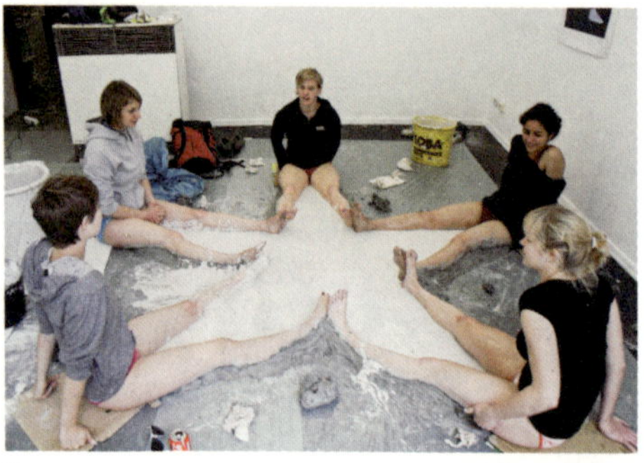

2

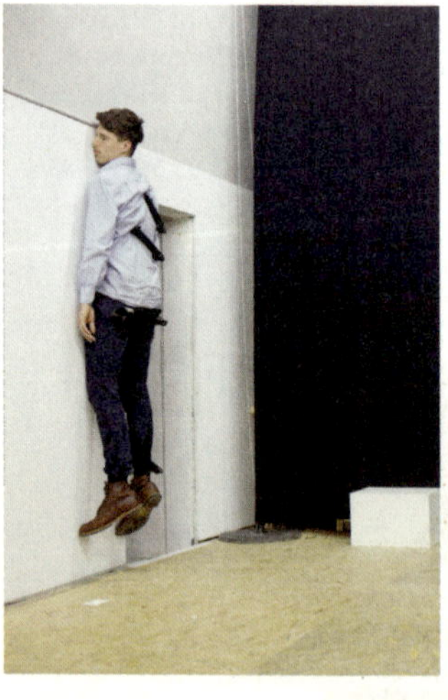

3

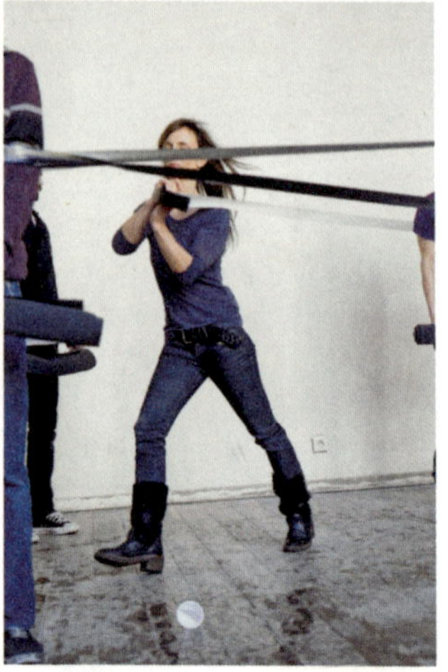

4

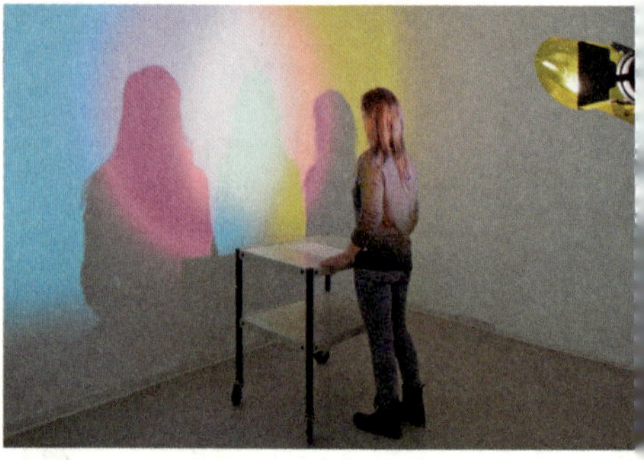

5

1/2 Exhibition: EXPANDED EGYPTED, Kunstraum Praterstraße 15, Vienna, 2010

3 Exhibition: AN:ORDNUNGEN, Liquid Loft Studios, Vienna, 2012

4 Workshop: Elfie Semotan/Erwin Wurm, 2010

5 Workshop: Shady El Noshokaty, 2011

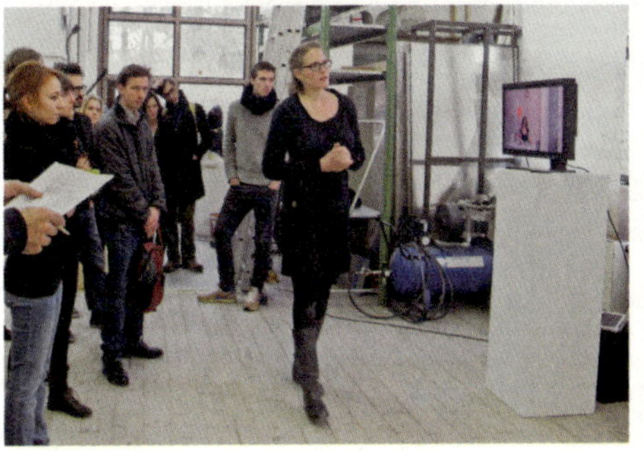

1

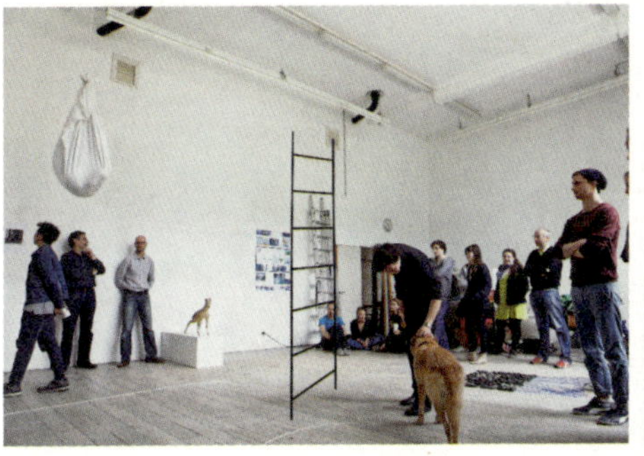

2

1 Semester presentation, 2013
2 Semester presentation, 2012
3 Lecture: Franz Schuh, 2011

3

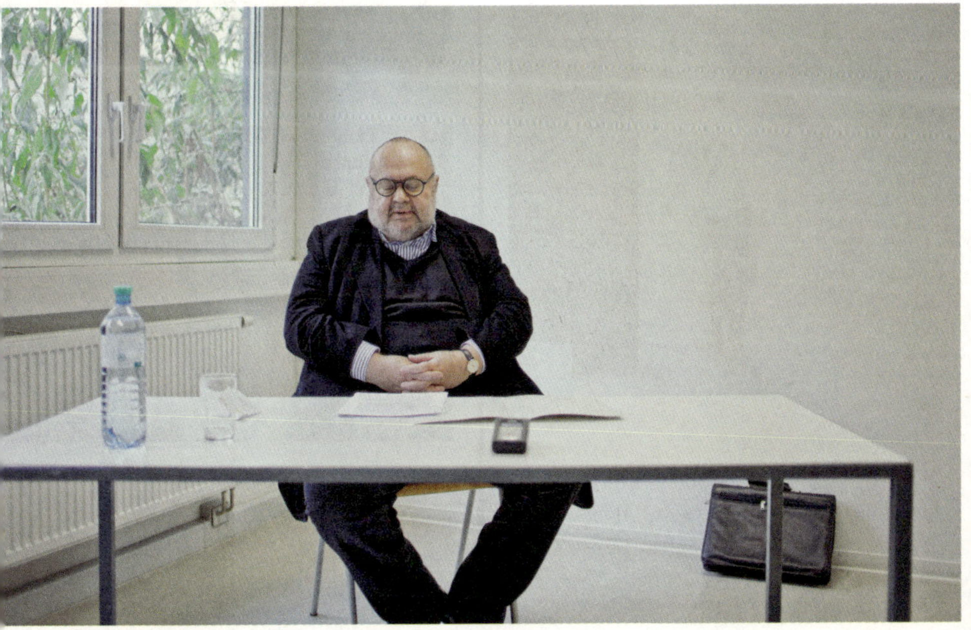

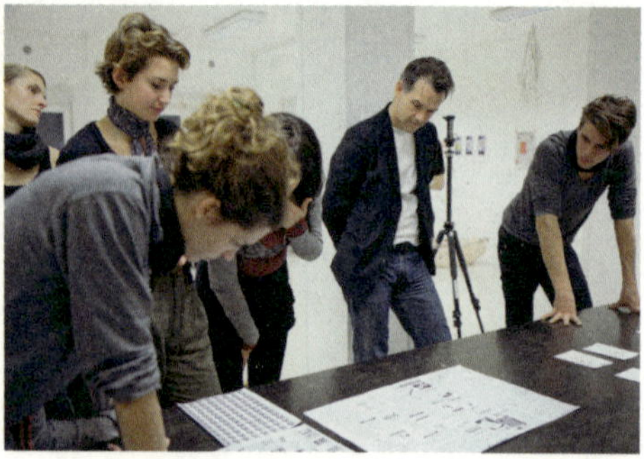

1

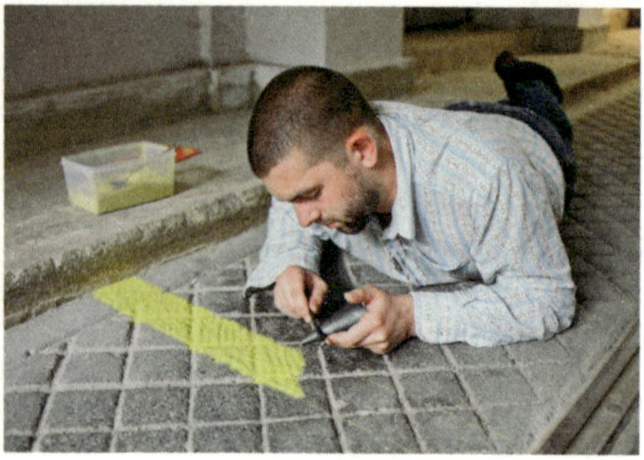

2

1 Workshop: Marc-Olivier Wahler, 2010
2/4/5 Exhibition: SITUAKTION, Krinzinger Projekte, Vienna, 2012
3 Workshop: Elfie Semotan/Erwin Wurm, 2010

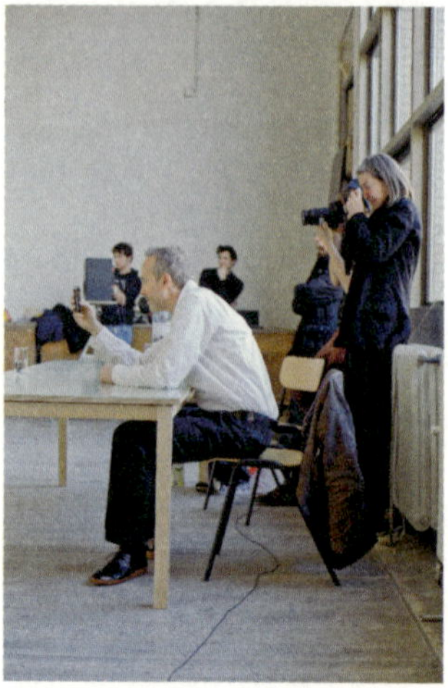

3

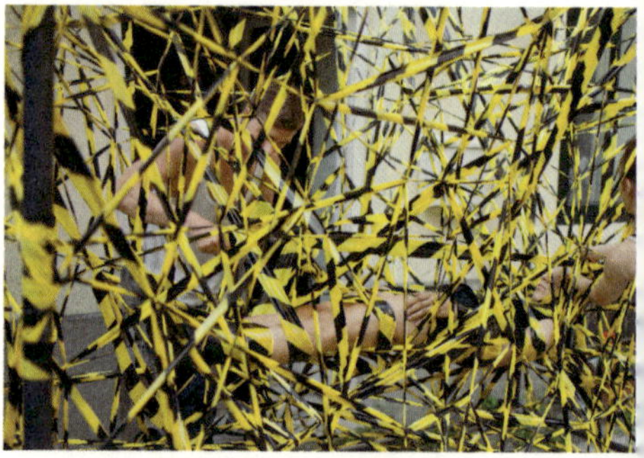

4

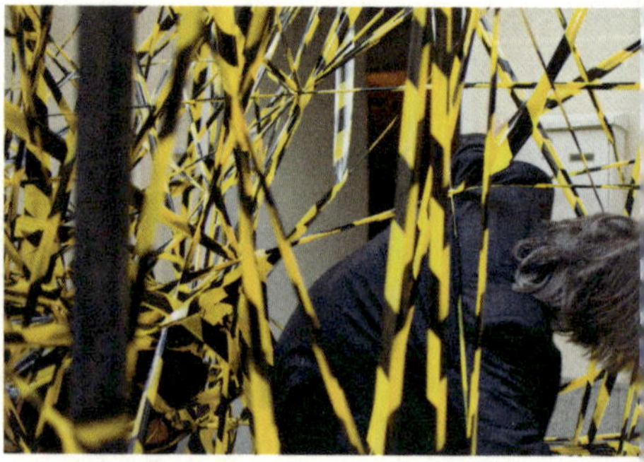

5

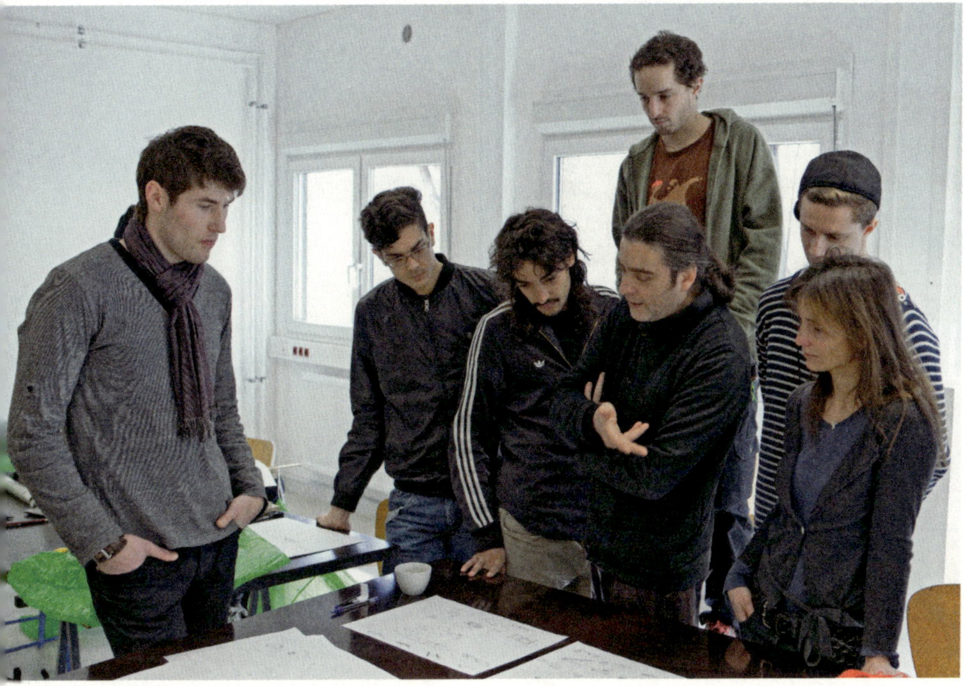

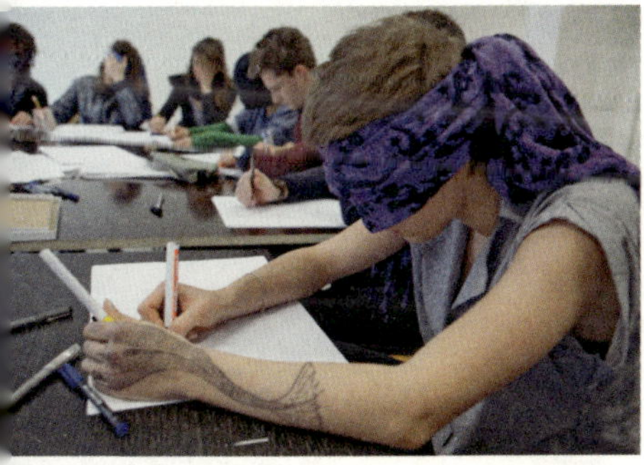

1/2 Workshop: Martin Walde, 2011

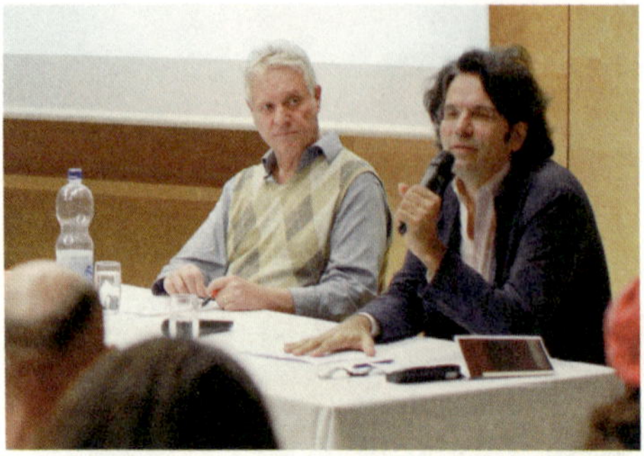

1

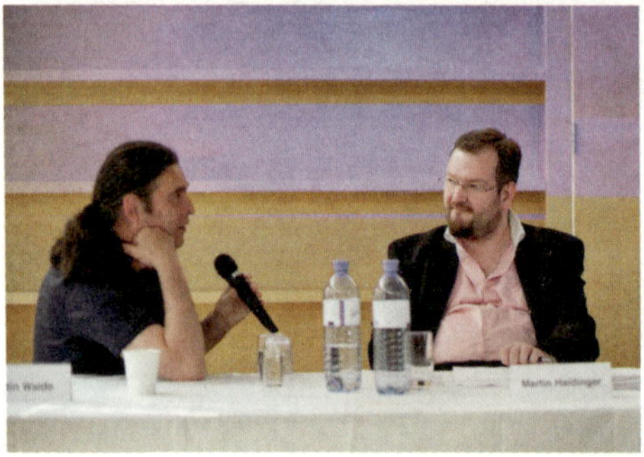

2

1 Round Table LET US DEMAND THE IMPOSSIBLE, 2012

2 Round Table THE IMPOSSIBILITY OF REALITY II, 2011

3 Round Table THE IMPOSSIBILITY OF REALITY I, 2010

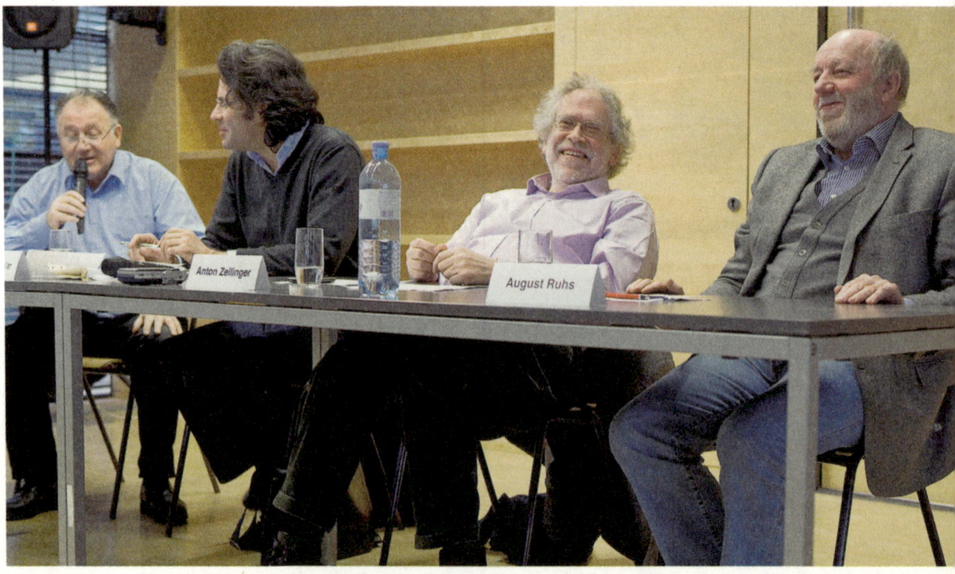

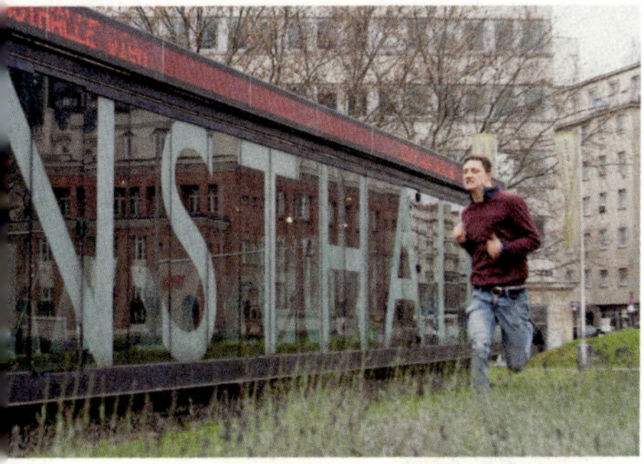

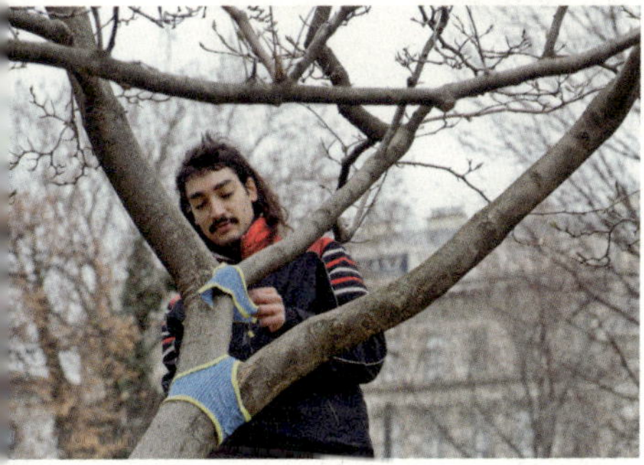

–4 Intervention in public space: AGAIN AND AGAIN, Karlsplatz, 2012
Workshop: Candice Breitz, 2011

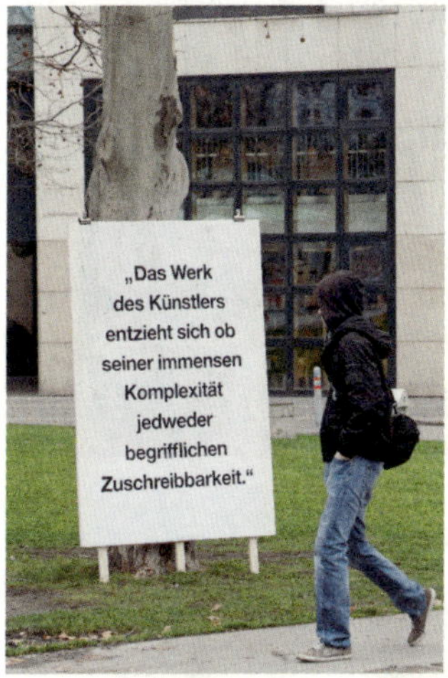

3

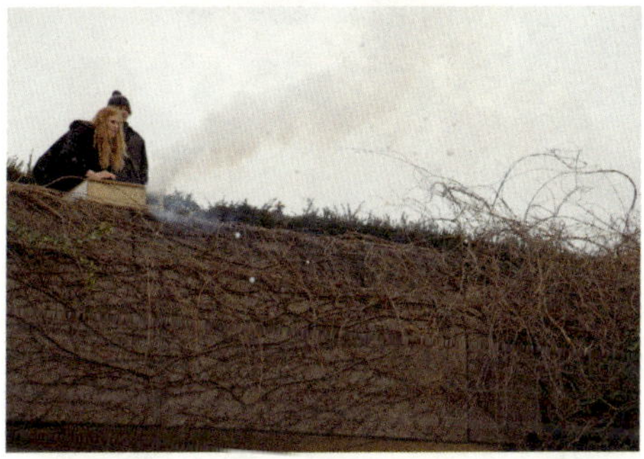

4

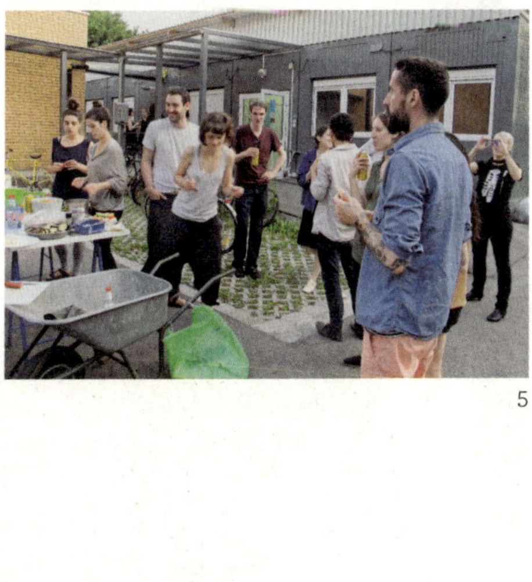

5

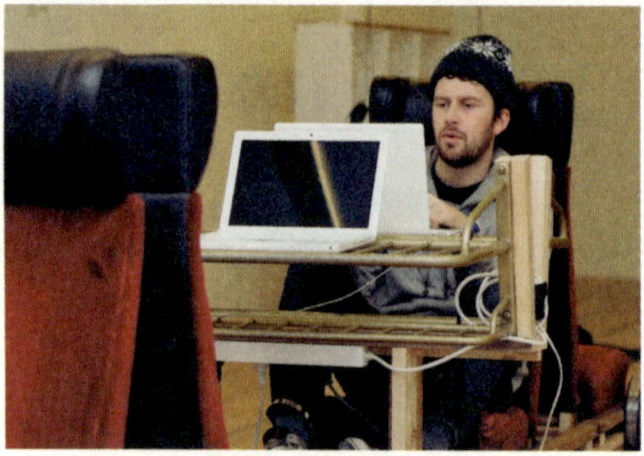

1

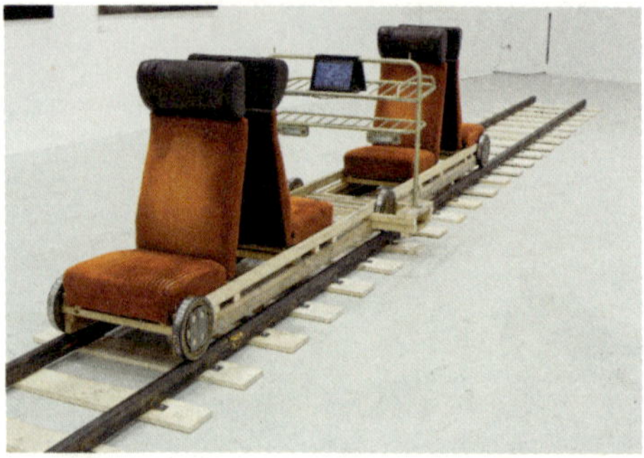

2

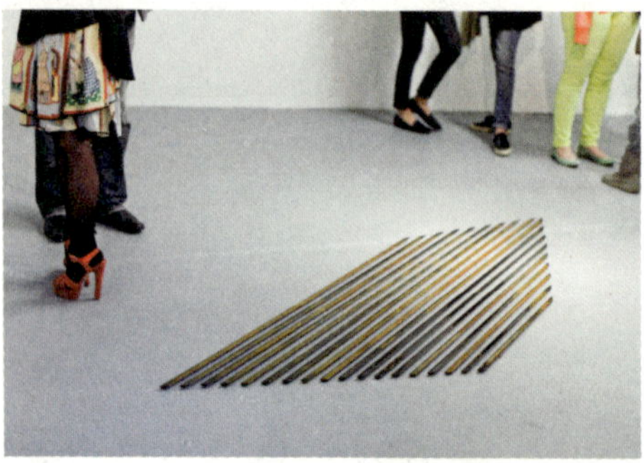

3

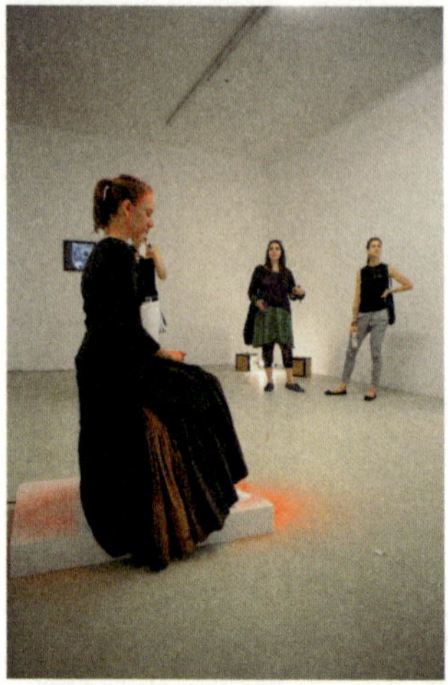

4

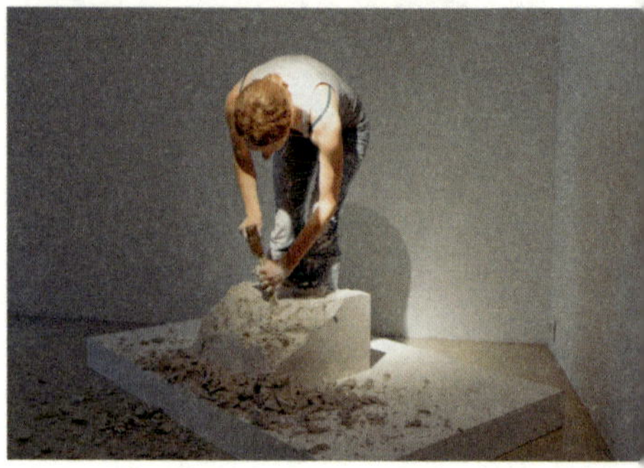

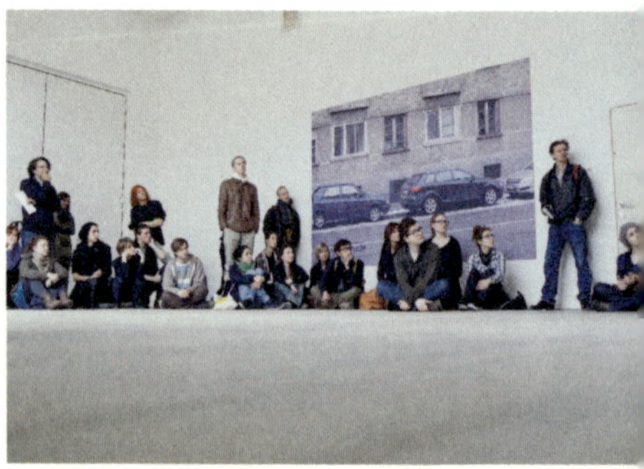

6

1 Exhibition: DON'T HAVE SEX WITH YOUR EX, Krinzinger Projekte, Vienna, 2010
2 Exhibition: ESSENCE 2011, MAK, Vienna
3 Exhibition: EPHEMERAL, Kunstraum am Schauplatz, Vienna, 2013
4/5 Exhibition: SITUAKTION, Krinzinger Projekte, Vienna, 2012
6 Semester presentation, 2013

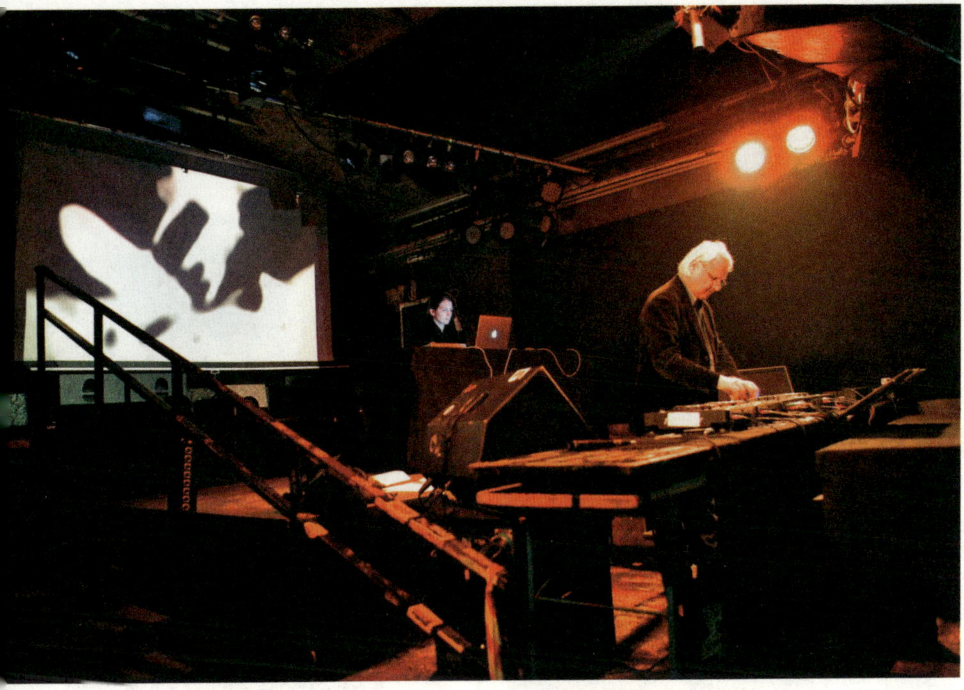

Performance: Bernhard Leitner, SOUND LIB, Fluc, Vienna, 2011
Lecture: Bernhard Leitner, 2011

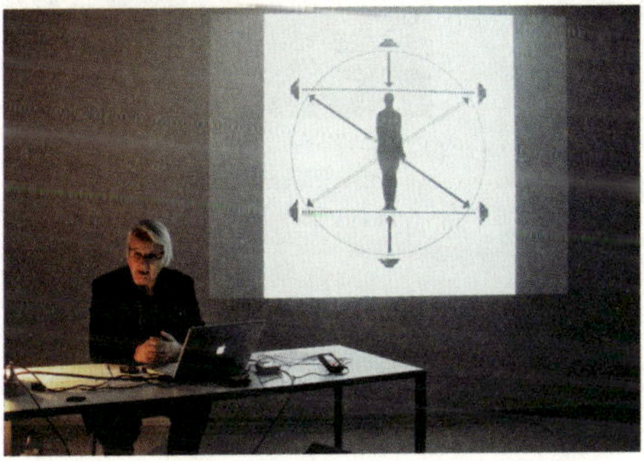

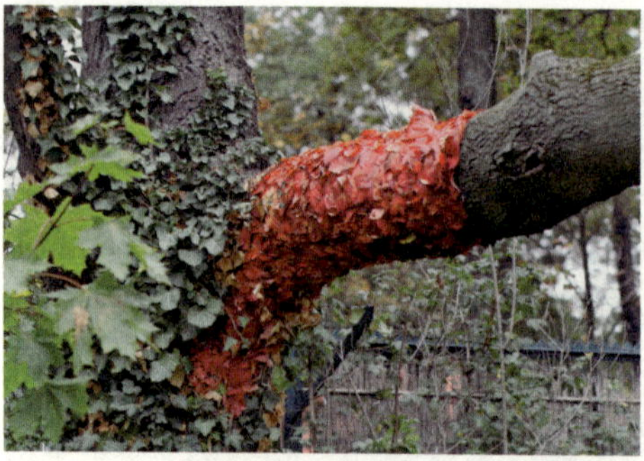

1

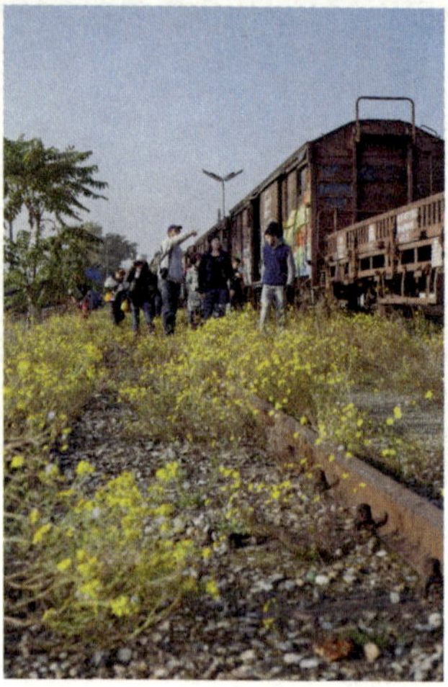

2

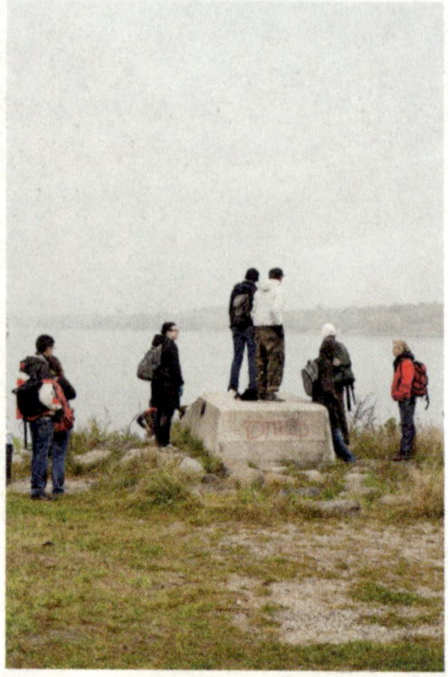

3

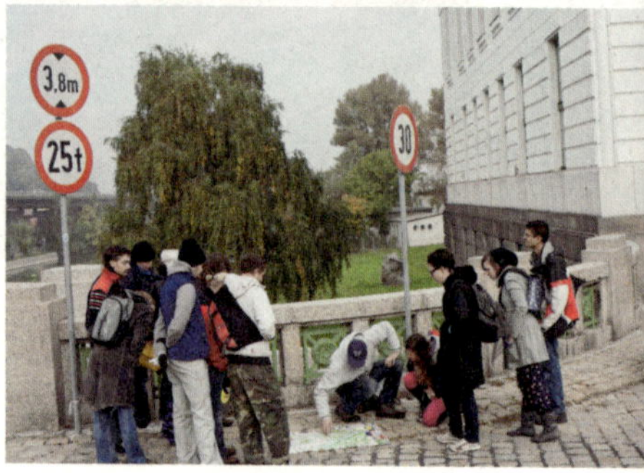

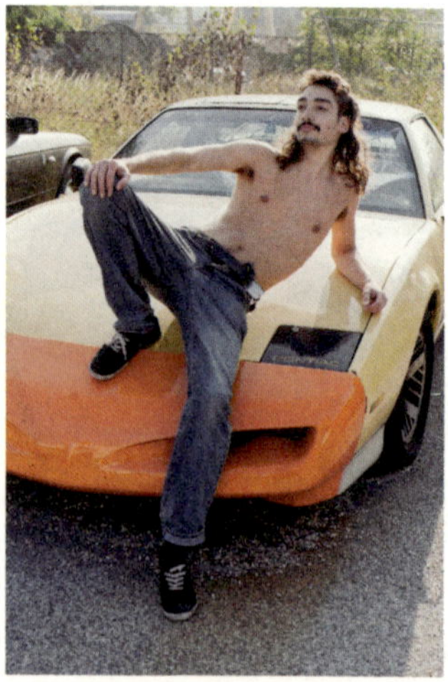

5

1 Workshop: Folke Köbberling, 2012

2–5 Workshop: Hans Schabus, 2010

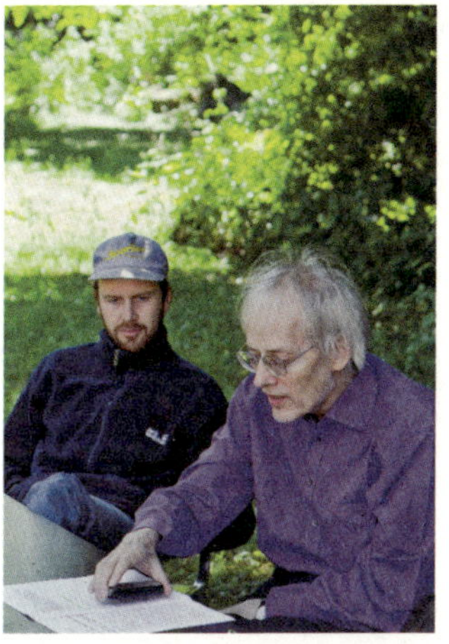

1

/2 Workshop: Timm Ulrichs, 2011

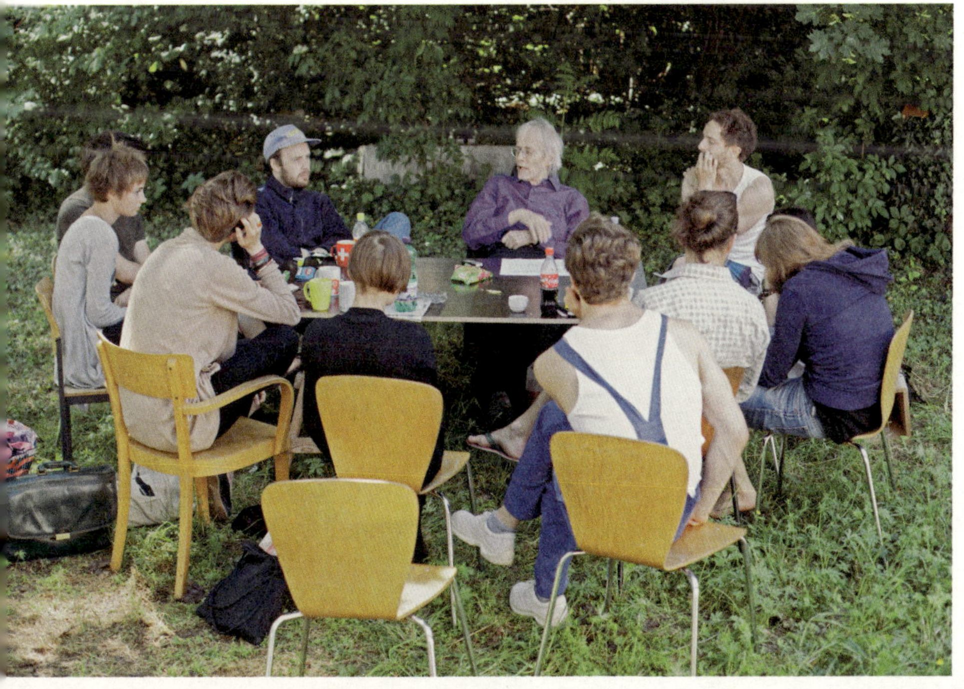

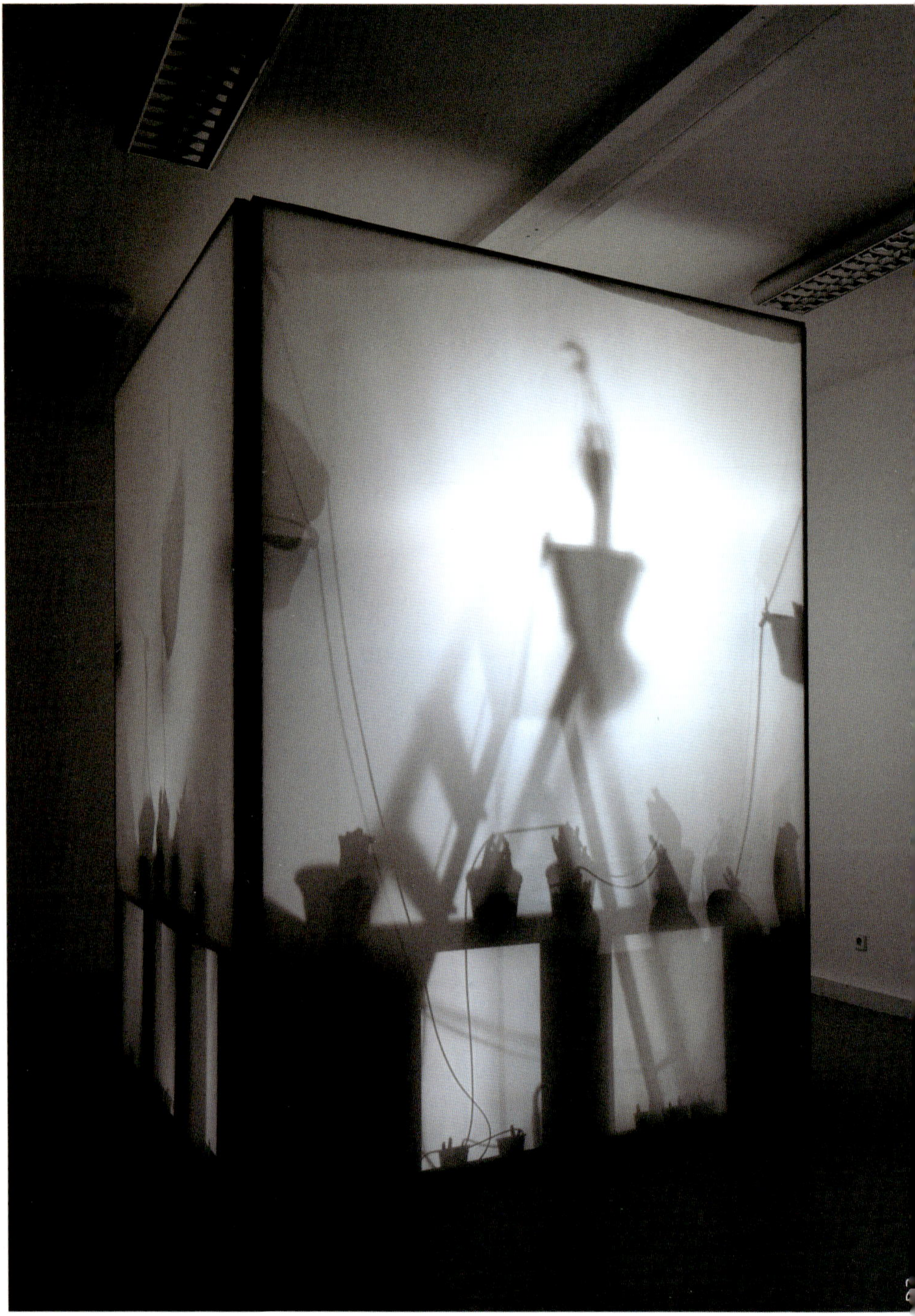

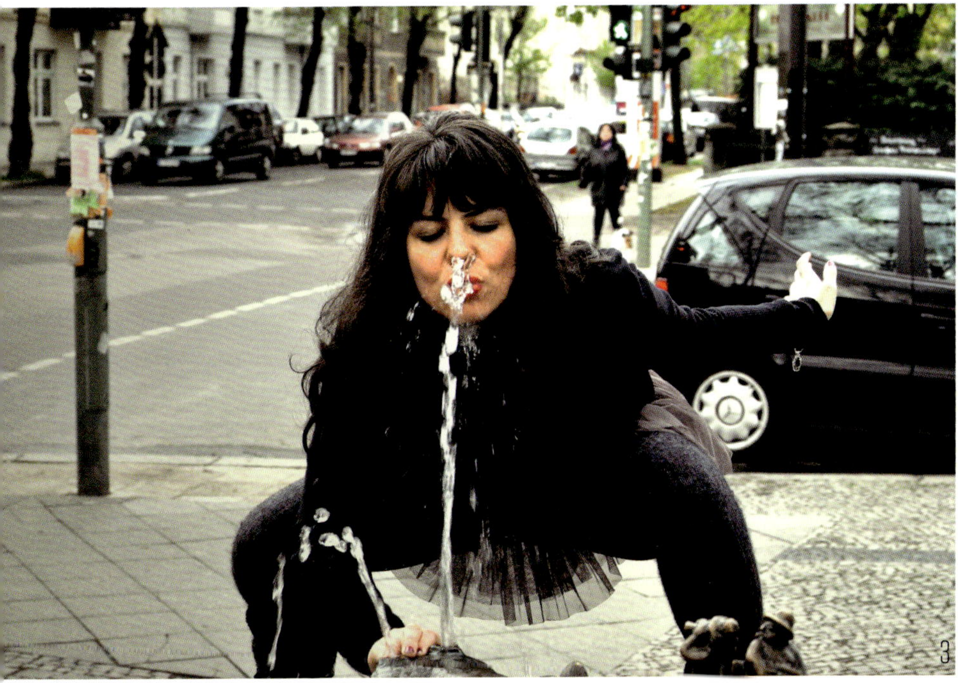
3

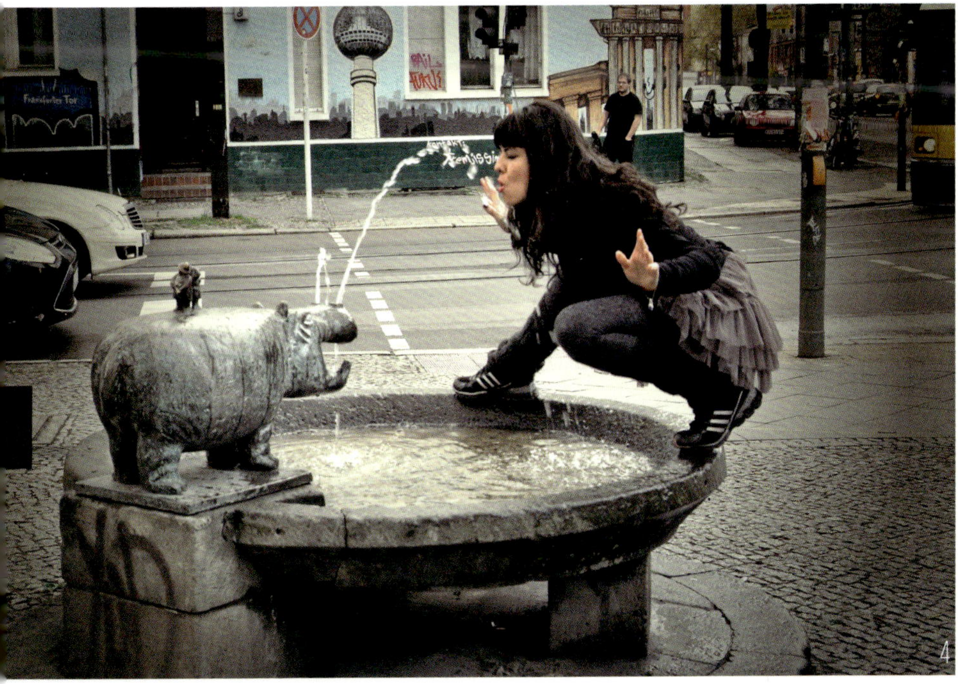

4

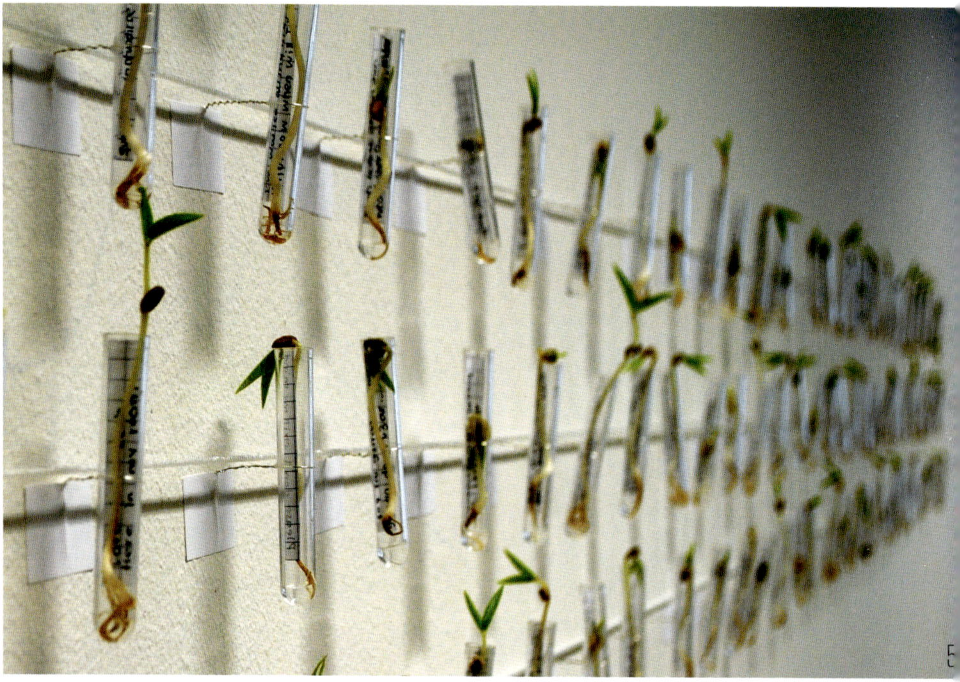

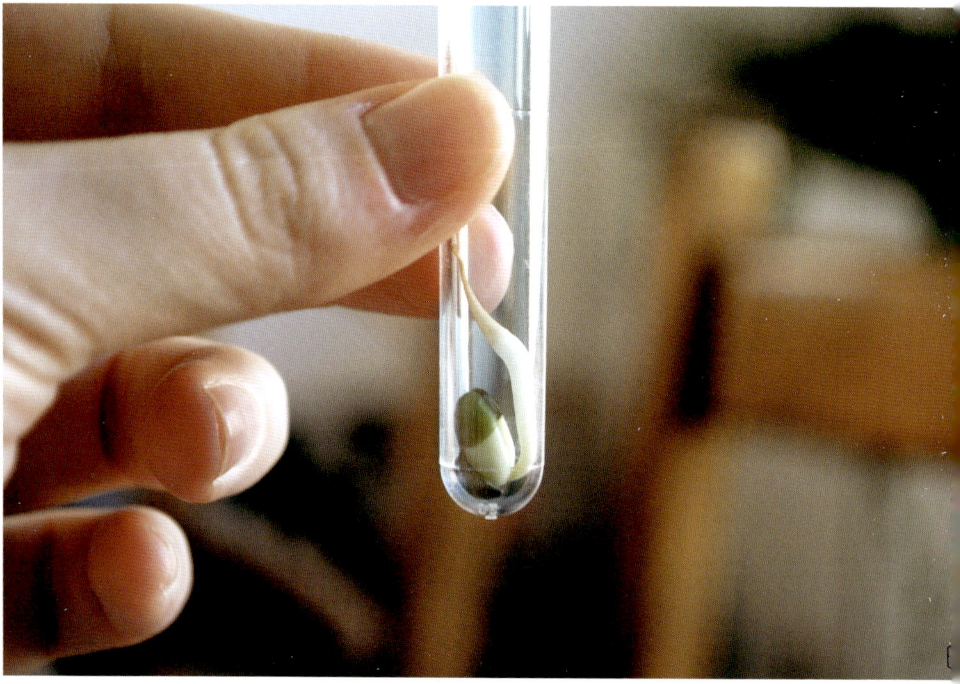

STRAWBERRY FRANKENSTEIN

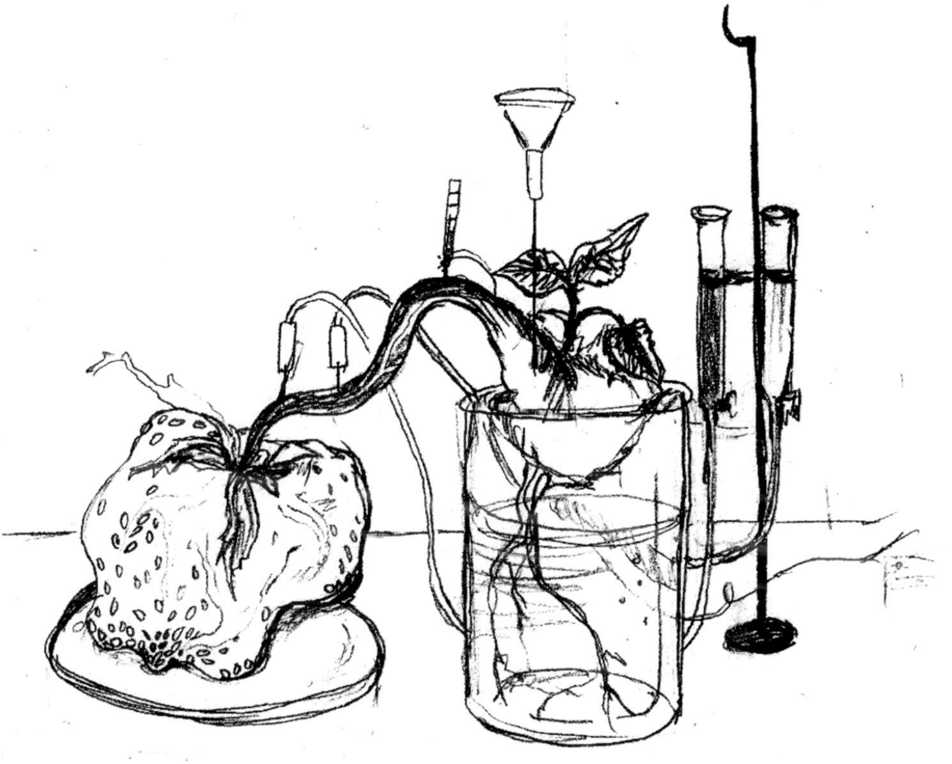

Created with the stem and roots from other plants for it to absorb more nutrients

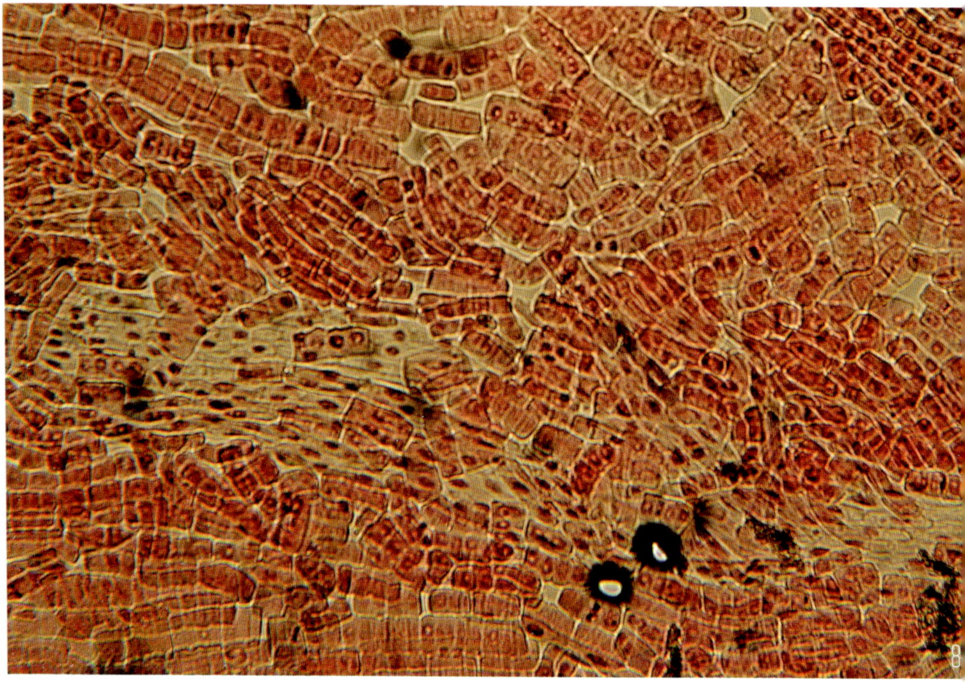

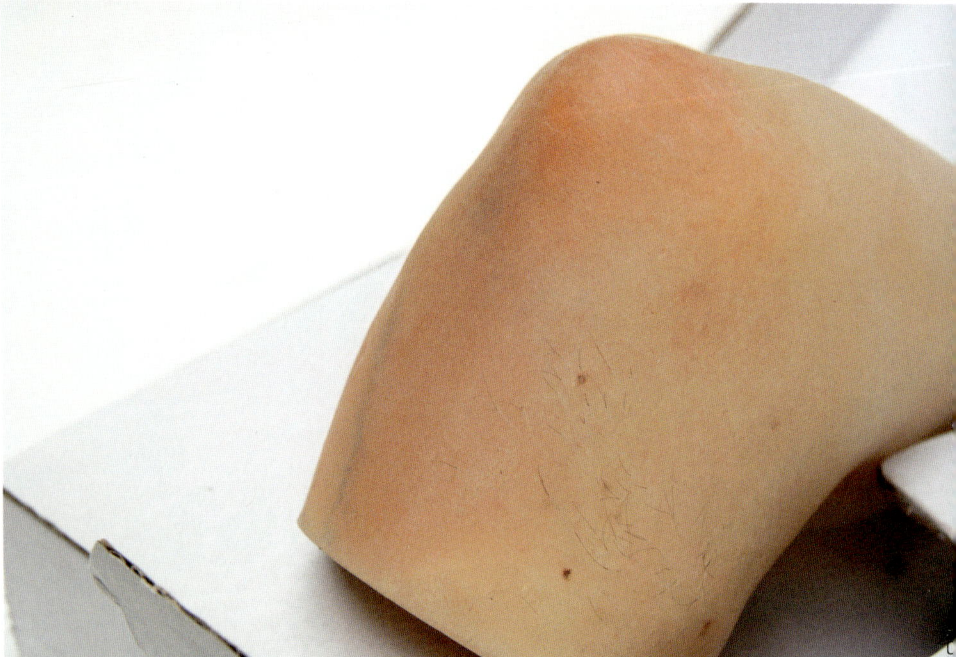

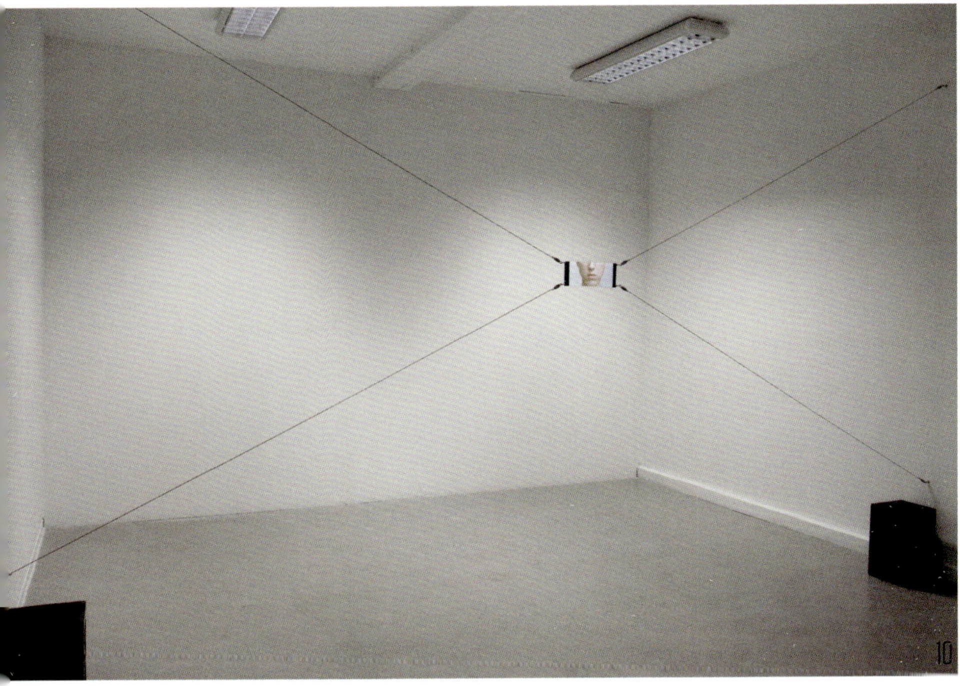

10

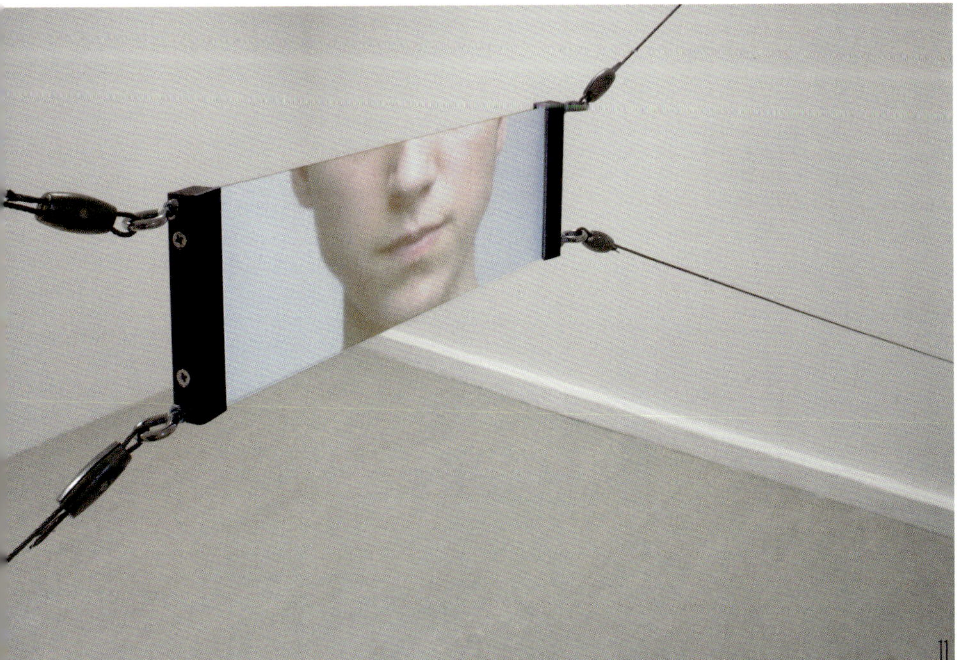

11

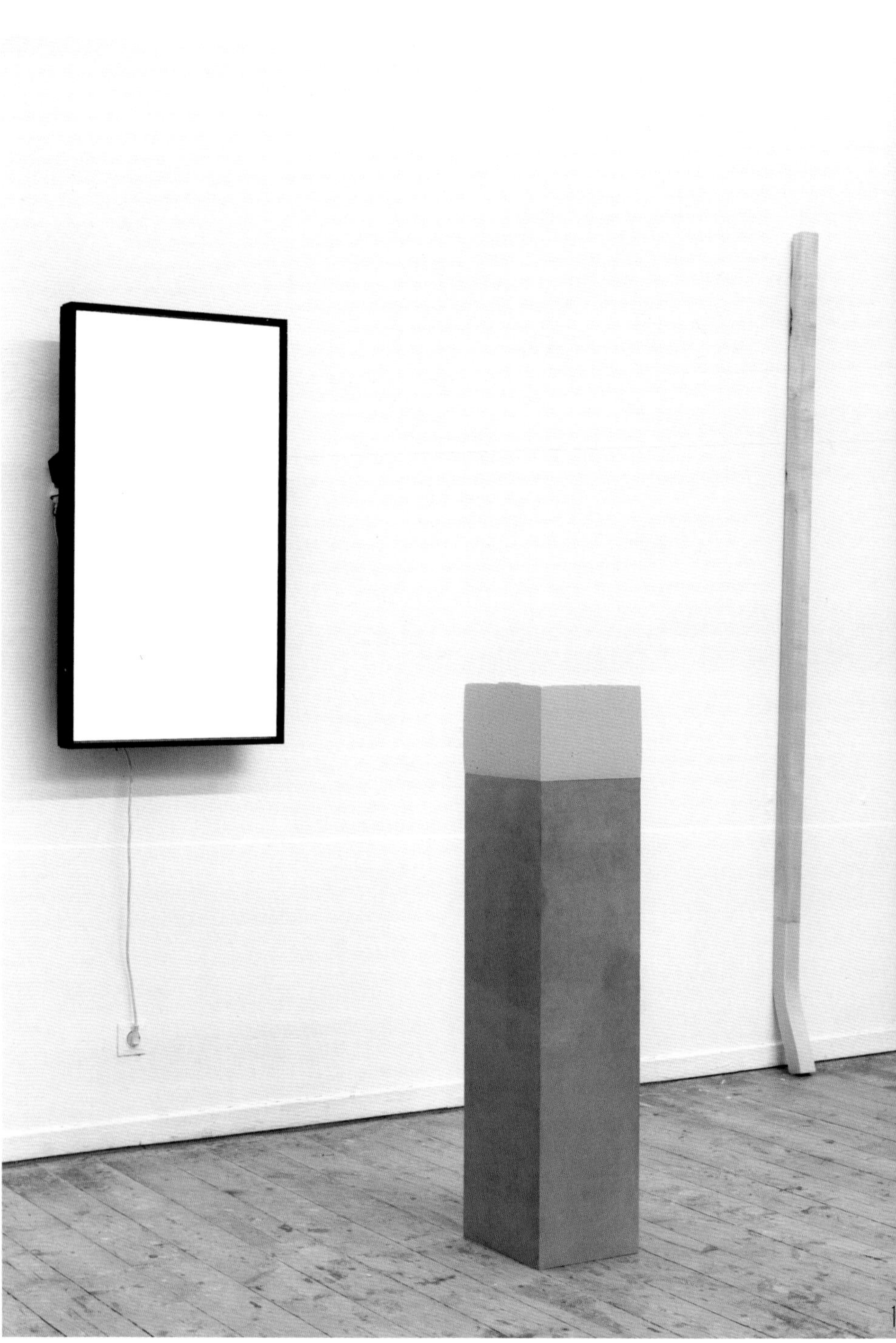

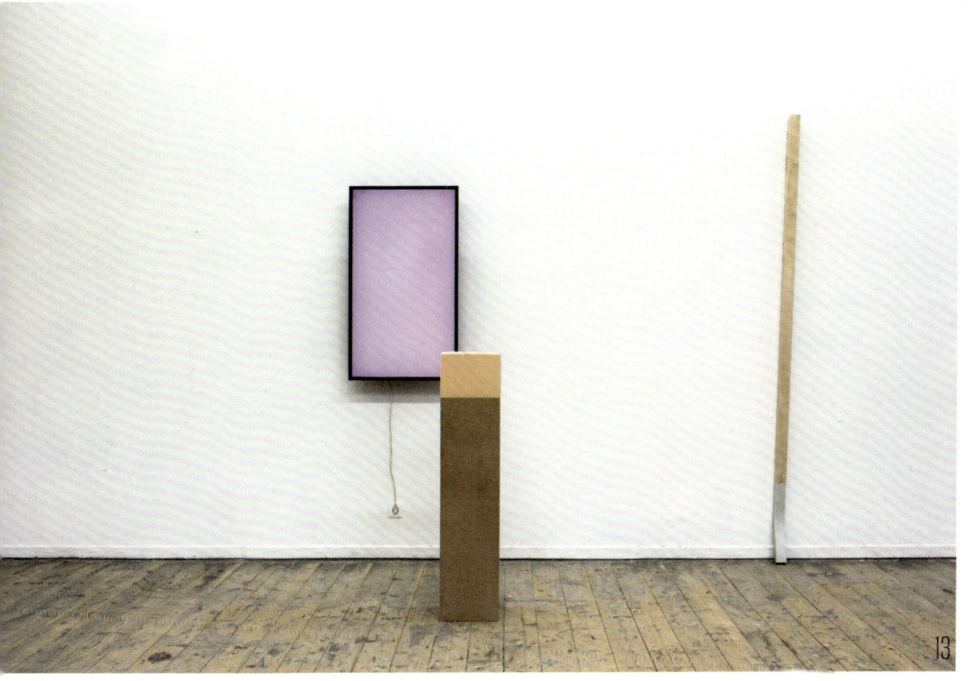

13

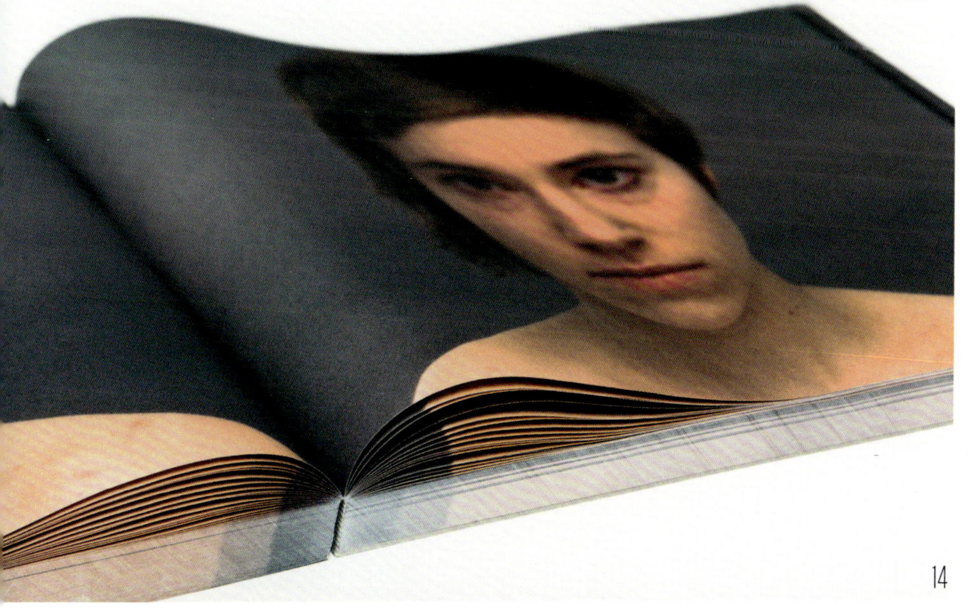

14

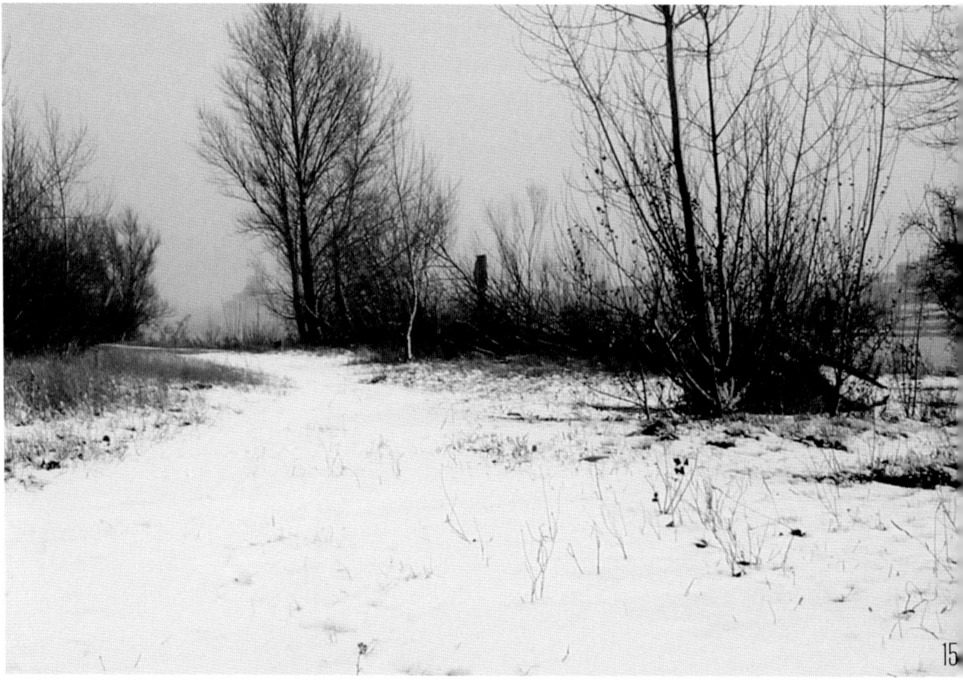

15

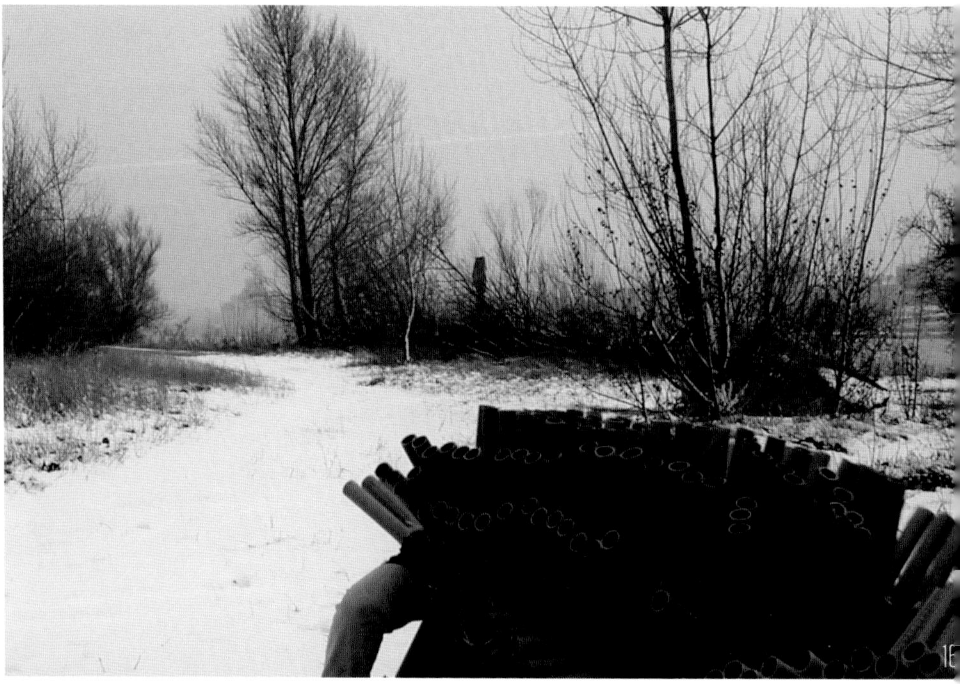

16

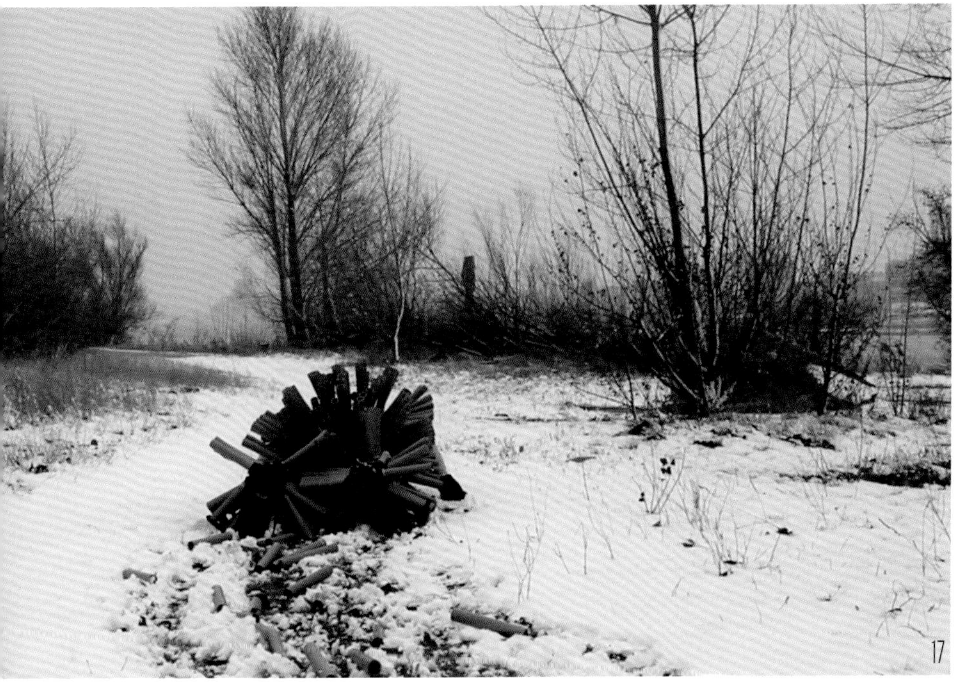

17

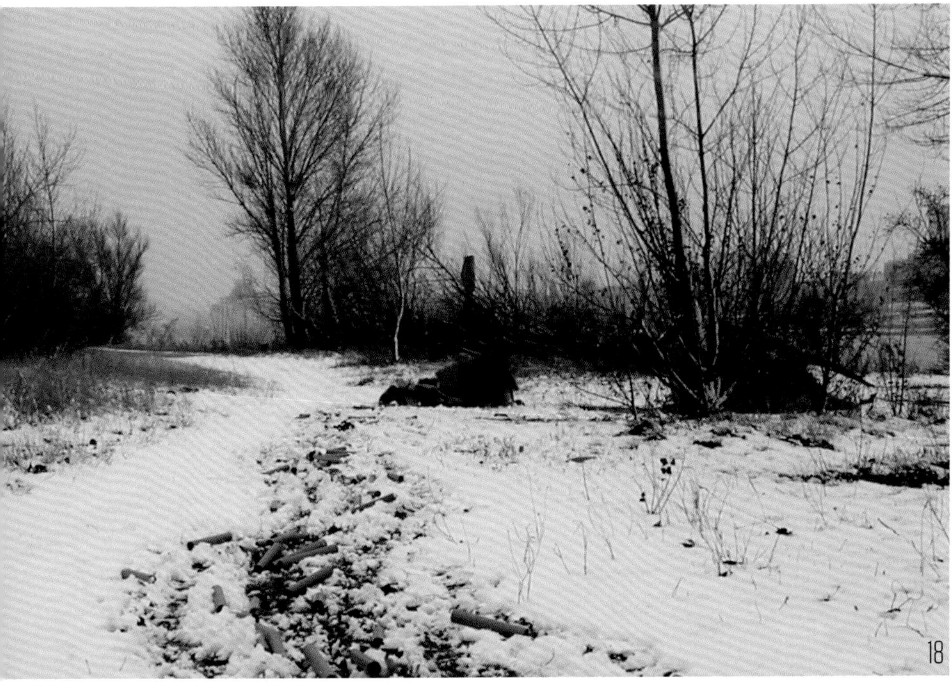

18

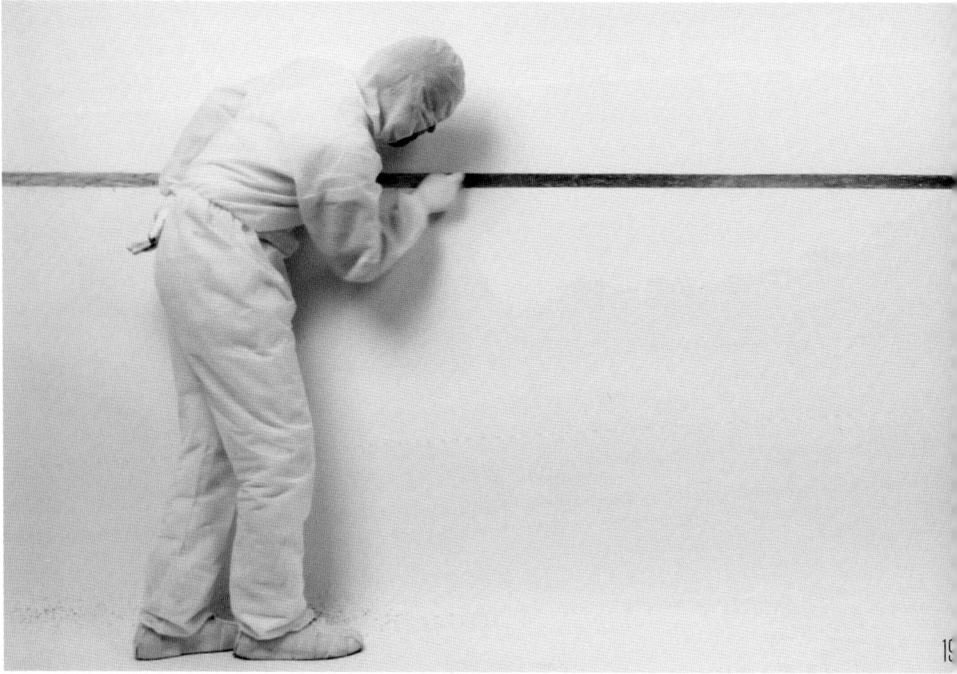

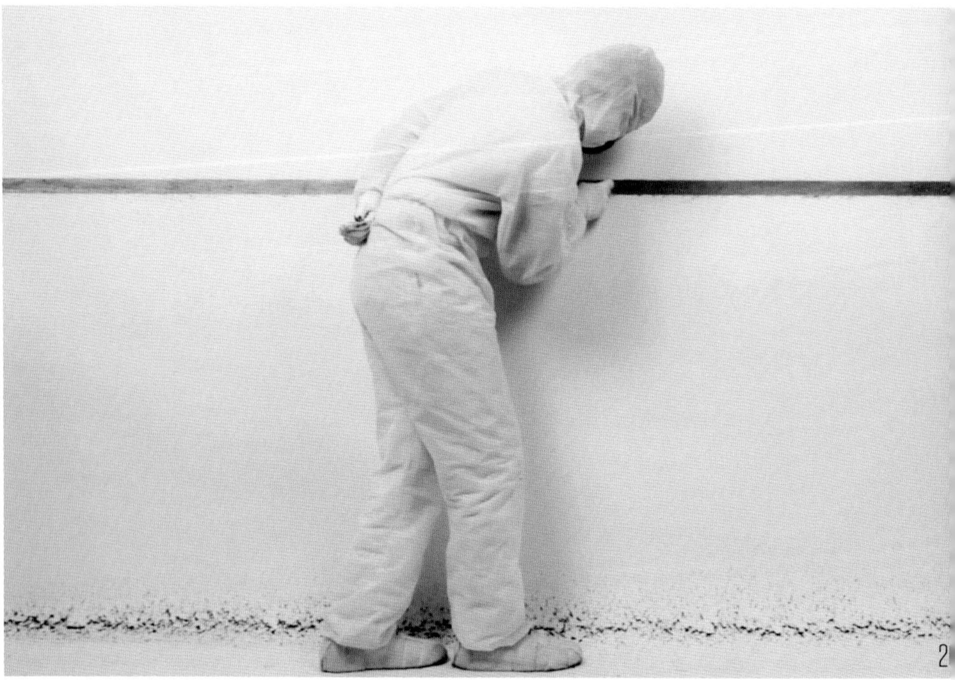

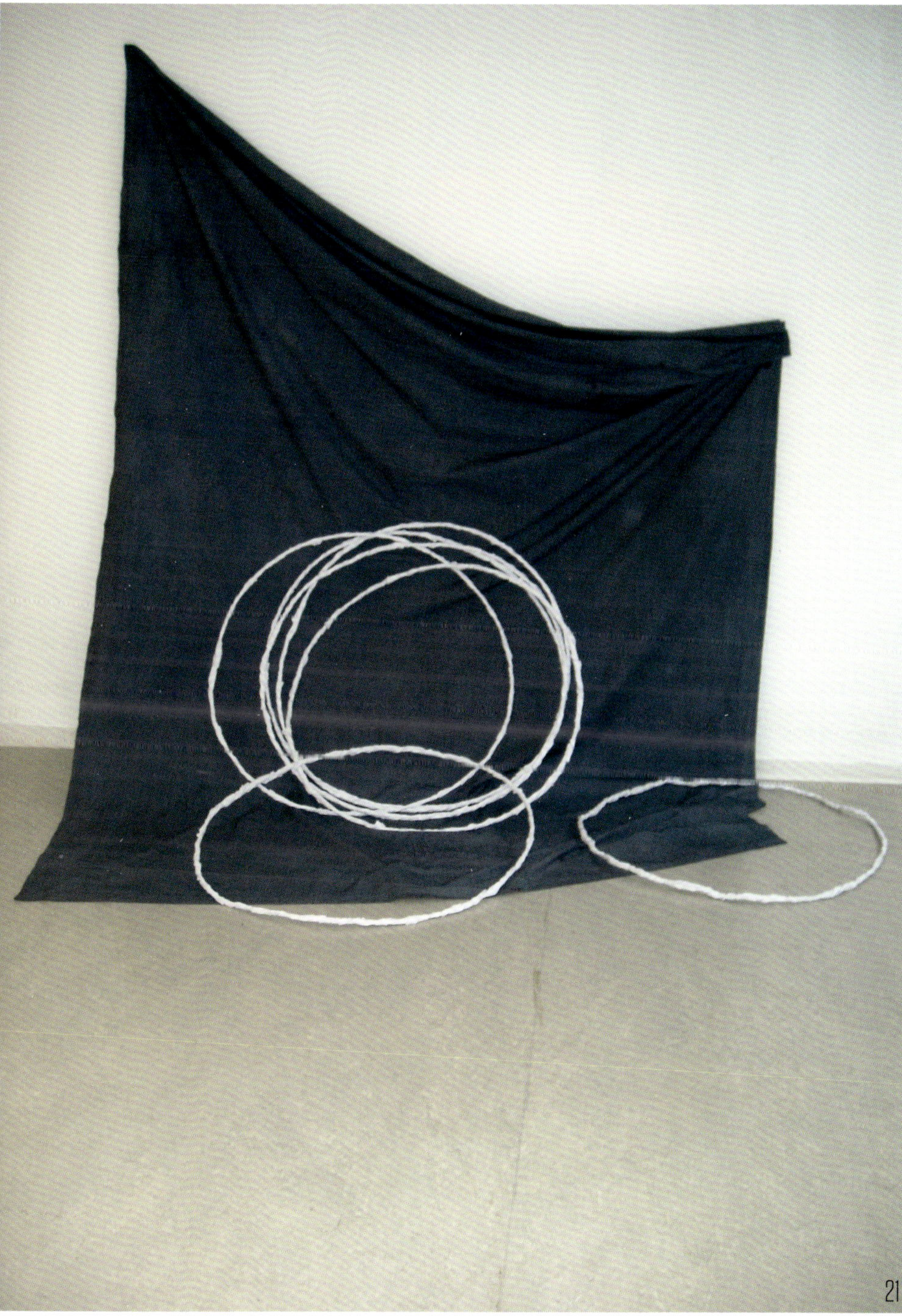

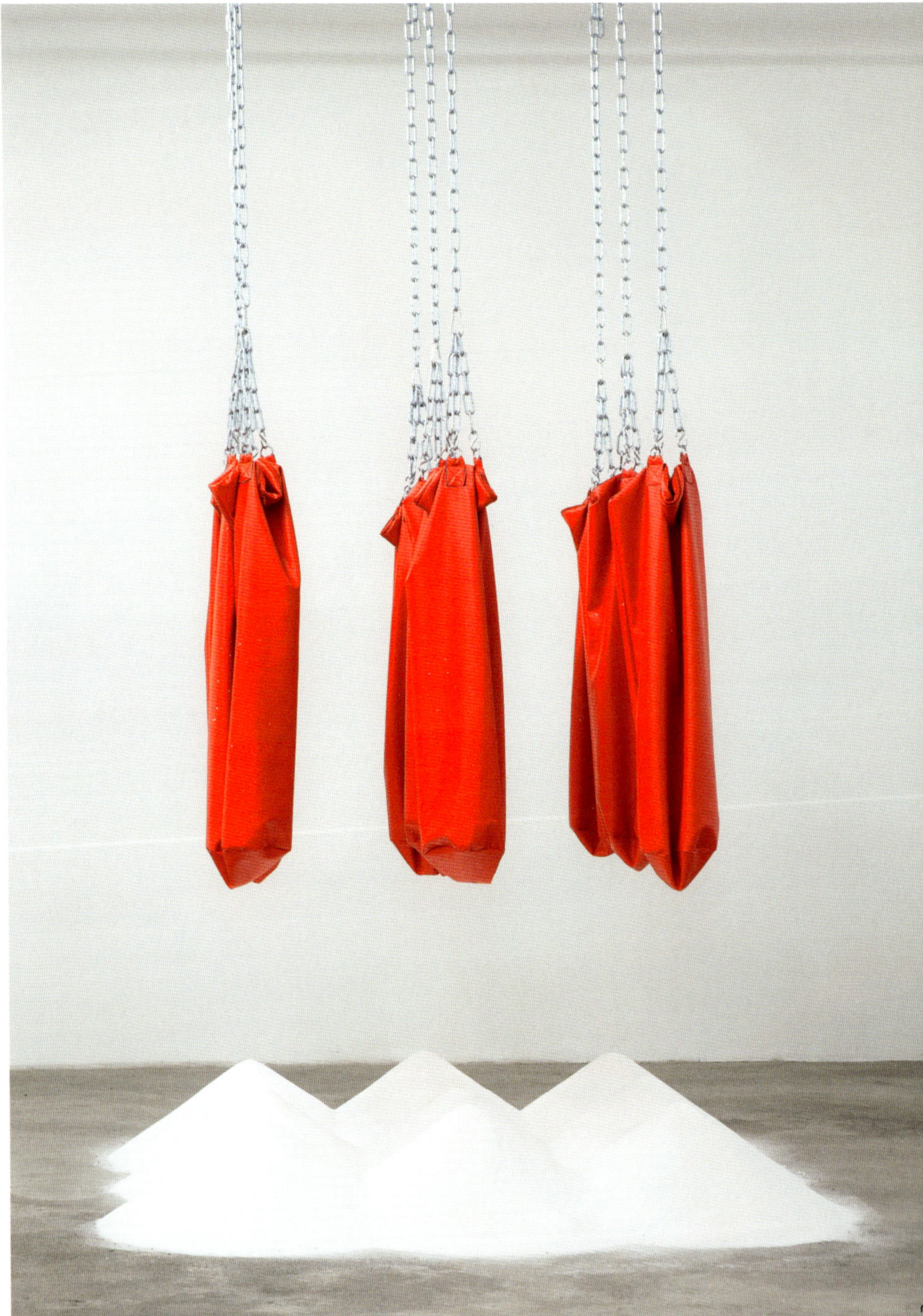

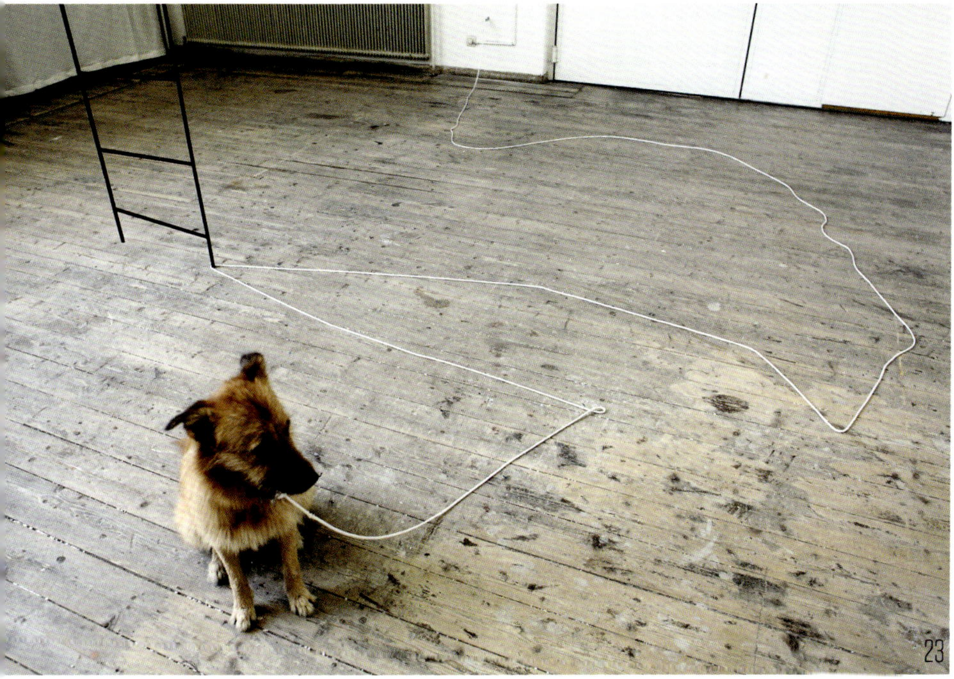

23

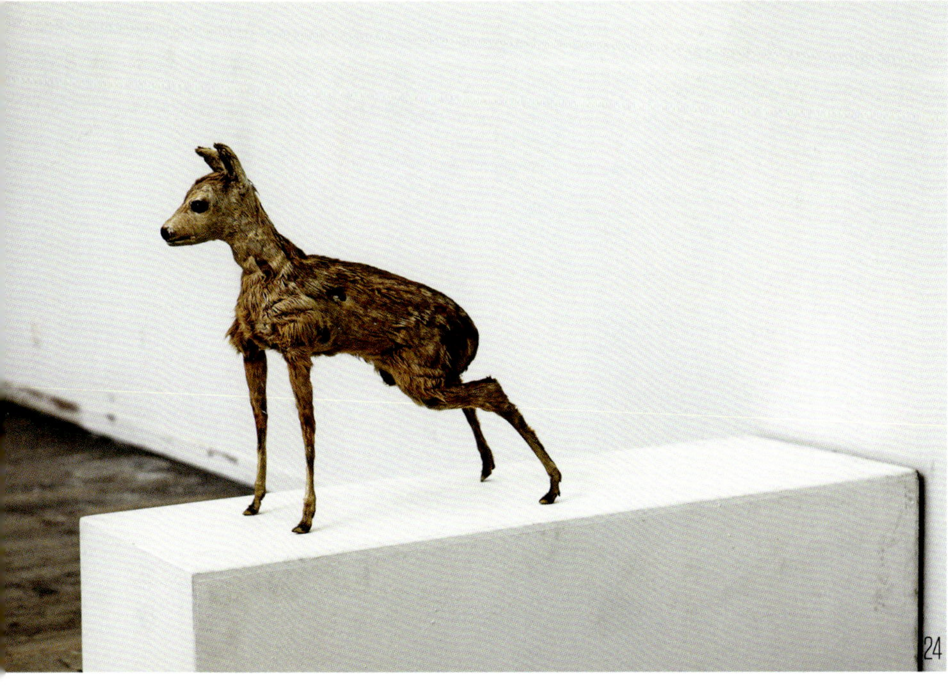

24

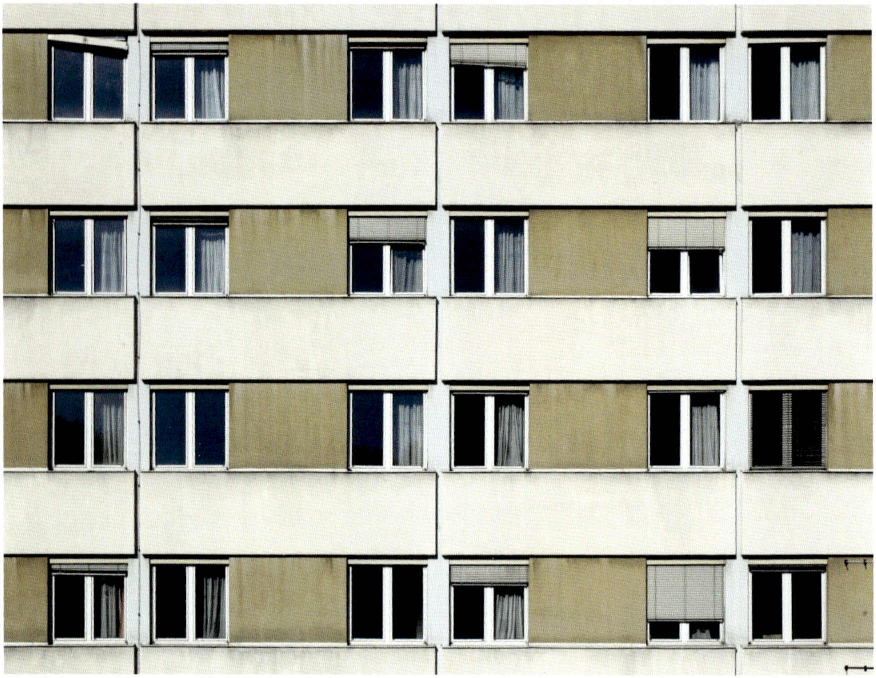

2

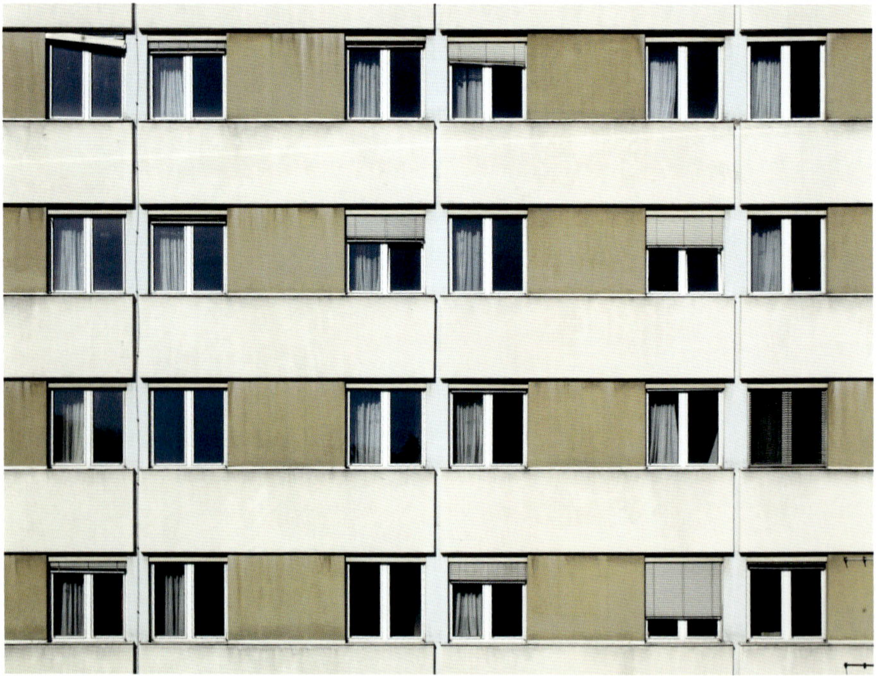

2

1 **Maria Cozma** 7776 2013

Video, 50 min.

The starting point for *7776* was the points of intersection on a plane. The work attempts to get round having to make a decision by offering all of the various alternatives. The decisions have no influence, however, on the beginning or the end as there is no beginning or end. This work obviates the recurrent question as to how the avoidance of choice or the various possible decision combinations influence the creation process and finally the resultant picture. The number 7776 is the total of possible combinations that I have for filming the given plane following a single line.

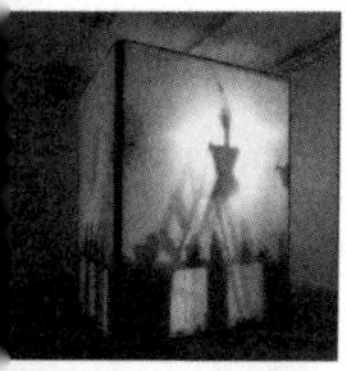

2 **Anna Baumann** Electrophoresis 2012

Installation. Photo: Birgit and Peter Kainz

The illuminated installation shows a surreal greenhouse in which four pictures are generated. It is a rectangular construction in a dark room adapted to the geometrical proportions of the exhibition room. A narrow passage leads around the greenhouse offering the recipient a view of one side at a time. Silhouettes are projected on the walls of the installation ...

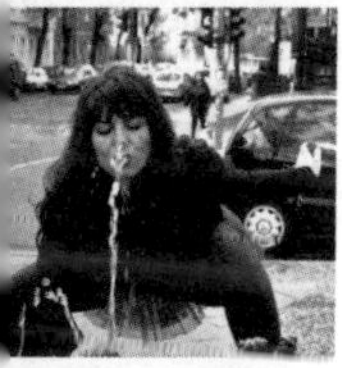

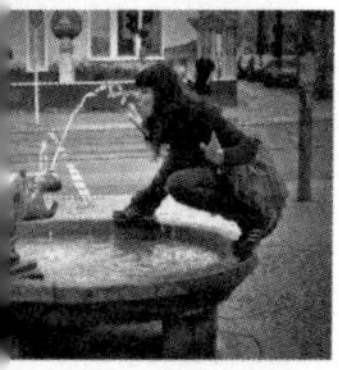

3/4 **Alessa Esteban** A Kiss to Naumann a Blink to Pina ... 2011

Performance. Photo: Sebastian Kraner

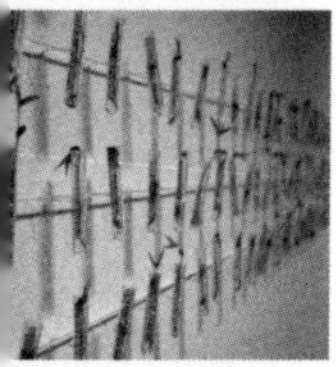

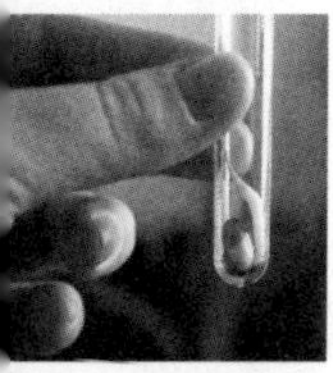

5/6 **Daniela Brill** Polyphony of the Roots 2011

Mixed media. Installation view

This project studies the growth of plants under different conditions. The plants are mungo beans, and each one (99 in all) has been cultivated with different music. As they are shown in test tubes, the difference, for example in the leaf growth and above all the roots, can be seen. The project started like a scientific experiment but the result is clearly a statement or better a poetic idea.

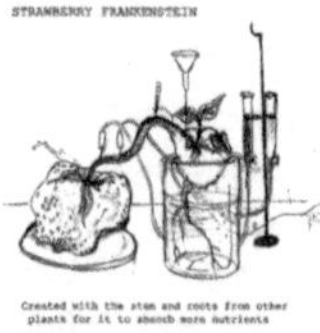

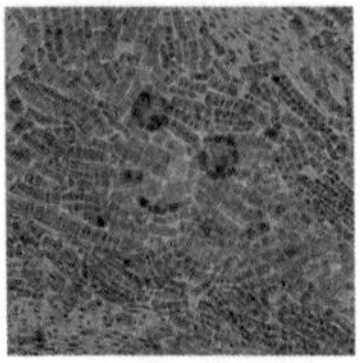

7/8 **Daniela Brill** How to make a strawberry the size of a watermelon 2010–2012

In collaboration with Juliana Canal, Biopop; Bogotá, Colombia
Material: Various

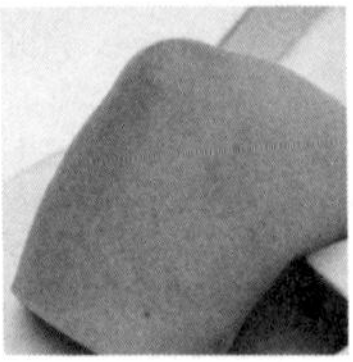

9 **Maria Grün I GrÜnsch AG (Maria Grün, Eva Grün)** ACCEPTANCE (ELBOW 1:1) 201

Silicon, pigments, cardboard, 24 × 24 × 11.5 cm

Part 4 of the reconstruction series by GrÜnsch AG Order No. 4
Articulatio cubiti, coxae, genus, femoropatellaris etc. for the first time also avai able in retail outlets, the latest technology made of high-grade HT 33 Transparen LT. Visit our new store.
GrÜnsch AG is moving to Schleifmühlgasse 12–14. Here from 29 September yo can purchase various parts of the musculoskeletal system and other small 'prac tical' parts of the body. Of course, our range also includes instructions for use an purpose and scientific presentations on the subject of prosthetics.
GrÜnsch AG – Your partner for reconstructions
In *ACCEPTANCE* phrases and situations such as forms, bureaucracy, precariou living, insurance, I & Co., 'start-ups', language, flexibility, self-exploitation, humou perception of the body in medicine, illness, decay, technical orthopaedics, iron etc., become part of the experimental arrangement.

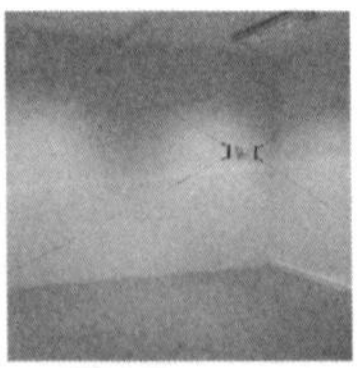

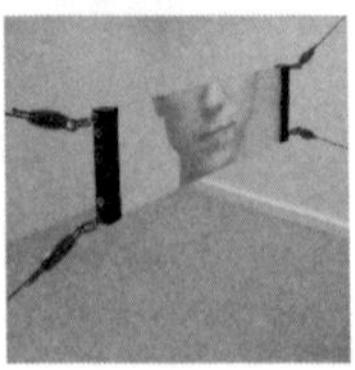

10/11 **Alina Helal** Untitled 201

Video loop

A video projected on a translucent foil fixed between tautly stretched steel rope shows the lower half of a face in actual size. The constantly tense jaw relaxes f only brief moments and quickly becomes tense again. The tensing and relaxin jaw itself produces the sounds accompanying the video, visible from both side

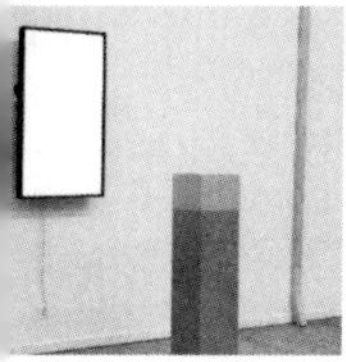

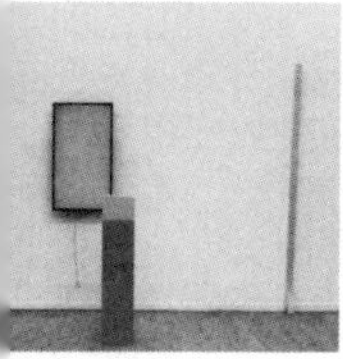

12/13 **Jonas Droste** before naming 2012

Hardwood, pigmented silicon, MDF, alginate, HD monitor. Installation view

The title *before naming* establishes a relational space where a number of material compositions are arranged. The installation brings together various positions on the stability of form – time here is seen as a non-linear structure constituted of moments of equal legitimacy.

A planed beam of Maplewood prolonged by a gray silicon extension: clear lines of a familiar geometry that is deformed by its own weight. The object as a whole begins to rob itself of form. The transition between different consistencies concurs with a structural break down of *function*. The extension however remains an attempt, an adumbration.

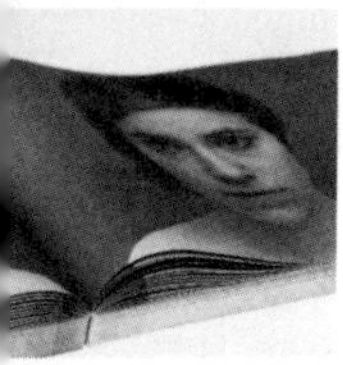

14 **Jonas Droste** zugunsten Gegenwärtigem 2011

Sculptural print object, DIN A3, reference monitor on plinth. Detail

'When I speak of time, it is not here yet. When I speak of place, it has disappeared. When I speak of a man, he is already dead. When I speak of time, it already is no more.'[1]

zugunsten Gegenwärtigem (in favour of presence) interprets the time-based medium film by translating it into the space-related form of sculpture. A stack of loosely bound prints as the structure of the work generates a fragile frame for engaging with the rectified sequence of moving images.

An additional film loop placed at a distance creates an omnipresence of moving images, an accompanying constant when engaging with the printed sheets.

[1] Baudrillard Jean: Why hasn't Everything already Disappeared. http://www.ubishops.ca/baudrillardstudies/vol-8_1/v8-1-why.html

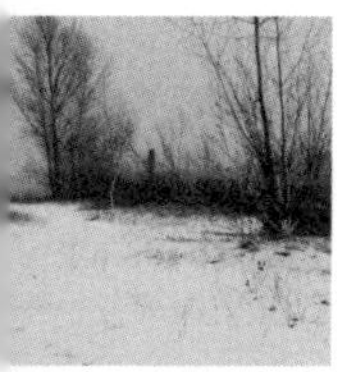

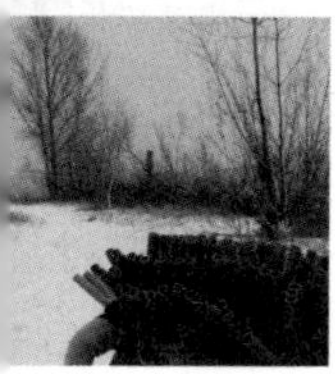

15–18 **Sebastian Gärtner** The porcupine similitude 2012

Video, 9:56 min.

In a suit made of black overalls, four zippers, 15 rubber door mats, 400 sewage pipes and 200 metres of nylon thread, I crawled over a snow-covered field. It was more tiring than I had thought. The new snow stuck to the tubes and made the suit heavier. After the first few metres I had already lost some of the tubes. I rested behind a stone, then continued crawling.

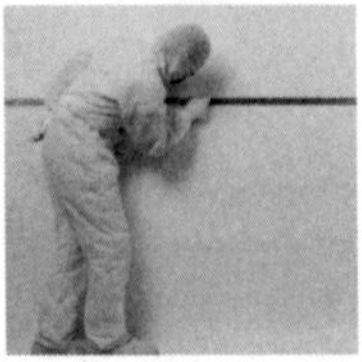

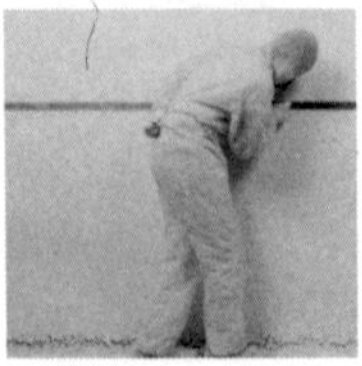

19/20 **Sebastian Gärtner** Arrearagerase 201

Video, 38:12 min.

The idea was to continually erase and redraw the line until what remained wa the same colour as the original drawing. After five attempts I gave up. A furthe line had been created at my feet. That was the problem: only a small deviation, small error, and it was necessary to start over.

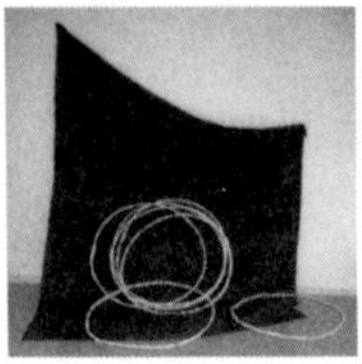

21 **Marie-France Goerens** In search of lost time 200

Hand-made rings made of white A4 sheets of paper, linen sheet dyed blue-black, 180 × 250 cm

In his work *In Search of Lost Time* Marcel Proust writes about suppressed mem ories that are revived by him through chains of association. I took up this idea t sketch autobiographical events. The linen sheet, normally white, our bed line from earlier, was soaked in dark dye. The hula hoop rings represent innocen childhood memories but also being captive and unable to escape. The thin whit sheet with which the rings are made gives the work a certain fragility, weaknes and frailty.

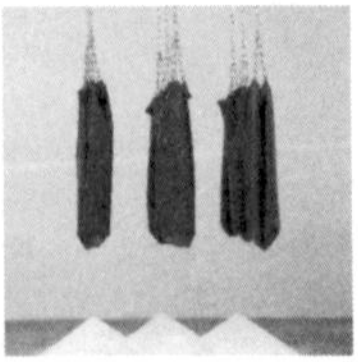

22 **Marie-France Goerens** Similes 201

Nine stitched punch bags made of synthetic leather, galvanized steel chains, salt from Salinen Austria
Installation, approx. 150 × 150 × 350 cm

The new red punch bags are filled with salt that gradually trickles out through hole in the bottom. Air pressure builds up inside and the bag empties in a line fashion. On the ground a landscape of salt hills is created. According to Jea Baudrillard, the poetic transfer marks a new beginning. After a boxing workou symbolizing effort, strength and stamina, there is emptiness; only now can a ne beginning take place.

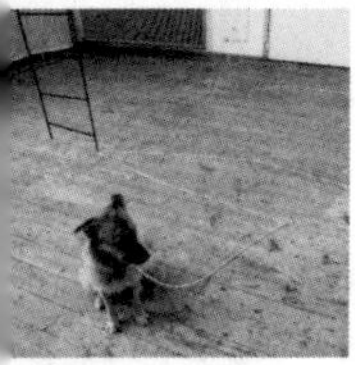

23 **Rick Lins** Work six 2012

Installation/performance

The dog (Kafka) is attached on a long leash (adapted to the size of the room). It can move throughout the entire exhibition room, creating short-lived drawings on the floor and also a continuously changing exhibition architecture in relation to the works and people in the room, which changes dynamically thanks to the dog's unbending liveliness.

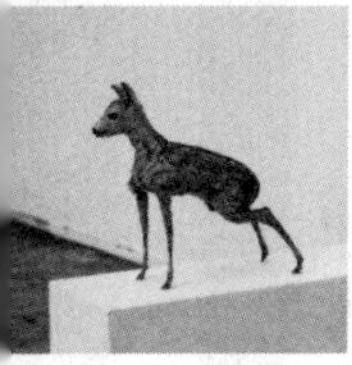

24 **Rick Lins** Work five 2012

Preparation, 70 × 70 × 20 cm

The deer is what we have made of it. We make something out of everything. What do we care about this naturalness when we ourselves give it a name? Formation and deformation are the same thing; there is no need for two words. What is there to talk about?

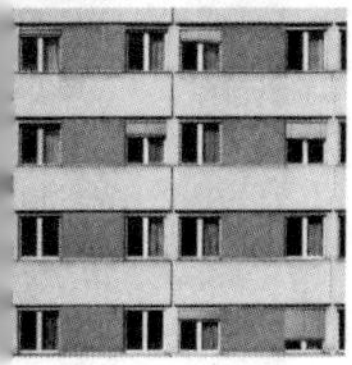

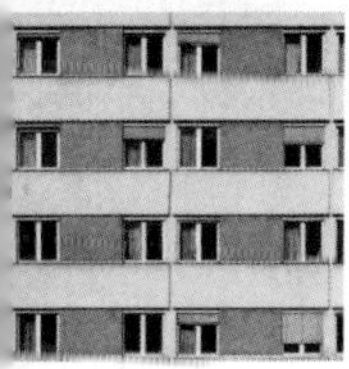

25/26 **Miriam Hamann** Morgen kommt Besuch 2012

C-print, 45 × 60 cm each

Morgen kommt Besuch (We have Guests Tomorrow) addresses the principle of the series. Four apparently similar house façades seem to be identical. This impression is however interrupted by almost invisible changes in the image that are an irritation to the viewer or urge them to search for differences.

visiting professors

HANS SCHABUS Artist, Vienna

OCTOBER 2010

Zwischenbrücken

Workshop

& lecturers

MARC-OLIVIER WAHLER Director Palais de Tokyo, Paris **NOVEMBER 2010**

Improve your Schizophrenic Quotient

Lecture and Workshop

AUGUST RUHS · PETER WEIBEL · ANTON ZEILINGER · ROBERT PFALLER · JOSEF PENNINGER · MARTIN WALDE · MARTIN HAIDINGER · JUDITH EISLER · JENNIFER FRIEDLANDER · HENRY KRIPS · HANS SCHABUS · MARC-OLIVIER WAHLER · RAINER METZGER · PETER NAGY · ELFIE SEMOTAN · ERWIN WURM · ANDREAS STADLER · UWE JONAS · HANS WINKLER · KÖBBERLING / KALTWASSER · TIMM ULRICHS · ELSY LAHNER · CANDICE BREITZ · INGEBORG STROBL · NICOLE SIX / PAUL PETRITSCH · FRANZ SCHUH · BERNHARD LEITNER · SHADY EL NOSHOKATY · CHRIS

RAINER METZGER Professor at the Academy of Fine Arts, Karlsruhe **NOVEMBER 2010**

Metropolises and their Interaction with the Arts

Lecture

HARING · KATHRIN RHOMBERG · DAVID MALJKOVIC · URSULA MARIA PROBST · MANFRED WIPLINGER · EDGAR LISSEL · JUDITH FEGERL · LIDDY SCHEFFKNECHT · ZILVINAS KEMPINAS ·ULI KÜHN · FOLKE KÖBBERLING · ALMUT RINK · KLAUS MOSETTIG · ELECTRIC INDIGO · WERNER REITERER · CHRISTIANE MÖBUS · MARKUS HANAKAM & ROSWITHA SCHULLER · ANNA JERMOLAEWA · CHRISTIAN HÖLLER · OLAF NICOLAI · MATTHIAS MICHALKA · LUCAS CUTURI · SYLVIA ECKERMANN · HANS PETER KAMMERER · HELGA KROMP-KOLB · FRIEDRICH STEINHÄUSLER

PETER NAGY Artist, Gallerist, Curator, New Delhi

NOVEMBER 2010

Don't have Sex with your Ex

Workshop and Exhibition

ELFIE SEMOTAN Photographer, Vienna / New York
ERWIN WURM Artist, Vienna

DECEMBER 2010

Runways

Lecture and Workshop

TRANSCENDENCE AND INTERCONNECTION OF DIFFERING ARTISTIC AND SCIENTIFIC DISCIPLINES

MARTIN WALDE Artist, Vienna

MARCH 2011

The Continuity Game

Workshop

projec

MATTHIAS MICHALKA Curator for New Media, MUMOK, Vienna

MARCH 2011

Museum and Medium

Lecture

t work

ANDREAS STADLER Director of the Austrian Cultural Forum, New York **APRIL 2011**

Culture and Foreign Policy

From the paradigmatic shift in cultural diplomacy to transversal collaboration

Lecture

PREFACE

In complex social systems it is more than ever the task of educational institutions, particularly art universities, to create bridges and synergies between artistic disciplines, theory and practice, concept and artistic technique, artistic production and communication. TransArts is a new offensive in this regard by the University of Applied Arts.

TransArts is an art course whose content and structures are adapted to the dynamics of art today: the separation of the theory and practice of art – while maintaining all the differences – is seen as arbitrary and even obsolete. TransArts teaches the common and distinctive features of theory and practice and takes account of the fact that different artistic disciplines are not only mutually dependent and reinforcing but are also in competition with one another. Art is taught and studied not only through traditional forms of teaching but in particular through communication, inven-

---

ANDREAS STADLER Director of the Austrian Cutural Forum, New York **APRIL 2011**

On Public and Private Funding of Artists Projects with a Focus on Foreign Policy

Workshop

tiveness, reflection and the exchange of ideas between teachers and students. TransArts attempts to consolidate these creative processes by means of a new study architecture that breaks with the disciplinary limitations traditional to universities to create a radical innovative and in many regards unique approach to art education. Instead of direct teaching and organizational and thematic fragmentation, the coursework focuses on project orientation, individual responsibility and communication.

This pluralism in the course content is reflected in the organization of the teaching and the students that ensures both continuity and variety. In addition to the continuous supervision of students by the teaching staff, lectures and workshops with visiting professors and renowned international figures are also offered. In this way the diversity of modern art and art theory will be effectively communicated. Continuity and different perspectives – in TransArts and elsewhere – permit project-based, contemporary and future-oriented education in keeping with the University's guiding philosophy.

This publication describes the principle of TransArts at the University of Applied Arts. The depth and breadth of the

---

UWE JONAS Artist, Curator, Berlin

APRIL 2011

City Rules

Workshop held in Berlin in cooperation with Lichtenberg Studios

course in the first three years are clearly documented. At the same time, it shows the functioning of the TransArts concept of radical project orientation, interdisciplinary work and systematic defragmentation of the course of study. The course depends on highly motivated and quality-conscious teachers and students who regard initiative and the possibility and need for improvisation primarily as an opportunity for individual and institutional development. I should also like on this occasion to express my sincere thanks to all students and particularly to the TransArts staff, Stephan Hilge, Roman Pfeffer and Nita Tandon, for their outstanding commitment to the implementation of this internationally acclaimed course of study.

Gerald Bast, Rector

HANS WINKLER Artist, Berlin

APRIL 2011

Public Art

Lecture

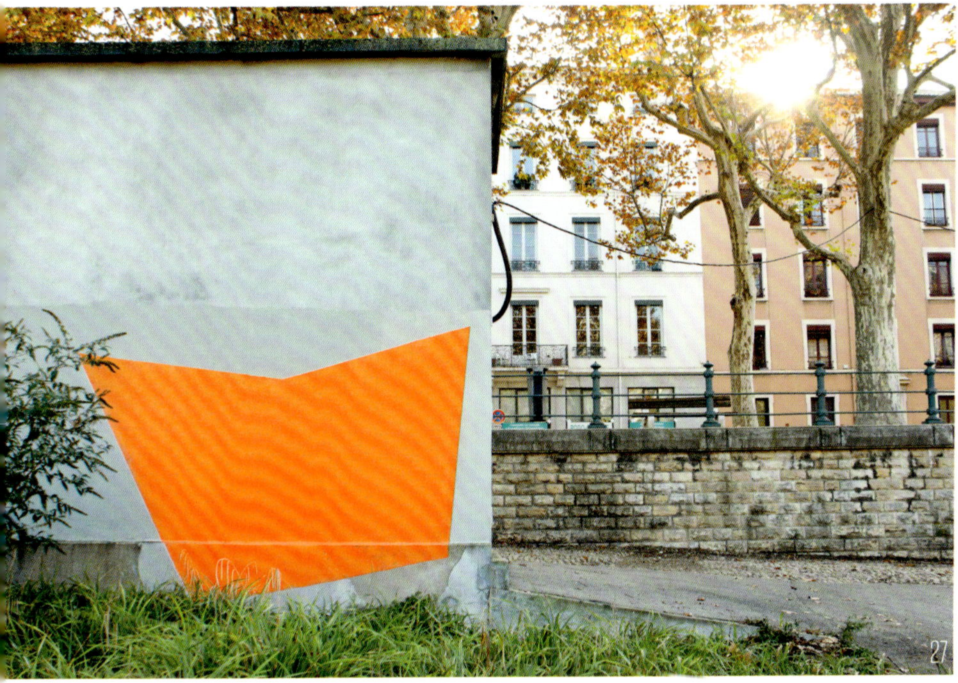
27

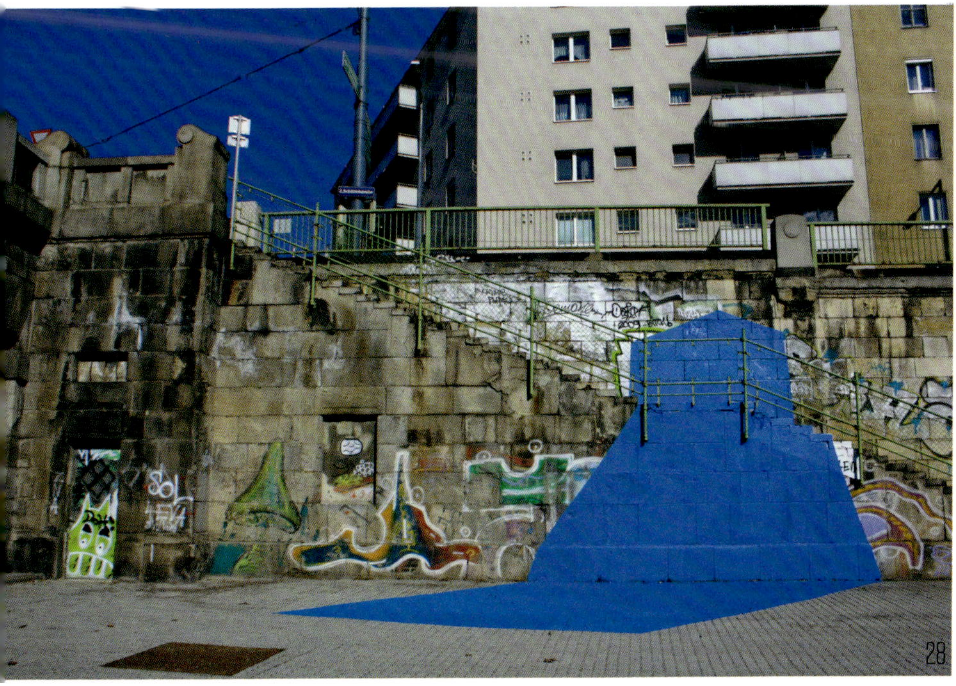
28

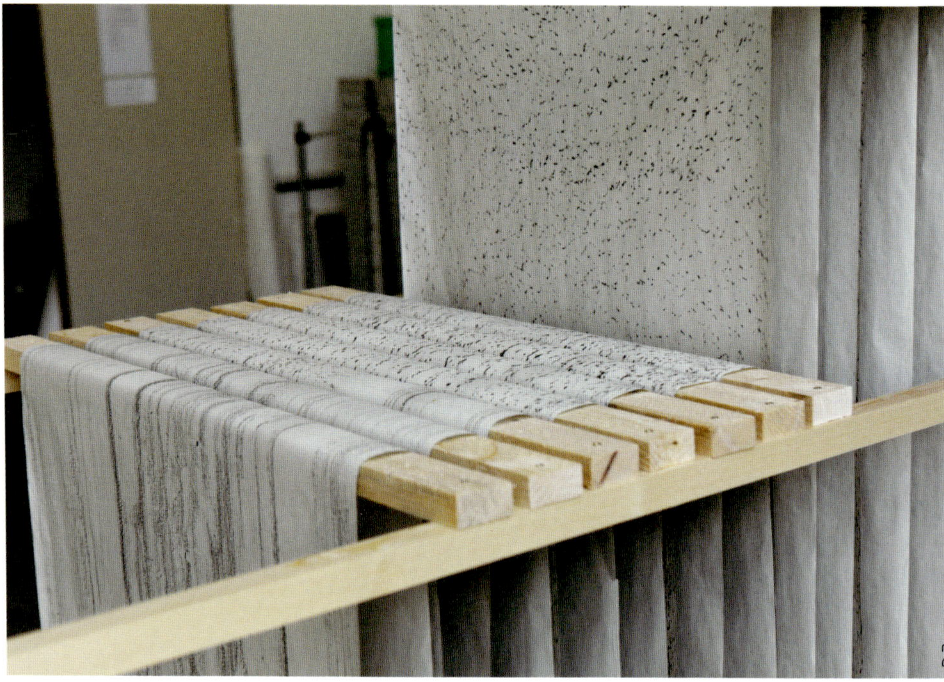

29

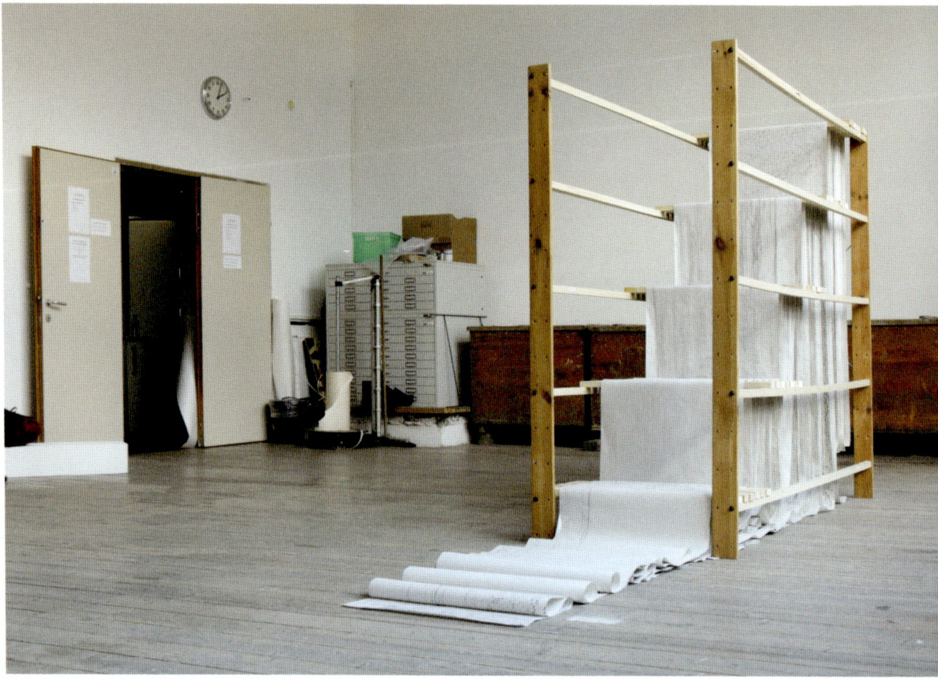

3

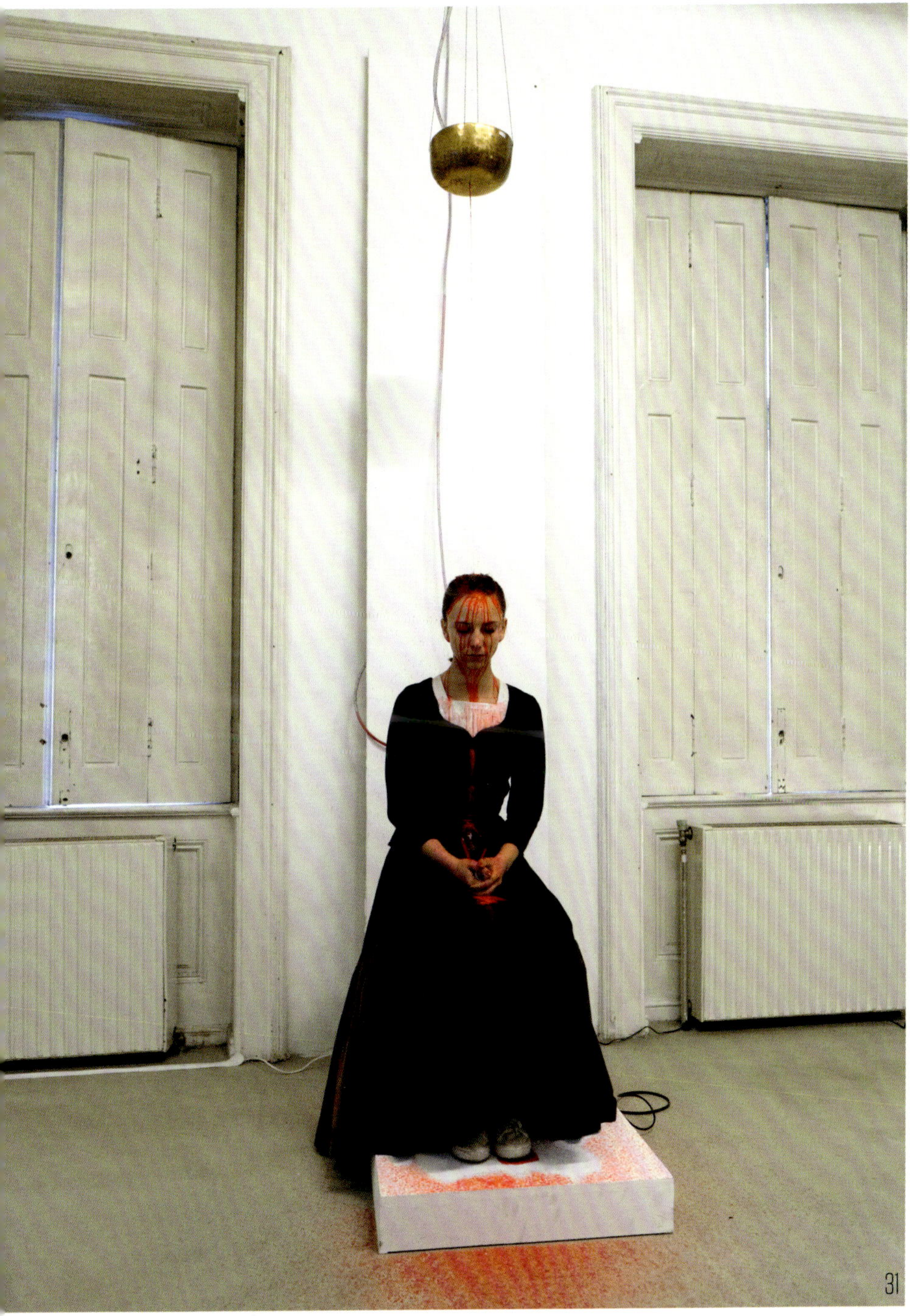

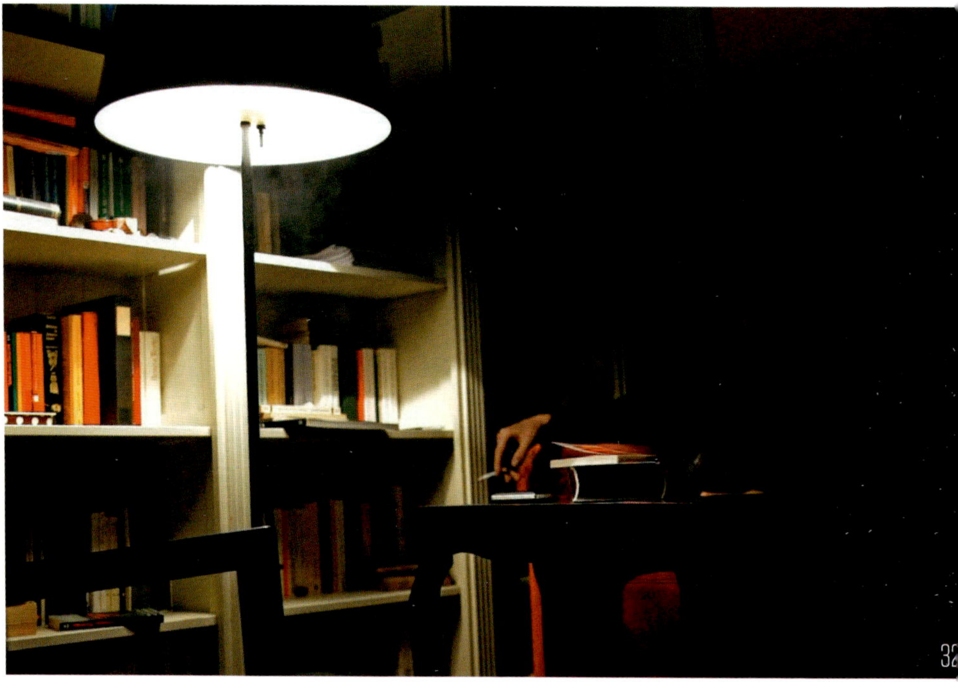

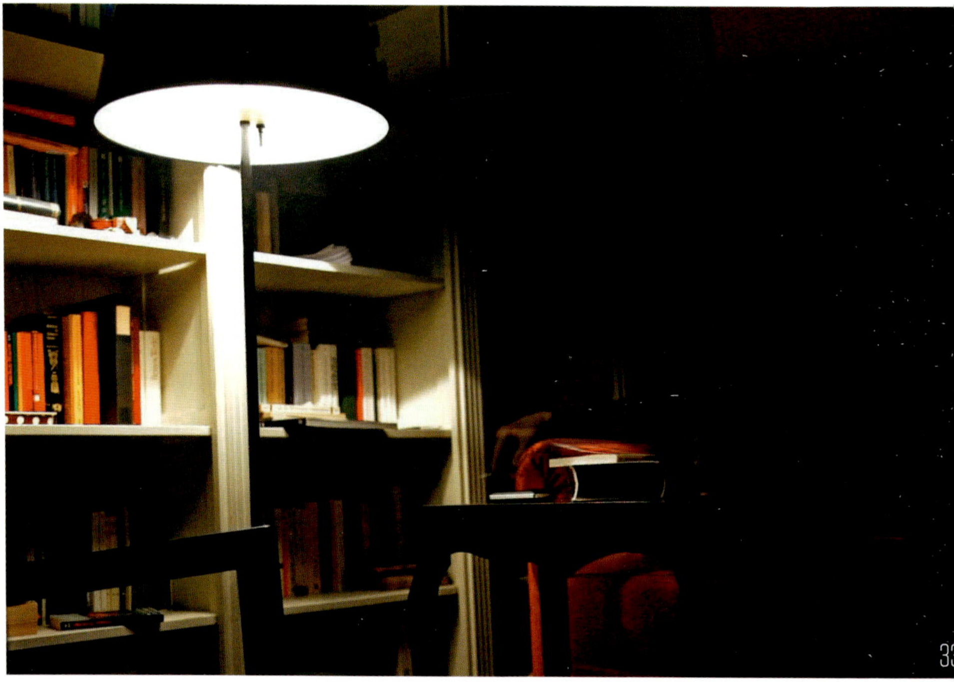

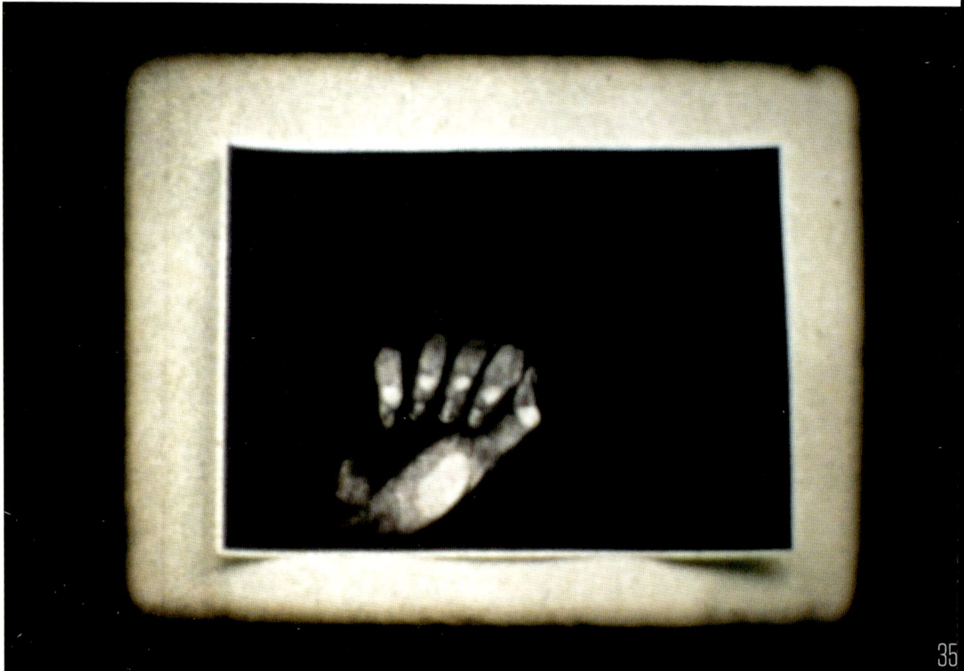

35

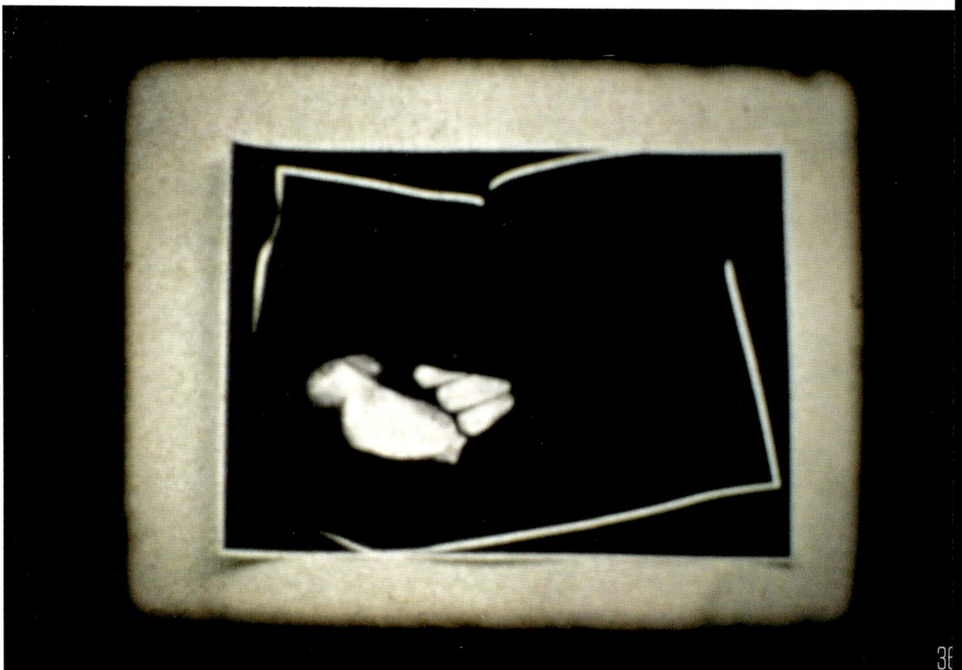

36

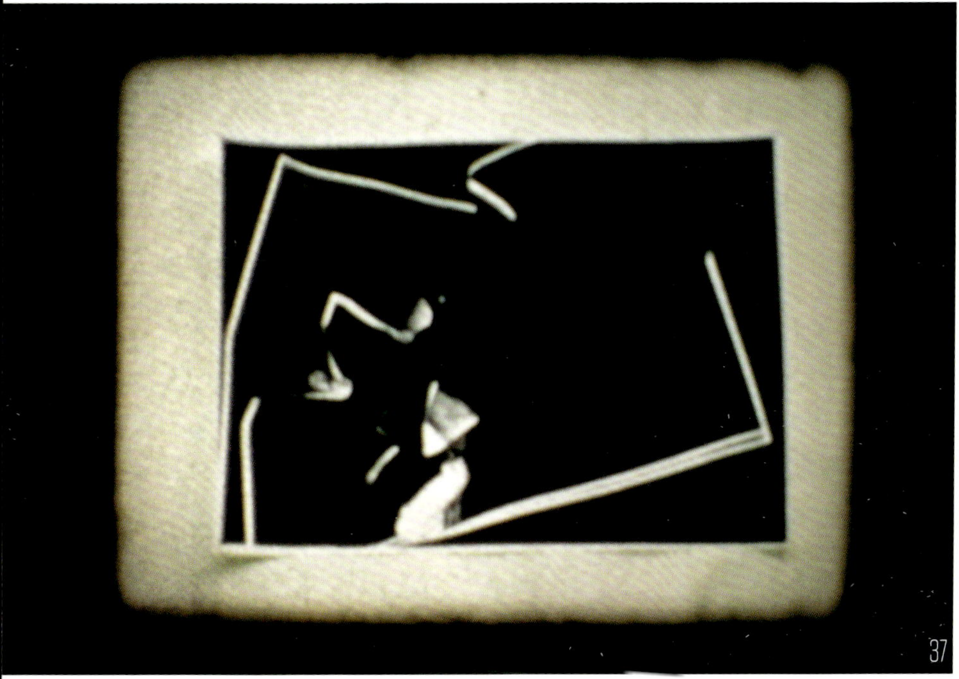

37

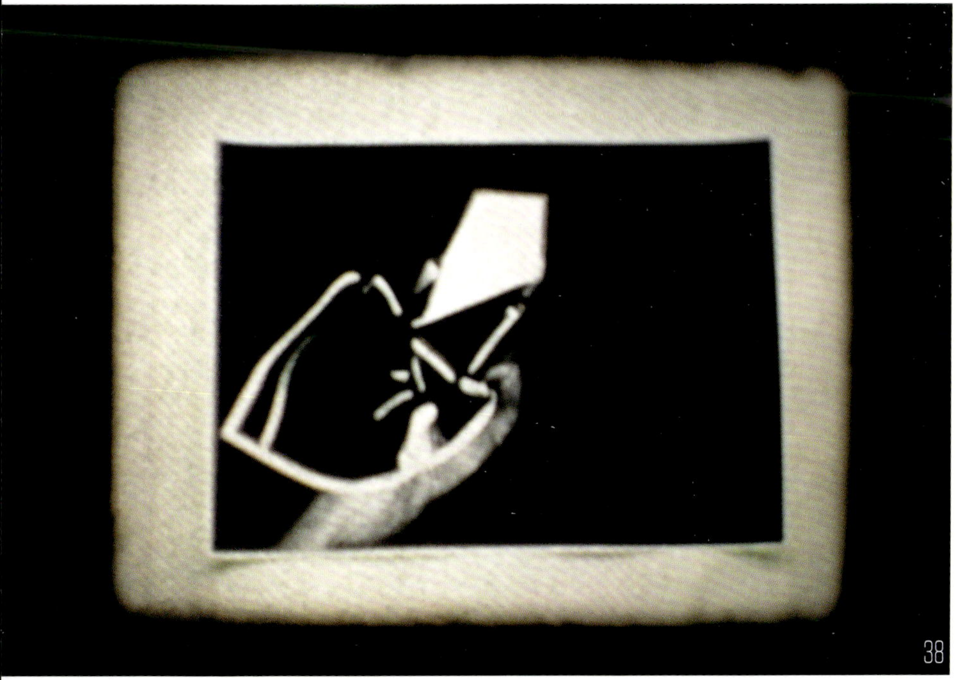

38

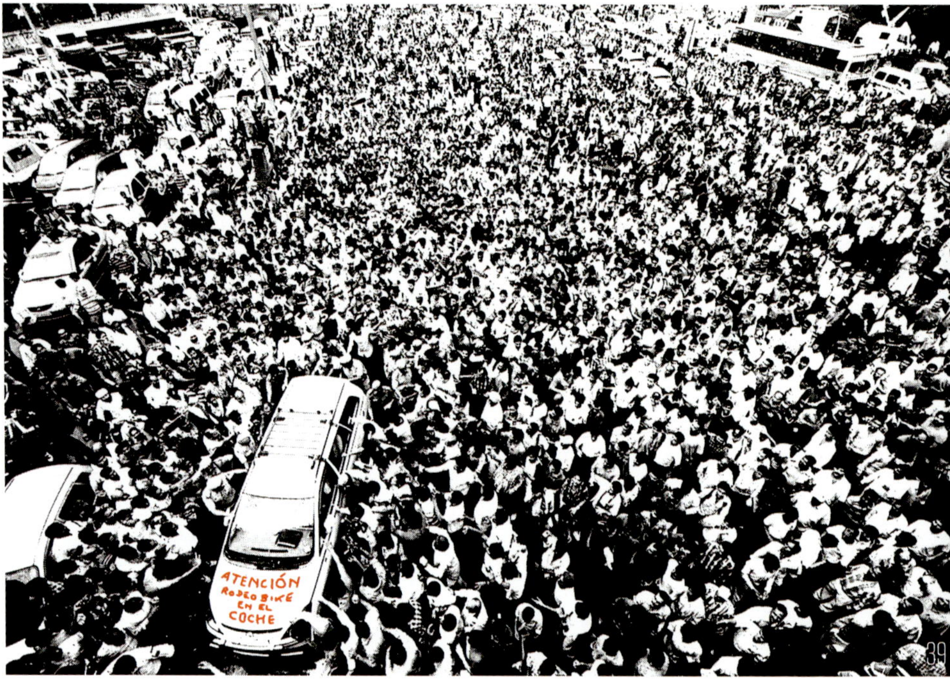
ATENCIÓN
RODEO BIKE
EN EL
COCHE

39

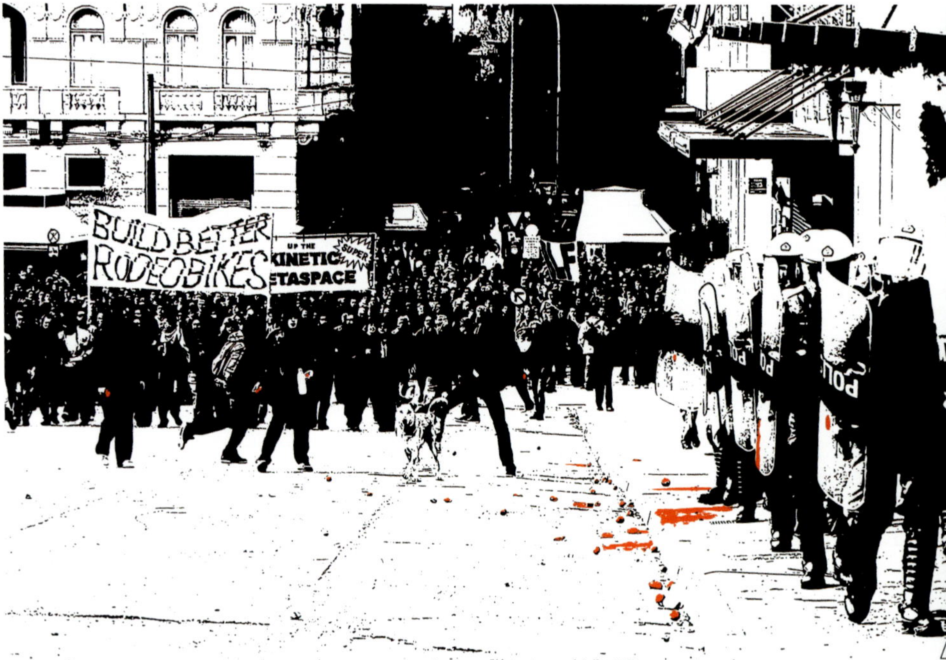
BUILD BETTER
RODEOBIKES
UP THE
SUPER
KINETIC
ETASPACE
POL

4

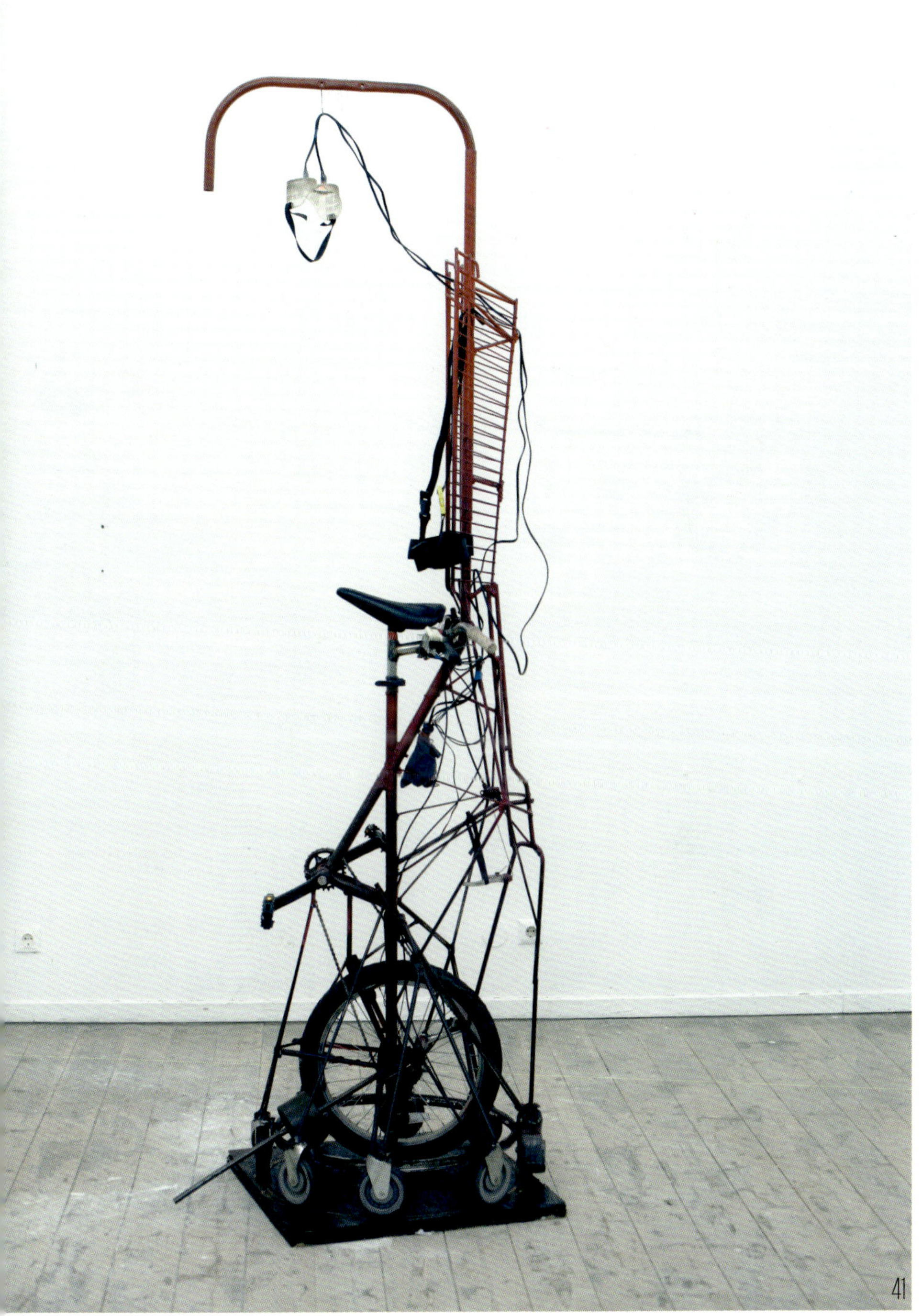

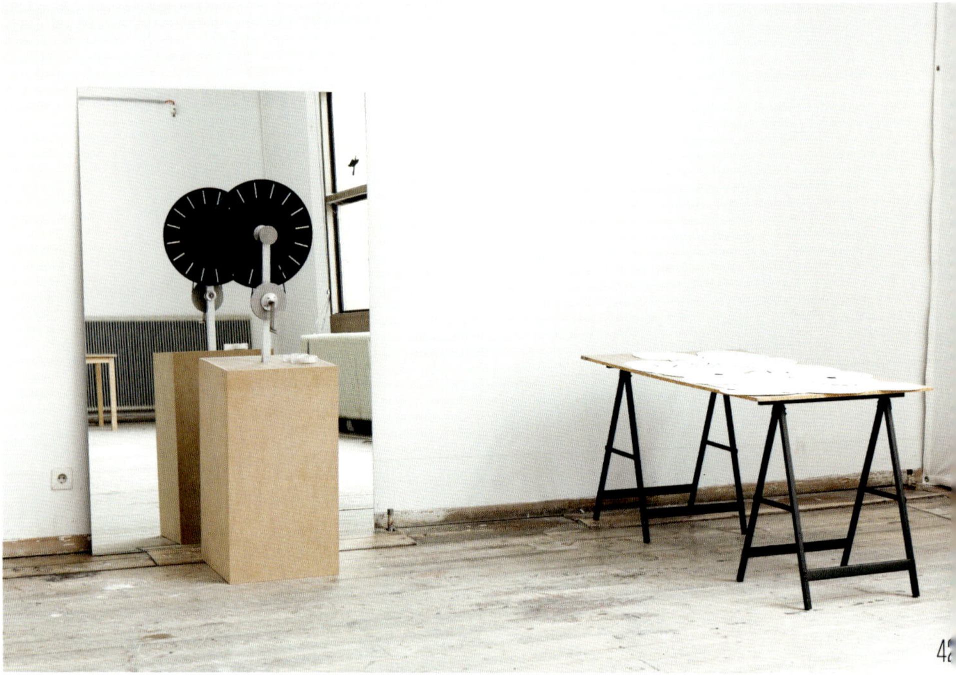

42

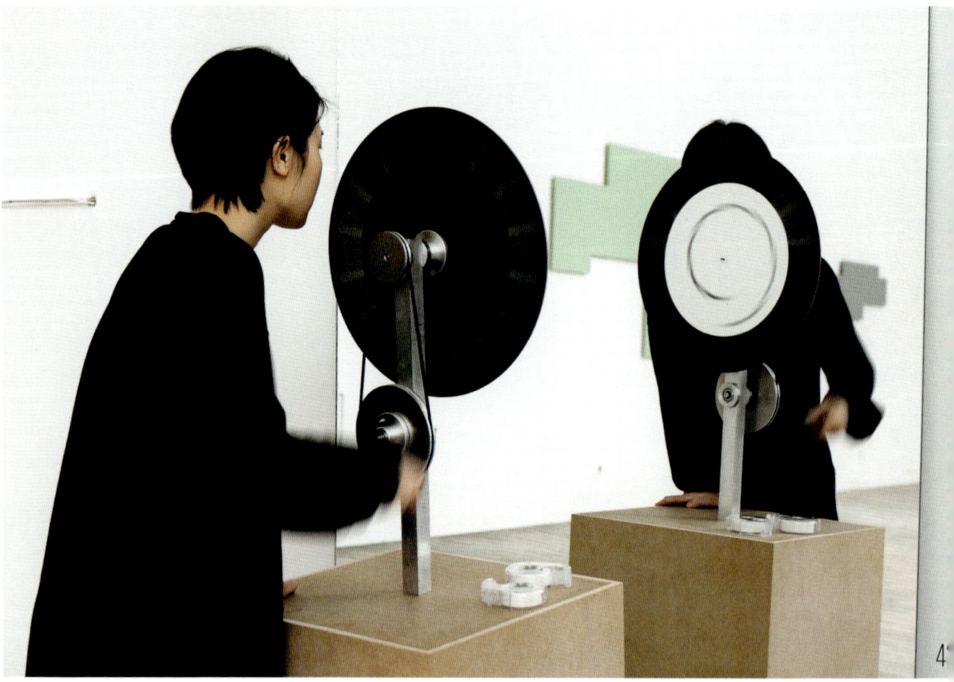

4

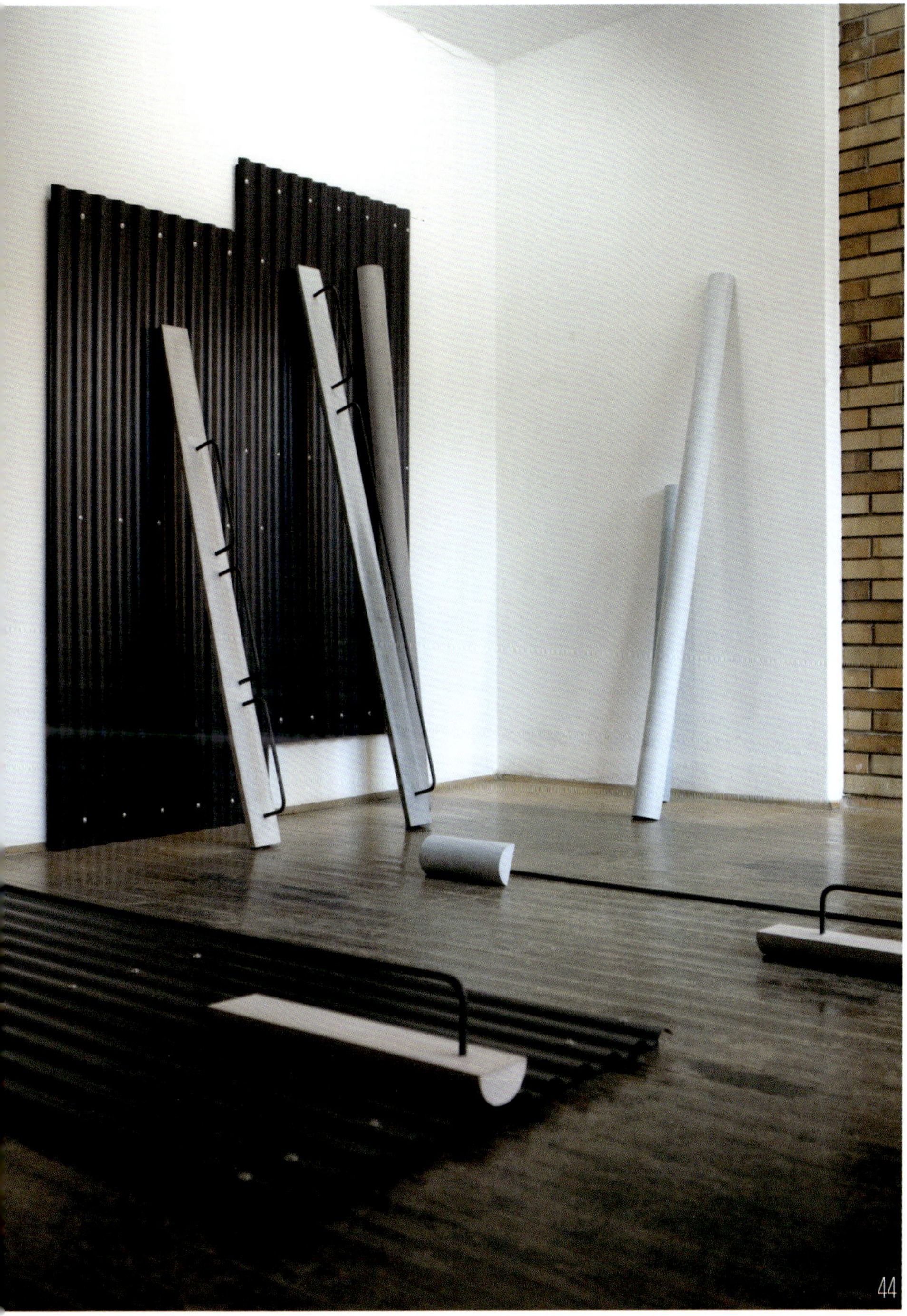

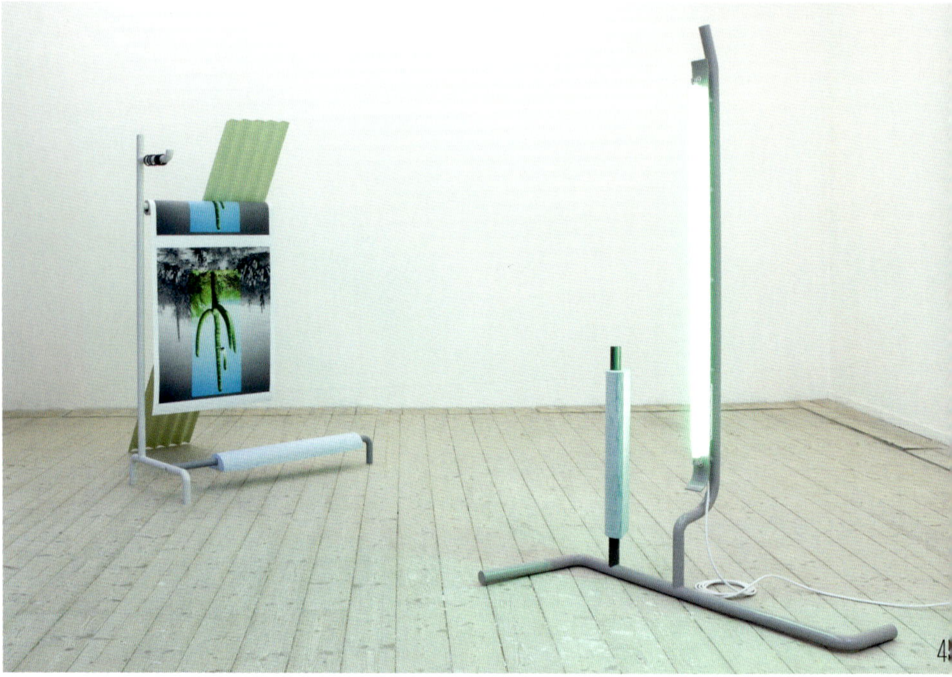

4

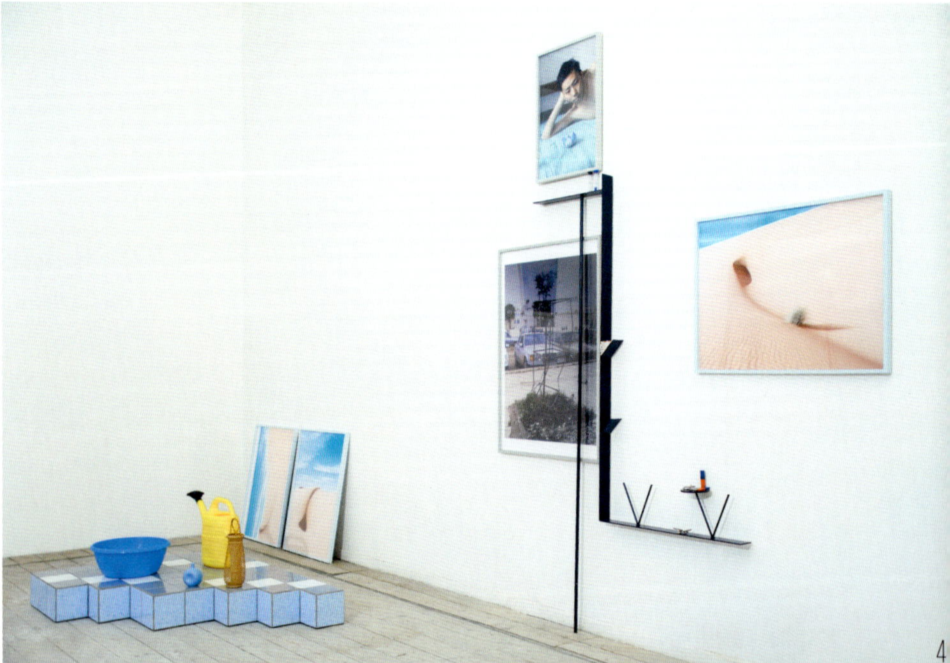

4

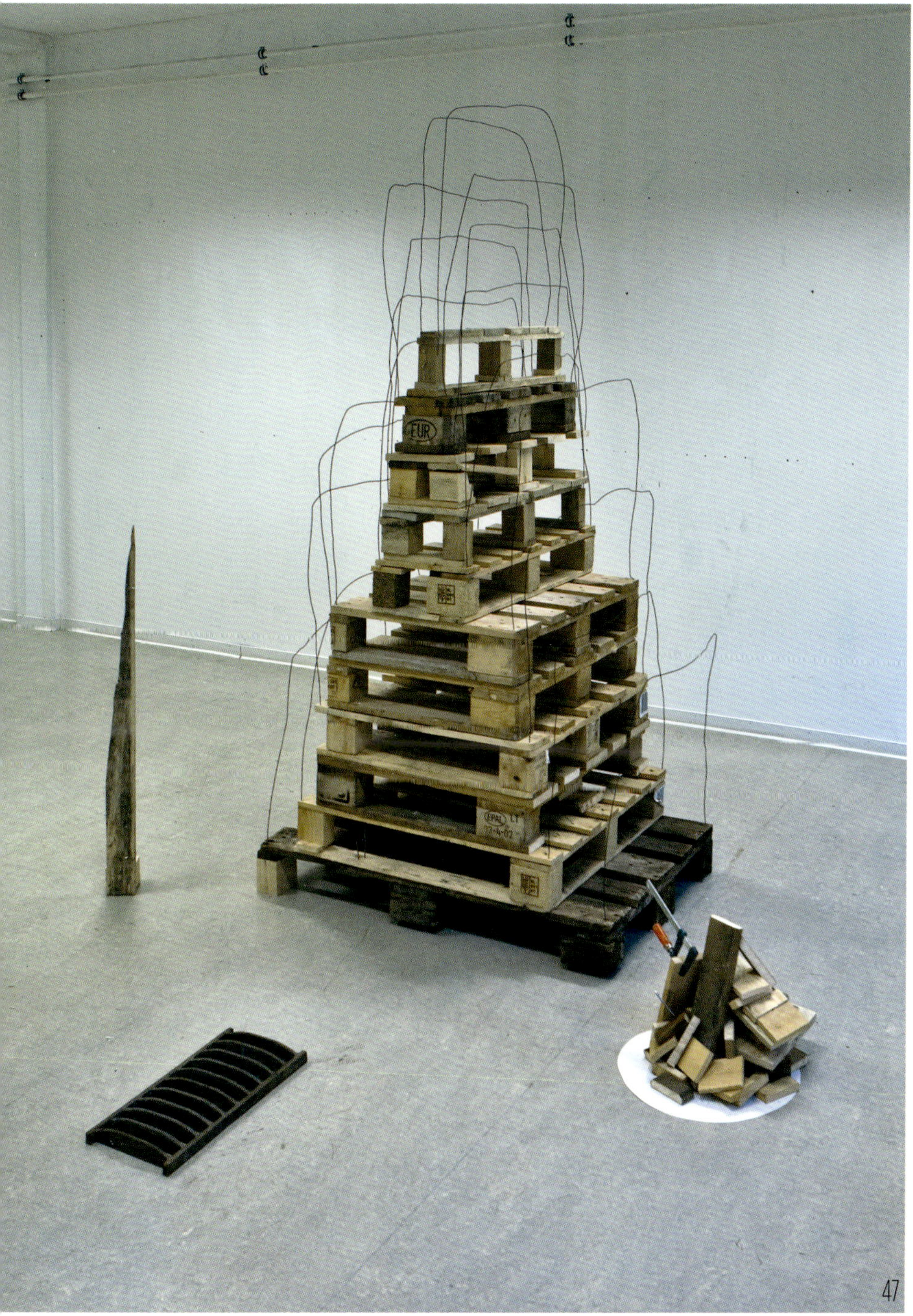

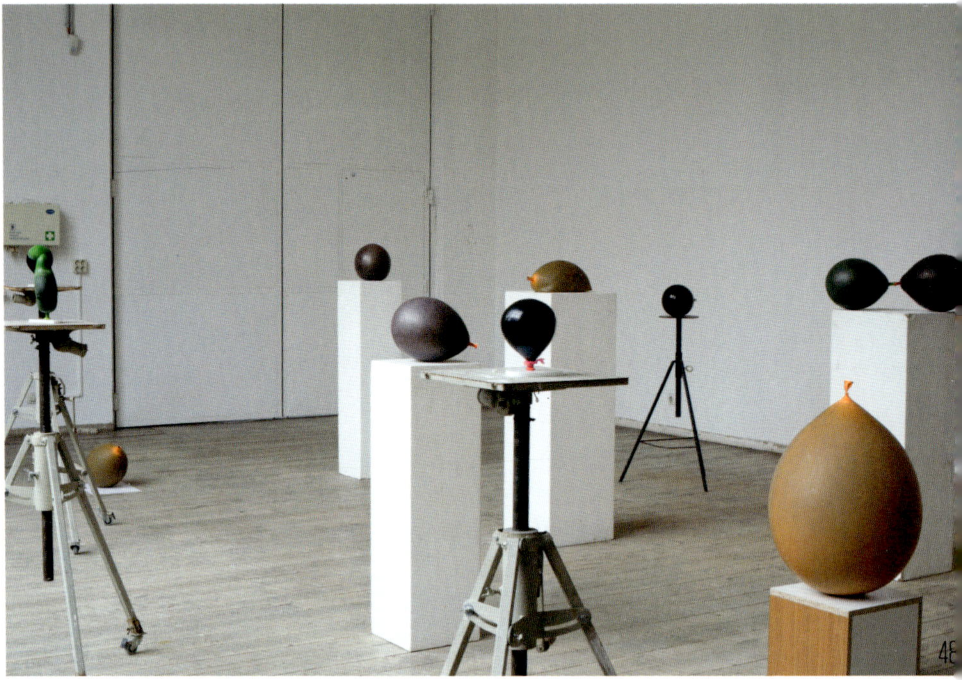

48

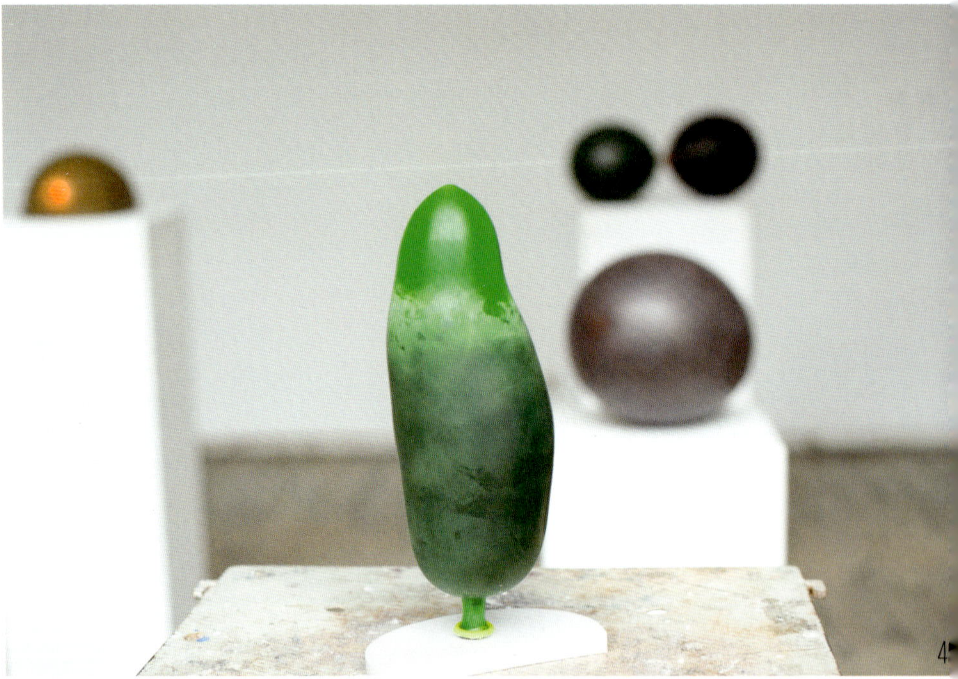

4

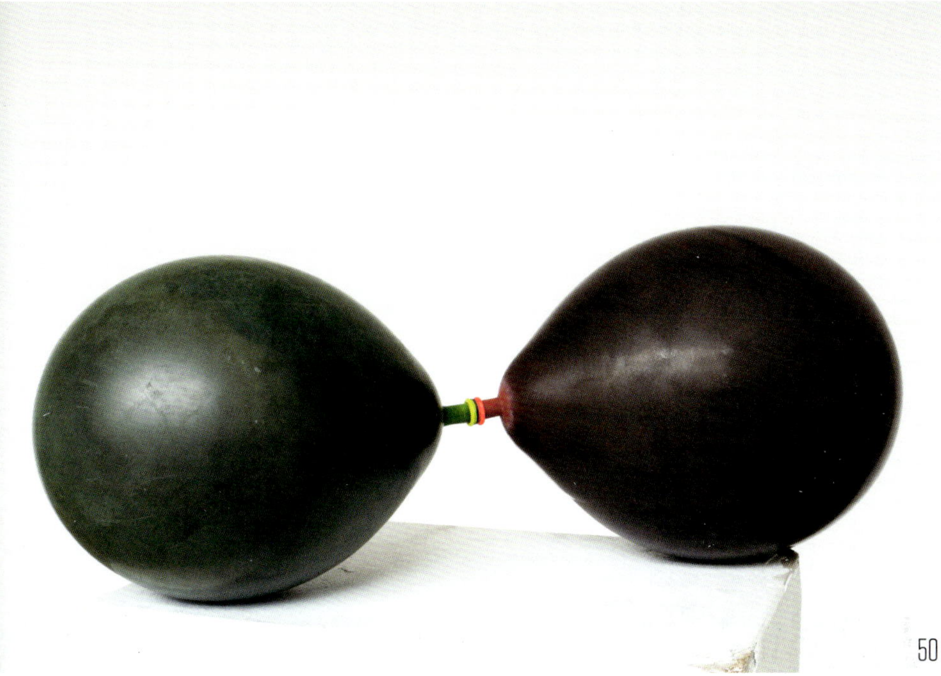

50

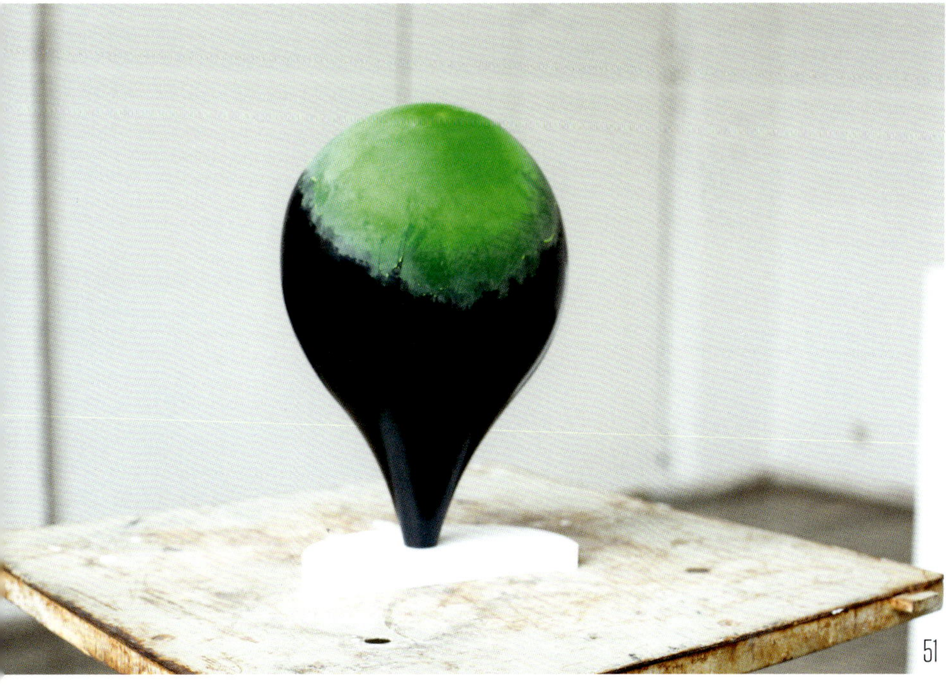

51

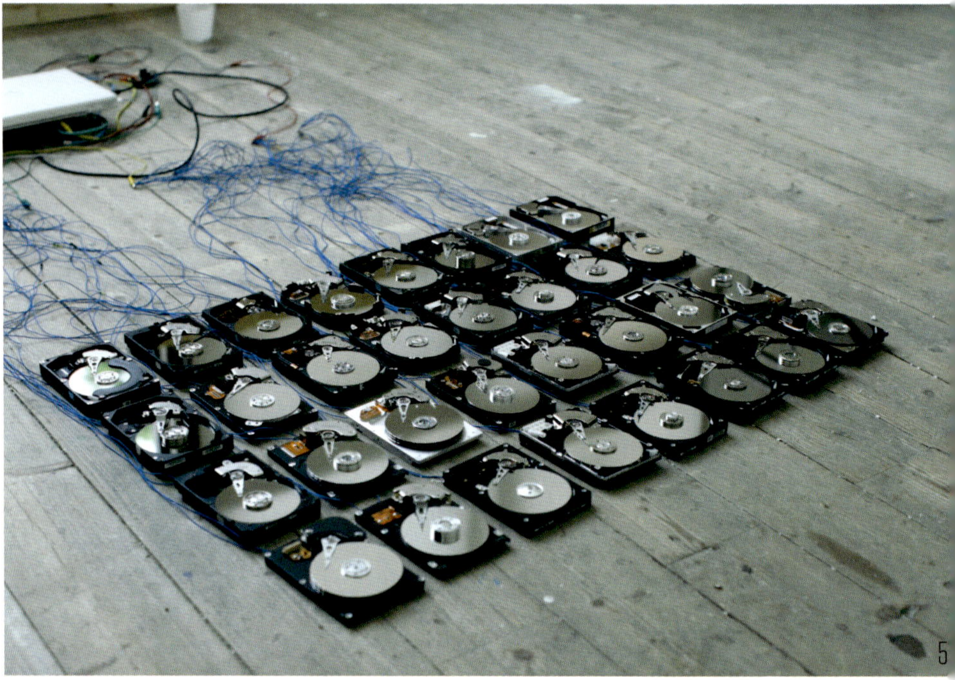

5

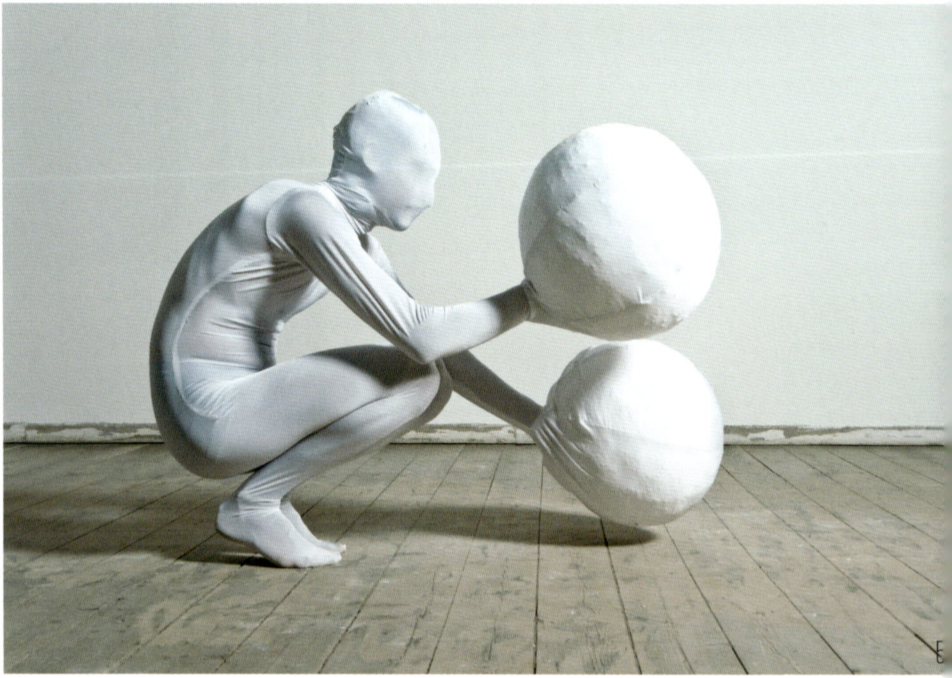

6

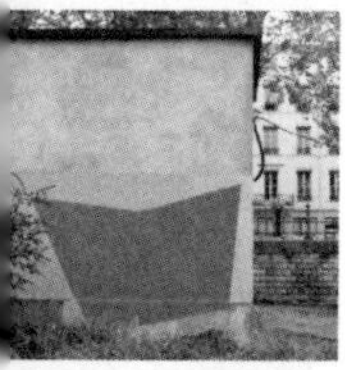

27 **Merlin Kratky** I Think I Think, Lyon — 2011

C-print, 66.5 × 100 cm

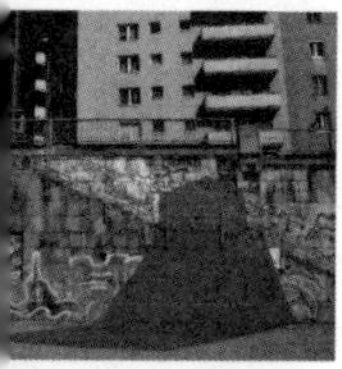

28 **Merlin Kratky** I Think I Think, Vienna — 2010

C-print, 66.5 × 100 cm

Maximum reduction of form allows the viewer to freely interpret every situation in public space that is normally predetermined or informs the public about something specific. This method is used here to make unrestrained consumption or association possible.

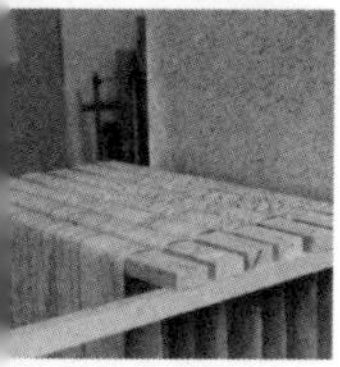

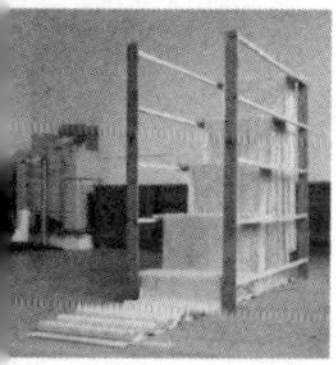

29/30 **Lisa Langeder** Gestettengasse 4a/30, 1030 Vienna — 27 February 2012

Wood, blank newsprint, graphite, 60 × 210 × 175 cm

The five-part storage system consisting of an elongated IKEA shelf is a snapshot of my bedroom wall and floor. I made a graphite rubbing of the wall and floor structure on a blank endless web of newsprint. The work considers the transfer of the private sphere to a material and system with public character.

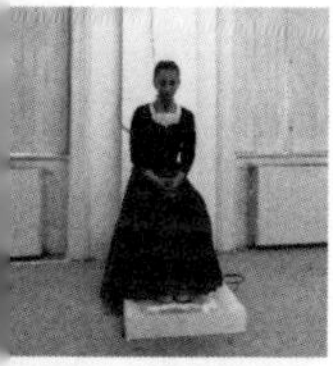

31 **Rebekka Hagg** inspirationsinitiation — 2012

Perfomance

Copper, stage costume, red colour

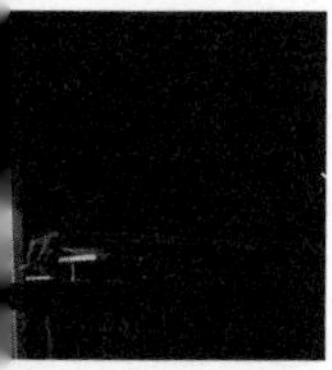

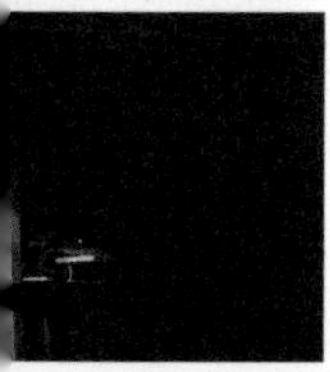

32/33 **Andreas Müller** Dissolution — 2011

HD video, 4:50 min.

The video shows a subject-object shift, which not only reflects their human references but also the need for the presence of humans. In this context the ideas of Jean Baudrillard and his book *Why Hasn't Everything Already Disappeared* are taken up and an extract from it spoken in the video.

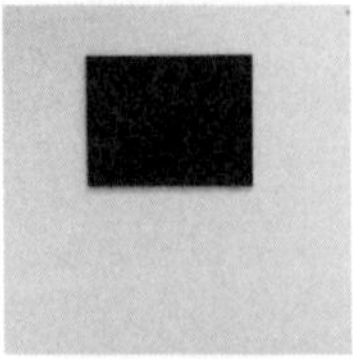

34 **Malin Schoenberg / Florian Regl** I don't love you any more (no.1) 200

Wood, paint, chalk. Size variable

No. 1 shows the end of a relationship. The chalk doesn't love the board any mor and breaks off the relationship by falling. The work shows a variation of the mc ment when the chalk and the board wanted nothing more to do with one anothe The traces remain.

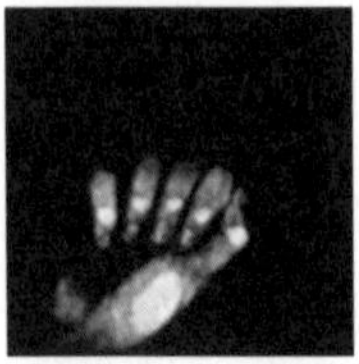

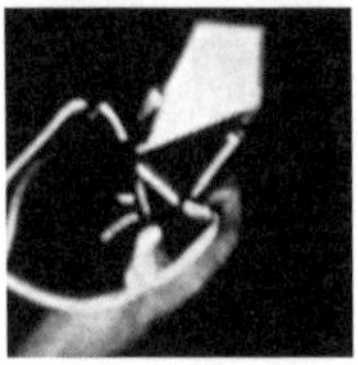

35–38 **Mara Novak** The copy of a copy of a copy as a unique object 201

Stop-motion film on 8 mm (with frames made with a copier), 1:16 min.

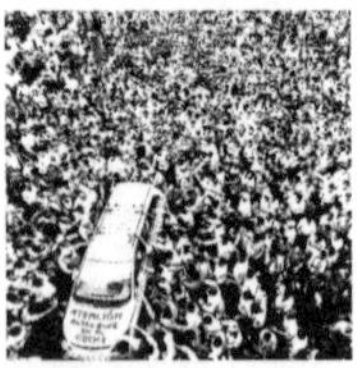

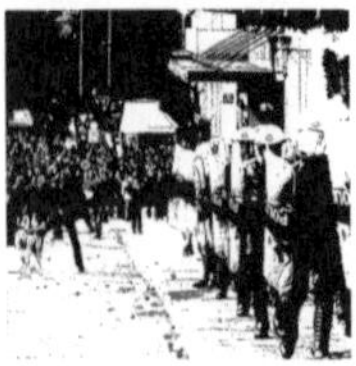

39/40 **Georg Sturmlechner / Gratis G. Strumpf** Before the Rodeo Bike riots, Vienna 1907 20

Silkscreen on linen, wooden frame, 71 × 50.5 cm

In spite of the explosive desire, the question of technical innovation, progres fairer distribution based more on quality and quantity characterized the aura earlier Rodeo Bikes. People knew that the utmost had to be demanded becaus compromises were always made at the expense of lost radicality. Following th worldwide attacks on manufacturers' headquarters, kidnapping of managers an day-long street fighting in cities, and after the deputy managing director 'gyrojoy' was injured by a letter bomb, the company intervened. Criticism wa seen thereafter as a stimulus and no longer regarded as being disruptive.

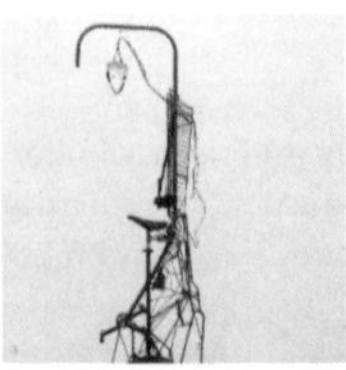

41 **Georg Sturmlechner / Gratis G. Strumpf** Rodeo Bike no. 3 20

Bicycle, supermarket trolley and other metal parts, approx. 75 × 75 × 320 cm

Kaboom ... you must test the improved Rodeo Bike 2.0, the ultimate tribute 'extreme physical sensation'. Now with alpha-wave drugs, safety racing belt ar accelerator weight on the brake lever. Because of massive protests in Centr Europe, North and South America, the Middle East and Asia the manufacture gyrojoy tm felt it necessary to review and improve the safety and excitement the second-generation Rodeo Bikes; the result is described by neuroscientists ar psychoanalysts as epochal. They say that the 'gyroscopic kinetic metaspace' hel recipients with depression, anxiety and neuroses as all sensory perceptions a guided into diametrically opposite paths to those experienced in normal life, pr ducing an objectifying effect and an extra-body sensation. The Rodeo Bike 3 offers limitless fun for young and old, a must for all homes, canteens and scho playgrounds. Test it for free today. You won't get enough of the spinning ecstas

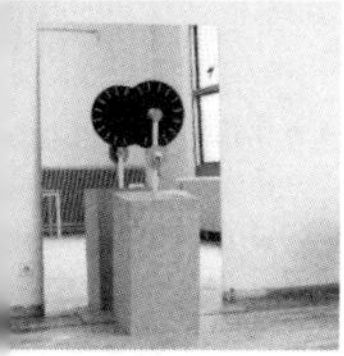

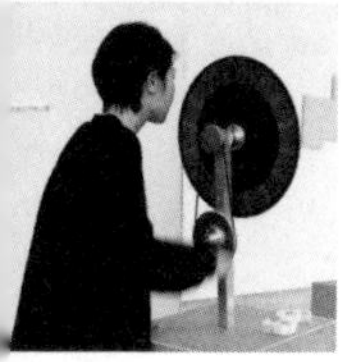

42/43 **Janine Schranz** Phantasmascope 2013

Phenakistoscope on base, 160 × 45 × 45 cm, mirror, table, paper stencils, tape. Installation view

Following up my interest in studying visual shifts in perception, I reconstructed a viewer which was the starting point for my artistic research. The phenakistoscope, also known as phantasmascope, is one of the predecessors of cinematography and is based on the after-image effect. The inventor Joseph Plateau developed the process in Belgium around 1832 to create an illusion of movement in a series of images. My work uses this process to construct and deconstruct images. Visual fragments are set in motion by the machine. They converge or decompose, depending on the speed of the machine. Within this process the viewer comes close to generating a static image. The desire to create a picture that is static is addressed through the movement. The physiological after-images seen by the viewer imitate the fragmented pictures and visualize the search for an image. I am interested in mechanically produced images, perception and illusion created by an analogue machine as a reaction to the overwhelming visual impressions in our digitized world.

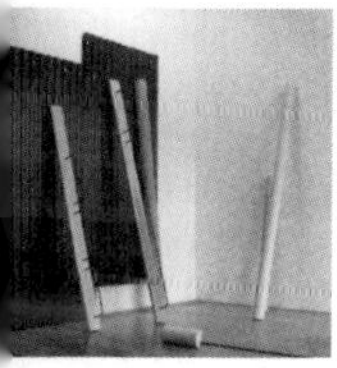

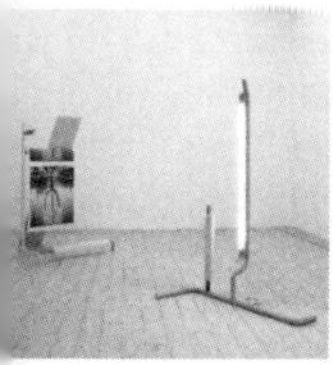

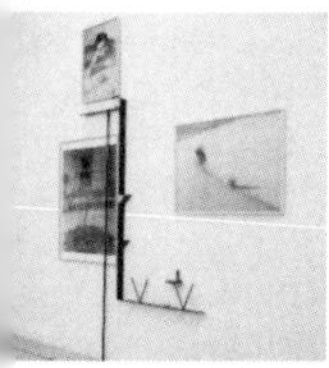

44–46 **Jumpei Shimada** Blind man's buff 2011

Steel, plaster, PVC, paint, pigment. Size variable

Jumpei Shimada Letter from Haniwa 2011

Steel, plaster, PVC, digital print on canvas, paint, pigment. Size variable

Jumpei Shimada Chlorophyll 2013

Steel, plaster, PVC, digital print on canvas, paint, pigment. Size variable

The large-scale installations and sculptures by Jumpei Shimada play with form and materiality. Our daily perception of objects and materials such as sealing and insulation material, foam or tiles and their functional arrangements is challenged by seeing them in new settings. The building materials, which are in fact quite inexpensive, appear shiny and expensive and seem to undergo an increase in value through this processing. The materials move from the outside, where they are functional, to the inside, where they are decorative. They are bare inferences and narrow references to the objective world without becoming concrete in themselves – a 'could be'. The formal strictness and clear, perfect processing suggest a grammatical interpretation, which is resolved by Jumpei Shimada's own material poetry. This repetitive interplay between free form and fixed structure thus defines our way of seeing, which alternates as a result between sense and nonsense, brittle aestheticism and pure beauty. They are endless works, optionally combinable – the resultant object always a reflection of its predecessor.

Text: Manfred Wiplinger

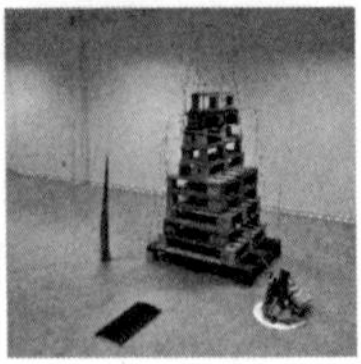

47 **Jakob Zacharias Steiner** What we worship 201

Mixed media. Installation view

This installation confronts visitors as they enter the room. A hierarchical peda
gogical mood is created by emphasizing the axis of vision and the arrangemen
of the rows of chairs. The inferred symmetry and height of the work underscor
this mood. A sculptural interpretation of a triptychon or an approximation of a
archaic heathen shrine. Europool pallets of different widths are positioned on th
bonfire of history or the sacrificial altar of identity. They represent the differer
terms of office of the Austrian Federal Chancellors of the Second Republic.
three-dimensional visualization of a precisely controlled approach to history a
the identity-forming element of a nation.

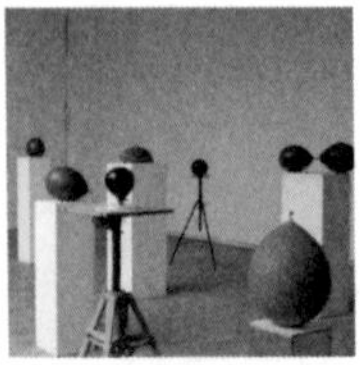

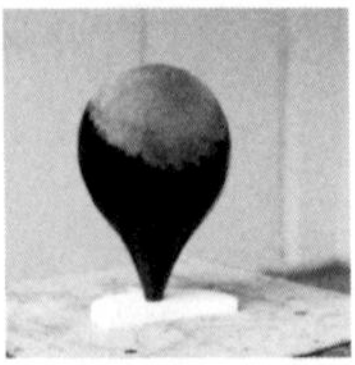

48–51 **Tim Wandelt** Untitled Series 20

Epoxy resin, balloon. Size variable

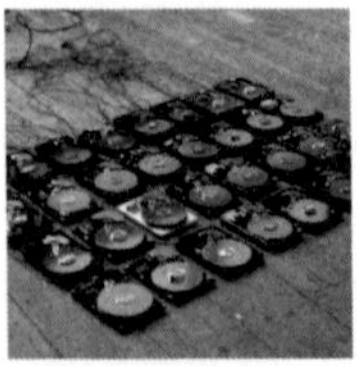

52 **Claus Diwisch** Hvar er lagið mitt 20

Hard disk drives, approx. 100 × 200 cm

In this work open hard disk drives serve as sound transducers. The coil that nc
mally positions the read/write head transforms the electrical sound informatic
into acoustic signals. The vibrations of the composition made specially for th
structure can be clearly seen on the R/W head and the sounds heard as throug
a conventional loudspeaker.

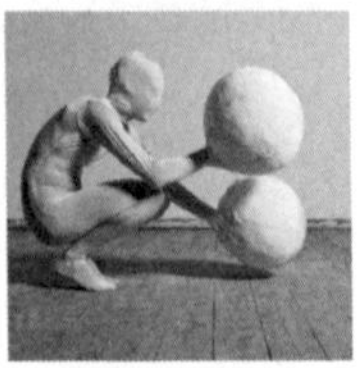

53 **Leander Schönweger** Fahel; Sirius A 2

Performance. Photo: Elfie Semotan

transdisciplinary thought

KÖBBERLING / KALTWASSER Artists, Berlin

APRIL 2011

The City as Resource

Lecture

LIBERATE THE SYNERGIES EXISTING BETWEEN ARTISTIC DISCIPLINES, THEORY AND PRACTICE, CONCEPTS AND ARTISTIC TECHNIQUES, PRODUCTION AND COMMUNICATION.

& action

TIMM ULRICHS Artist, Hannover/Munster/Berlin

MAY 2011

Life & Work Lecture

The Total Artist Speaks about his Work

Everyday Life as Adventure Workshop

transce

ELSY LAHNER Curator, Vienna

JUNE 2011

Portfolio Review

ndence

CANDICE BREITZ Artist, Berlin

JUNE 2011

Questions for a Stranger

Lecture and Workshop

CHRISTIAN HÖLLER

ELIMINATING THE HYPHEN

The Transdisciplinary Basis of Contemporary Art

For a long time one of the leading ideas in art was of expansion, of breaking down and crossing boundaries. Throughout virtually the entire twentieth century, one can identify phases characterized by an intention to dissolve and overcome established boundaries in genre, disciplines or media; phases driven with varying impetus and with differing goals. To recap briefly on three of these phases: Whereas the (first) historical avant-garde movement in the early twentieth century strongly aspired to dissolve art and reunite it with 'real life', from the 1950s onwards a trend towards expansion emerged, starting to confront art with the outside world and the field of *non-art* (drawing on Duchamp). Pop Art, Minimal Art, Conceptual Art, Performance, Video Art etcetera are all variations on this confrontation. In the more recent past, starting in the 1980s, a new breaking down of boundaries has come to the fore[1]: the unremitting attempts to expand art into other academic disciplines.

MARTIN WALDE Artist, Vienna

OCTOBER 2011

Alien Substance

Lecture

This endeavour has only recently been given the 'stamp of approval' under the buzzword of 'artistic research', with the outcome that there are increasing efforts to entrench this within institutional frameworks. According to a current creed, art is simply obliged to transcend existing limitations in terms of discipline, genre, and media; indeed as it strives to expand, it cannot help be anything but transdisciplinary. Yet what is the lie of the land as these single disciplines are seemingly being left behind? Haven't the disciplines (and similarly the 'discipliners') been overcome a long time ago? Should we really still be demanding a crossover when every core discipline seems to have long since been 'hollowed out'? Or is this primarily about invoking utopian potential that perhaps is not that easy to put into practice and quite possibly fulfils more of a rhetorical function?

These questions can perhaps only be answered by pausing for a moment and viewing the issue in a bottom-up way. The crux of the matter would then not be how art has set out to traverse other disciplines on a grand scale, however far removed these are, but something far more fundamental. How exactly does art initiate 'articulations' with a particular adjacent field? For a long time this bringing together, this bearing across into a *single* adjoining milieu, was known by the term 'crossover' and it produced a specific type of 'hyphenated

---

INGEBORG STROBL Artist, Vienna **OCTOBER 2011**

What We Know is What We See Lecture
The Subjectivity of Perception / Preference / Result
Workshop

figure': the artist-musician, artist-engineer, artist-ethnographer, even the artist-politician, and so on. This so-called 'hyphenated art' started to spread to such an extent that it gradually dawned on people that a true essence of art had possibly never existed but that in retrospect artistic practice had always consisted of an 'articulation' with one of its sister disciplines – an articulation that was aesthetically composed and for the most part media-reflexive.[2] The confusing part of this 'hyphenated syndrome', however, was that for the longest time there was a lack of clarity as to which criteria should be used to evaluate the results. Must an artist-DJ be judged by the standards of the music and clubbing industry? Or does he have his own set rules and can he work in something akin to a protected field? Moreover, there is the added difficulty that ethnographic or documentary works presented in the context of art can be easily extolled as a form of 'knowledge production' and yet still implicitly carry over the rules and assessment criteria from the corresponding field (ethnography, documentarism). One of the consequences of leaving your own discipline to return with 'foreign' wares is that criteria from the 'foreign' start to take effect in the original field. For a long time 'hyphenated art' wanted to dismiss this by presenting itself as the epitome of an up-to-the-minute avant-garde, breaking down and crossing boundaries, and deeming itself immune from non-art stan-

---

NICOLE SIX / PAUL PETRITSCH Artists, Vienna **NOVEMBER 2011**

Sound and Fury, Verticality and Free Fall

Lecture

dards of criticism. However, in a rather unforgiving field like contemporary art this only works (and worked) up to a point.

The positive side of this scenario is that the bigger picture, indeed the global relationship between the disciplines, no longer seemed set in stone but was guided towards a gradual change. Just as 'hyphenated art' could not merely combine the best of two worlds into something bigger and better (without lugging along some tiresome baggage from both), traversing boundaries between disciplines never just resulted in a superior, quasi 'vintage' mixture without affecting the constellation between the two fields. It is exactly at this point that the idea of transdisciplinarity starts to take effect. This was not devised in order to introduce a new theoretical field or a new method, as can be traced in the academic theories. Instead its proponents saw it as a 'research principle and an academic organizational form'[3], which perhaps in the long run will one day result in a new relationship between the disciplines. Transdisciplinarity is therefore not a new subject, and certainly not a separate discipline on a higher plane, but rather a 'research principle' that at best opens up the disciplines to one another. So transdisciplinarity – in contrast to multidisciplinarity – does not simply combine the best from the different parts into a cumulative hyphen 'daisy chain': the artist-as-philosopher-as-politician-as-social engineer etc. Instead, the *transdisciplinary*

FRANZ SCHUH Writer, Vienna

NOVEMBER 2011

Right Senses

Lecture

basis of today's art production heralds a changed constellation between all these fields (philosophy, politics, social engineering etc.), not as a fait accompli, however, but as a guiding although never truly attainable horizon. This would also render obsolete the variation of breaking down art's boundaries through selectively picking and choosing from the results of another field and then presenting these as a novelty or accomplishment in one's own discipline.

Therefore taking transdisciplinarity seriously as an extended basis, or indeed a research principle behind contemporary art production requires a change in the relationship between all these fields. Criteria from appropriated ethnography, music or film documentaries should not just be dismissed (as one imagines oneself on 'genuine artistic turf' where these criteria are not so strictly applied), but should be explicitly incorporated in the extended practice of art. Aspects from these disciplines should be directly linked with an aesthetic approach so that artistic and academic appear inseparable and ultimately the gravitational fields between the disciplines merge so completely as to create a new, shared plateau. The goal would not be 'art-*as*-ethnography', 'art-*as*-urbanism', 'art-*as*-welfare' etc. – all of this always smacks a little of an alibi case, so as not to say false labelling (treating something that works well elsewhere as 'art'; claiming X is Y). On the contrary, every-

---

BERNHARD LEITNER SoundSpace, Artist, Vienna

NOVEMBER 2011

SoundBodyBodySpace

Lecture

Performance SOUND LIB in Fluc

thing established within a single discipline and then incorporated in production should engender a completely unprecedented configuration where X does not stand for Y, but instead X, Y, Z head towards a *new* and shared whole in which the different ingredients cannot be identified as belonging to separate fields.

Being 'established in a single discipline' is the key phrase, partly because it contributes to countering the admittedly abstract nature of this concept. 'Disciplinary competencies remain … the fundamental prerequisites for tasks defined as transdisciplinary; yet they are no longer sufficient to successfully fulfil research tasks arising from classic subjects and disciplines.'[4] Jürgen Mittelstraß, who thus advocates a *methodological transdisciplinarity,* by no means wishes to abandon single disciplines, as is indeed true of the majority of this concept's champions. Similarly in the field of art, where centres and research units for transdisciplinarity are proliferating, there is an awareness of the difficulty in overcoming disciplinarity (in the sense of well-founded, methodologically distinct separate subjects). Florian Dombois, for instance, who founded the transdisciplinary subject 'Y' at the Hochschule der Künste in Bern, envisages an 'interdisciplinarity building

continued on page 102

SHADY EL NOSHOKATY Artist, Curator, Cairo

NOVEMBER 2011

Stammer – A Frozen History Lecture

Visual Creative Statements Workshop

From the Personal to the Global Game

TransArts stands for integrative project orientation instead of organisational and subject fragmentation as well as project work based on individual responsibility.

CHRIS HARING Choreographer, Art Director of Liquid Loft, Vienna **NOVEMBER 2011**

Eroticism of the Foreign Body Lecture

The Absent Body Workshop

From Impression to Expression

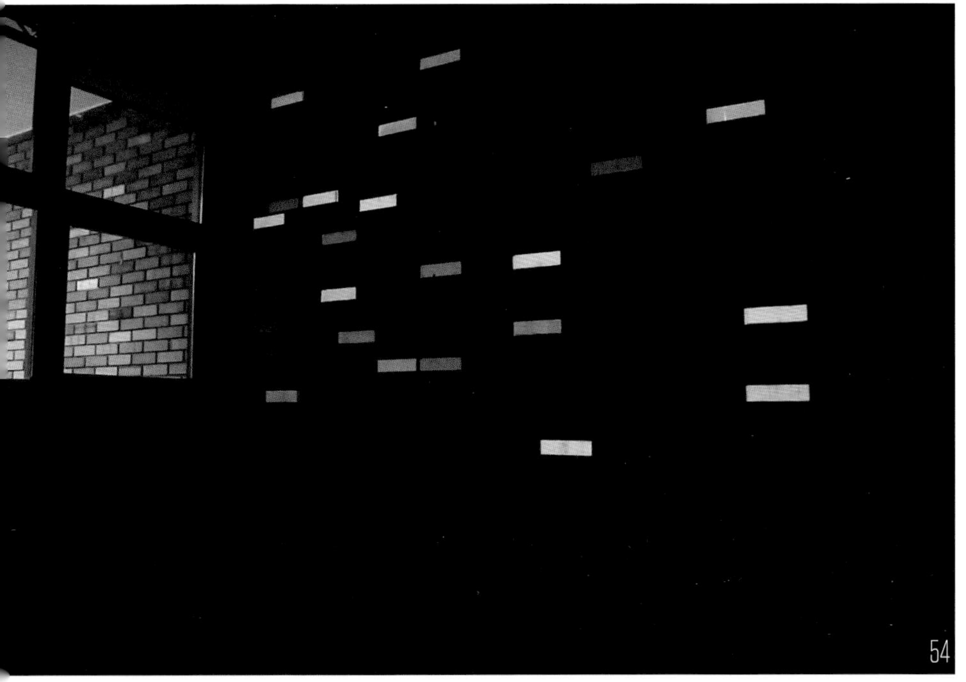
54

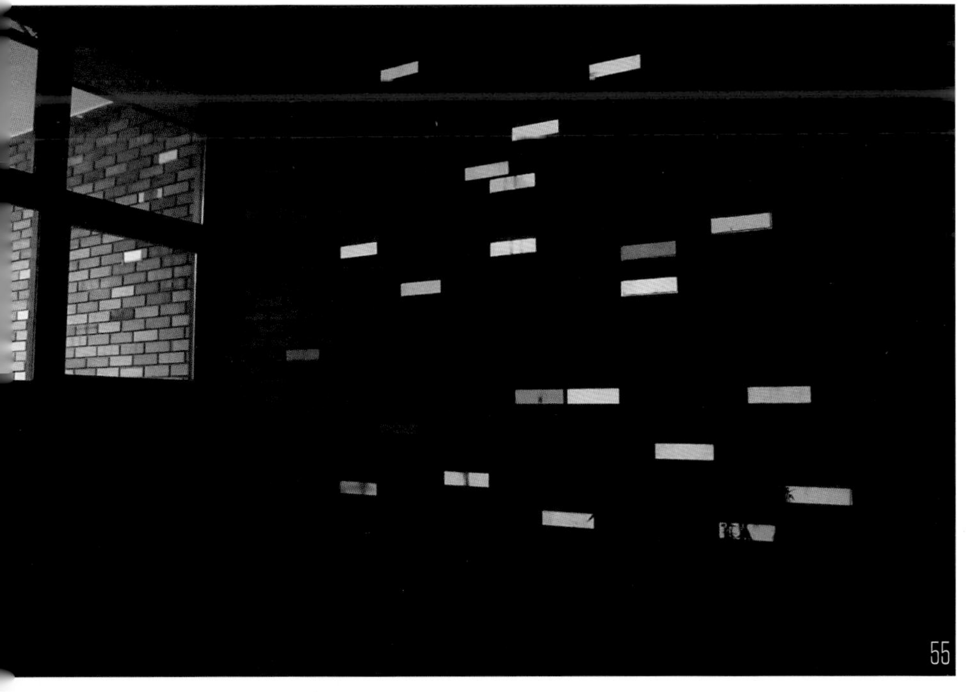
55

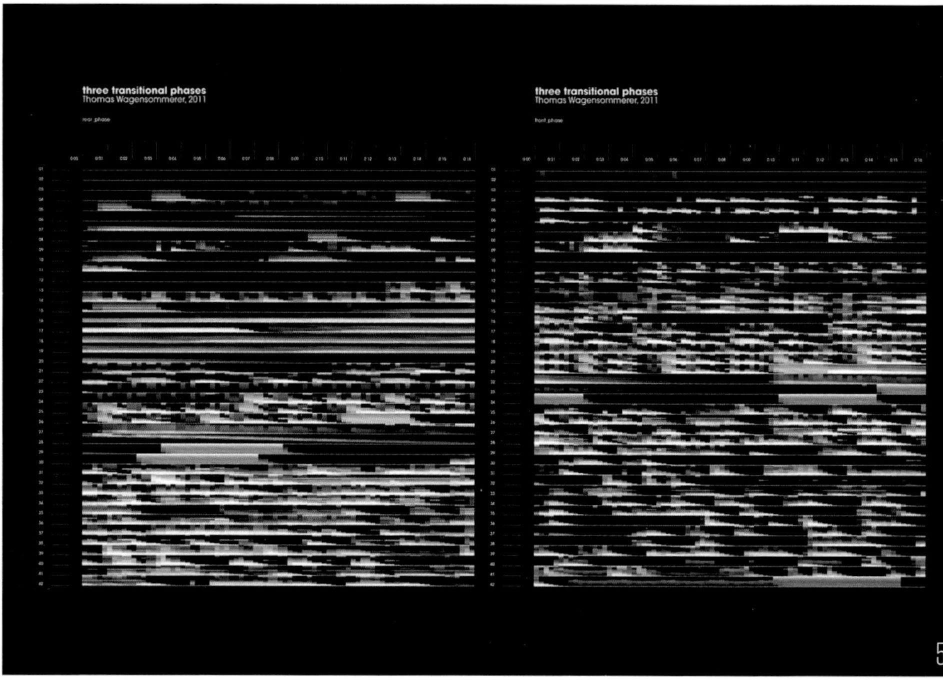
three transitional phases
Thomas Wagensommerer, 2011
rear_phase
three transitional phases
Thomas Wagensommerer, 2011
front_phase

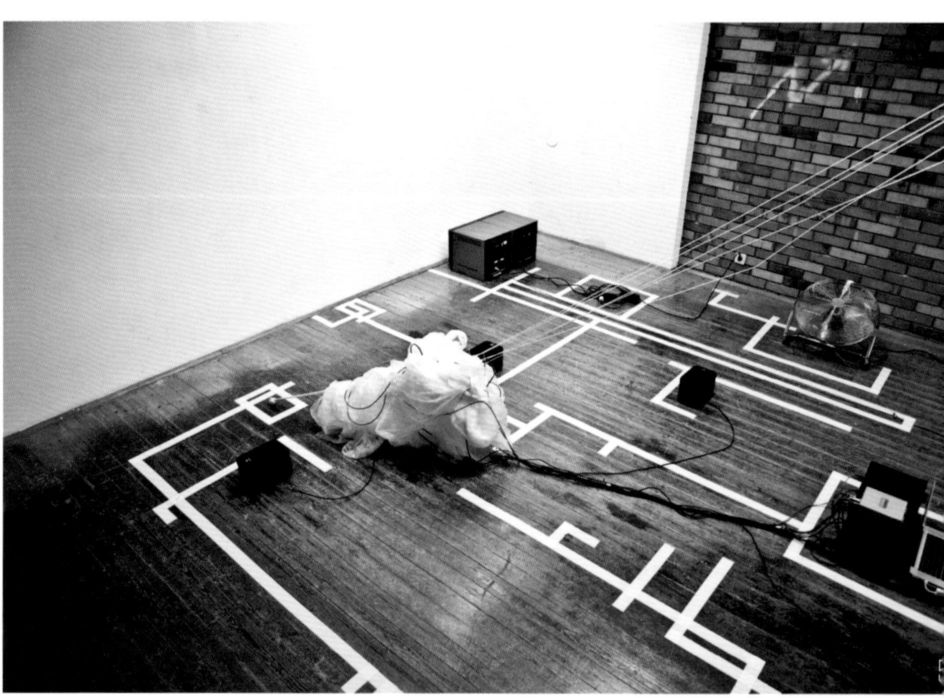

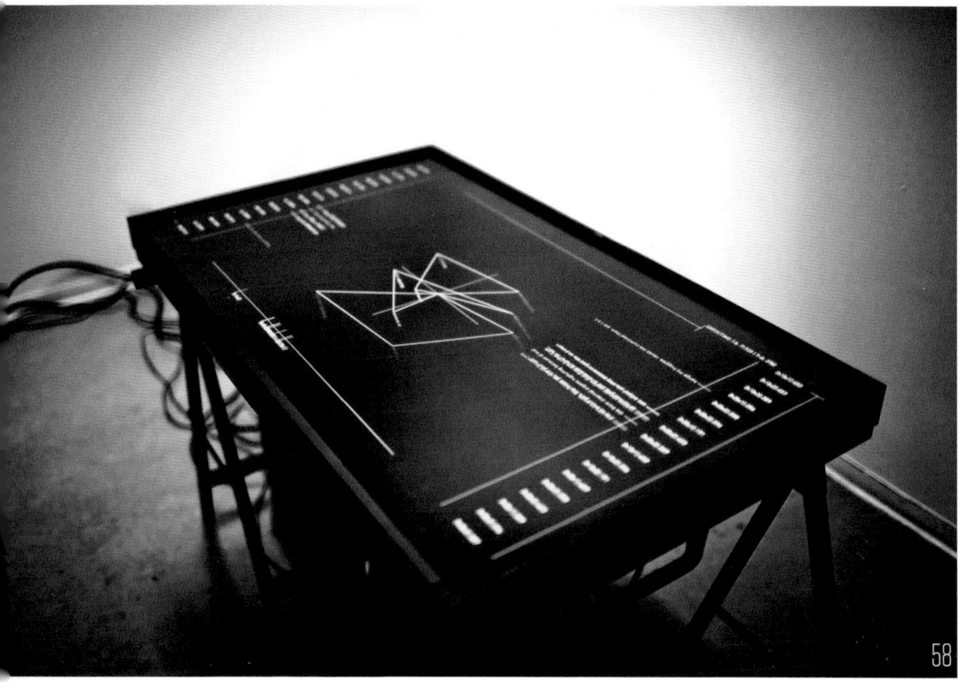

58

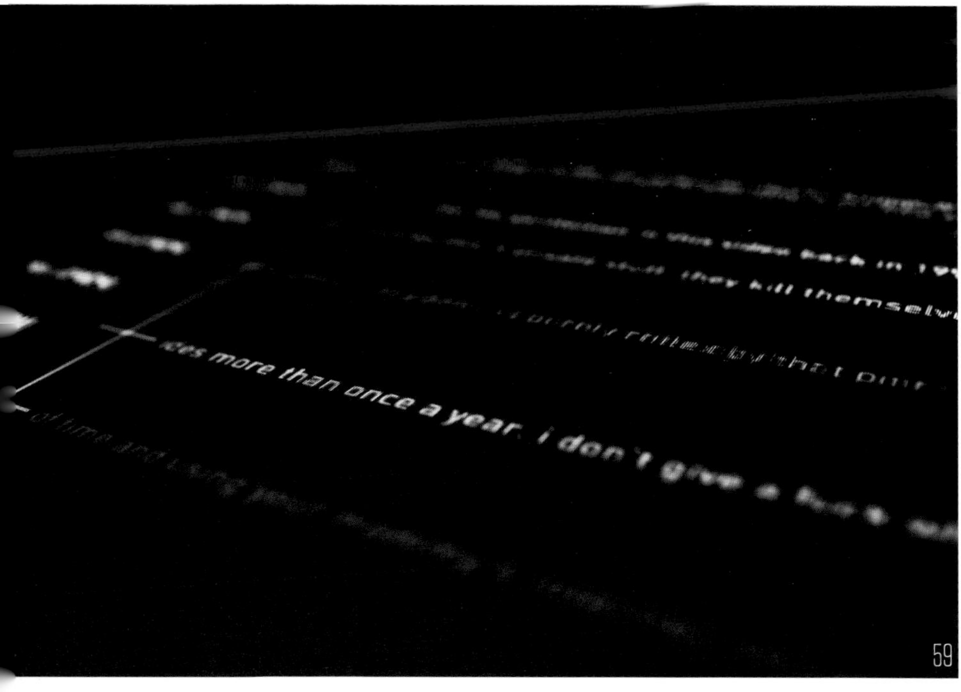

59

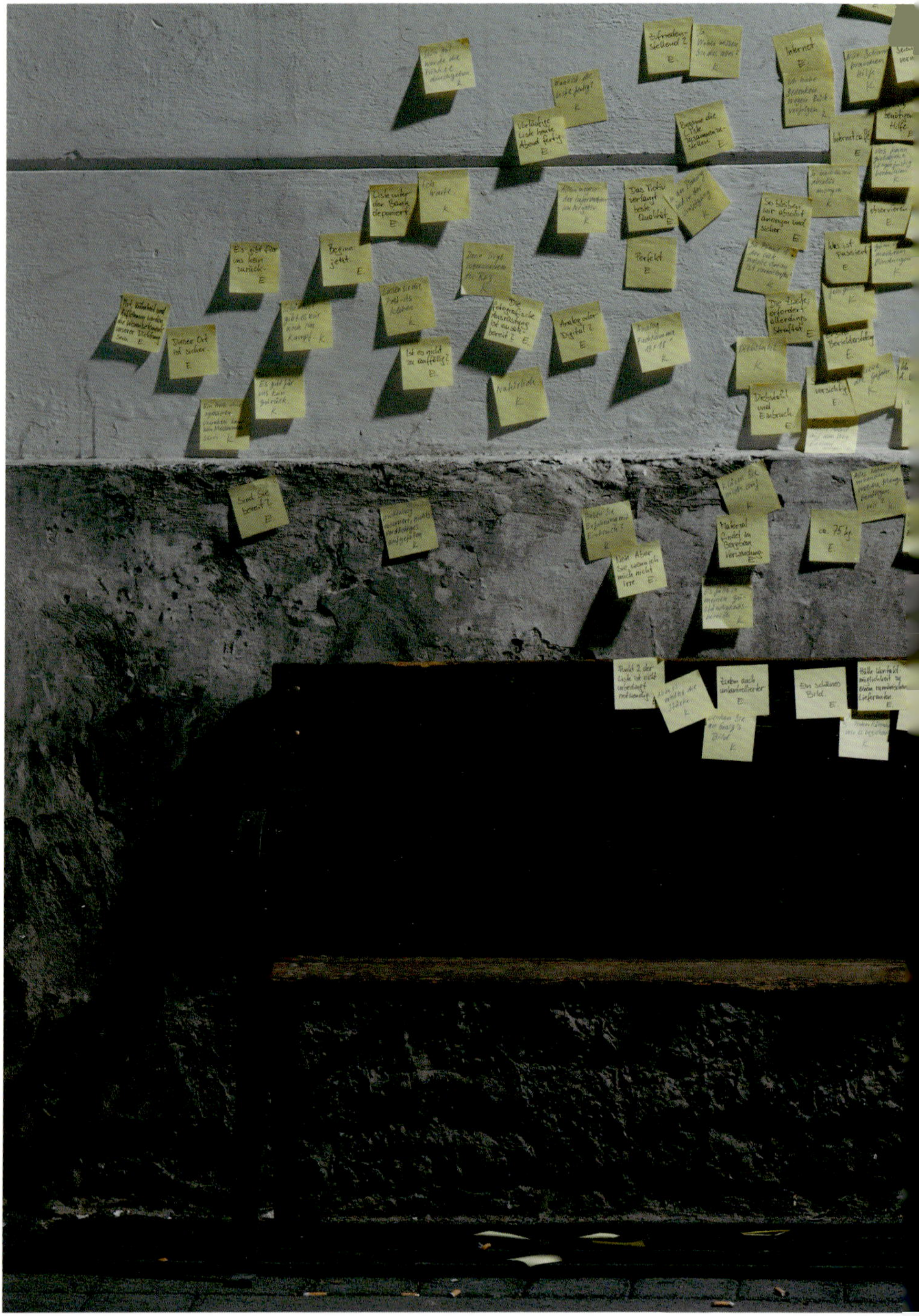
Internet
Perfekt
Natürlich
Sind Sie bereit?
Ein schönes Bild.
ca. 75 kg
Diebstahl und Einbruch
Dieser Ort ist sicher.
Beginn jetzt.
Analog oder Digital?
Das Motiv verlangt beste Qualität

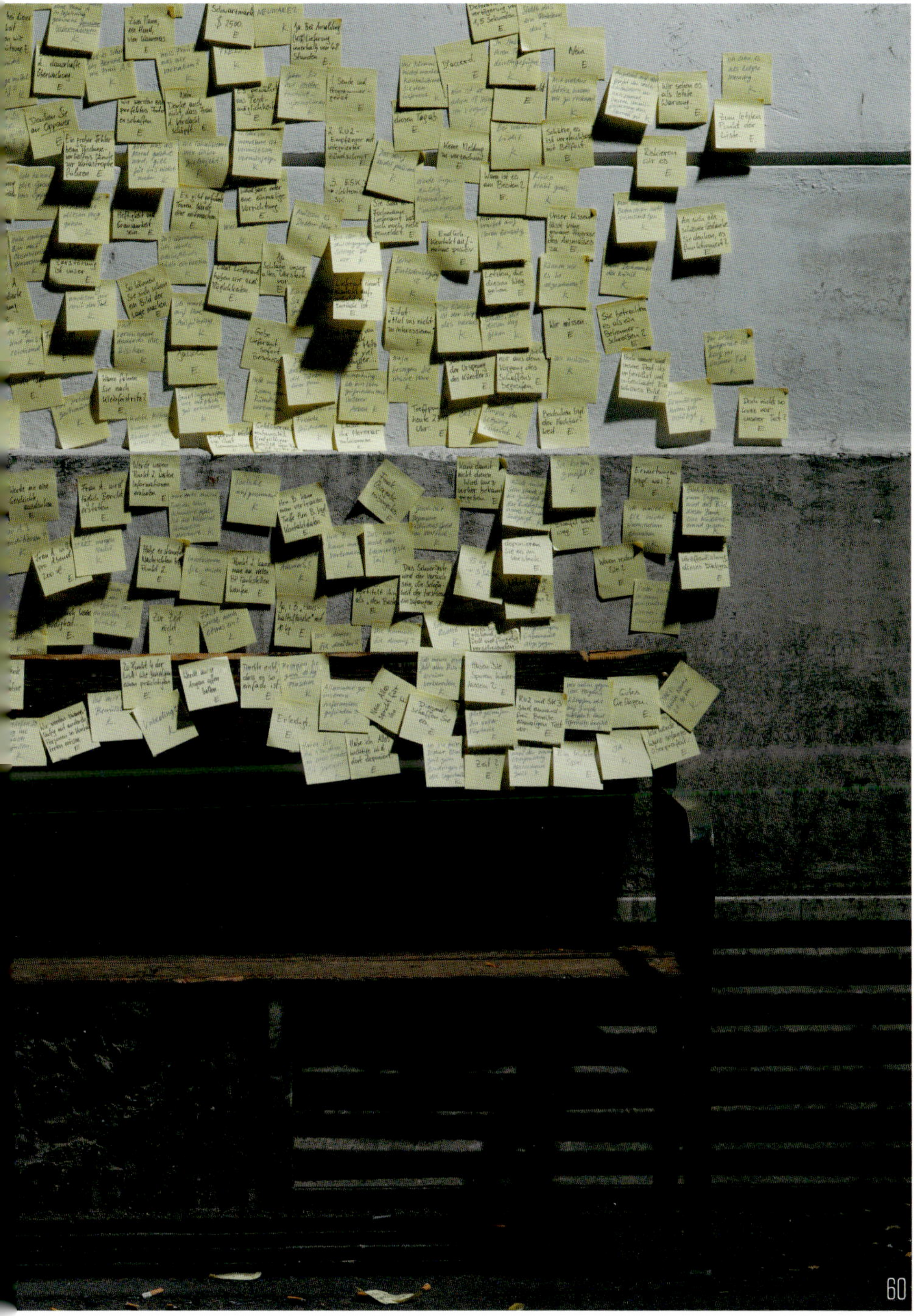

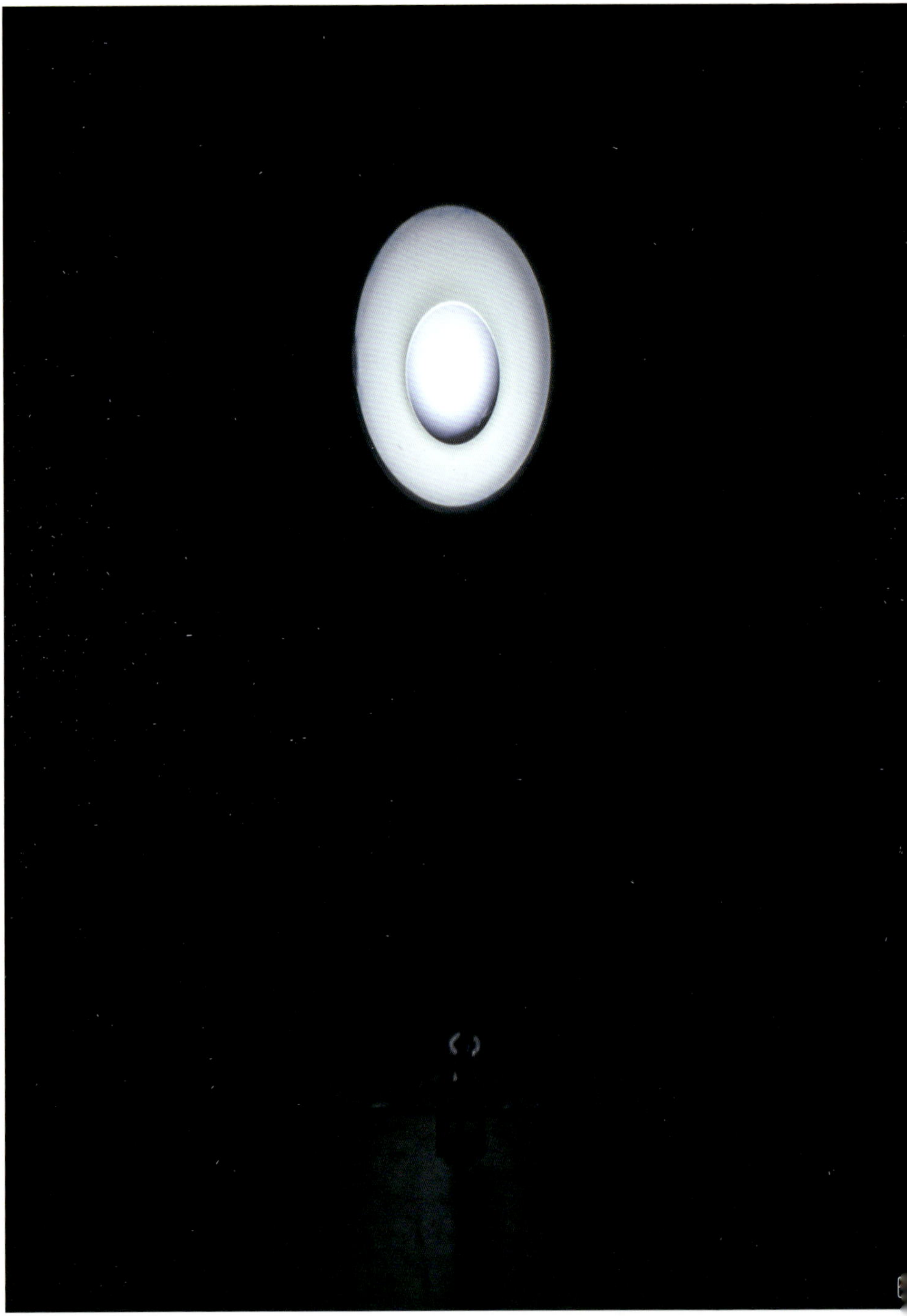

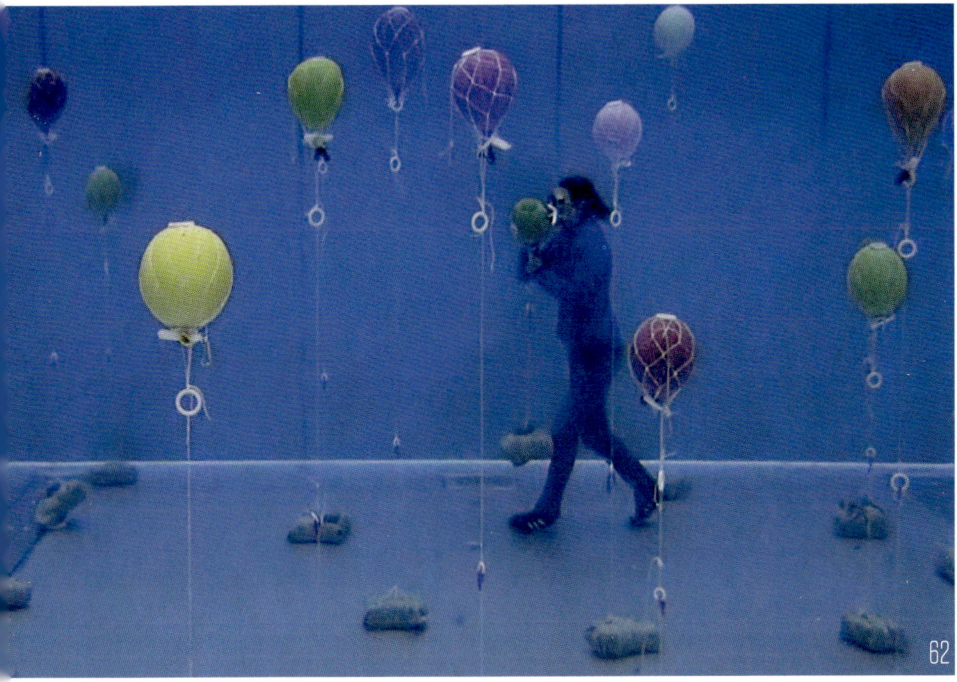

62

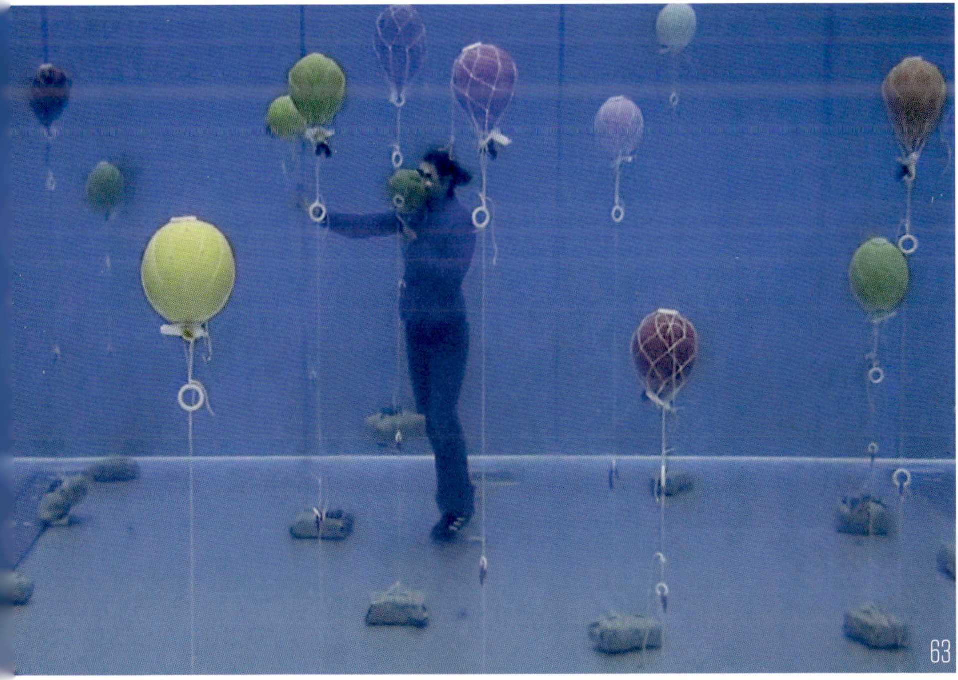

63

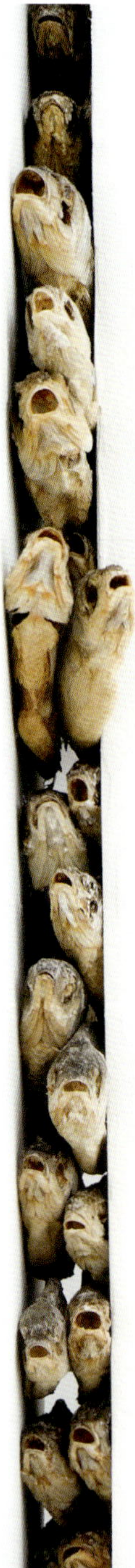

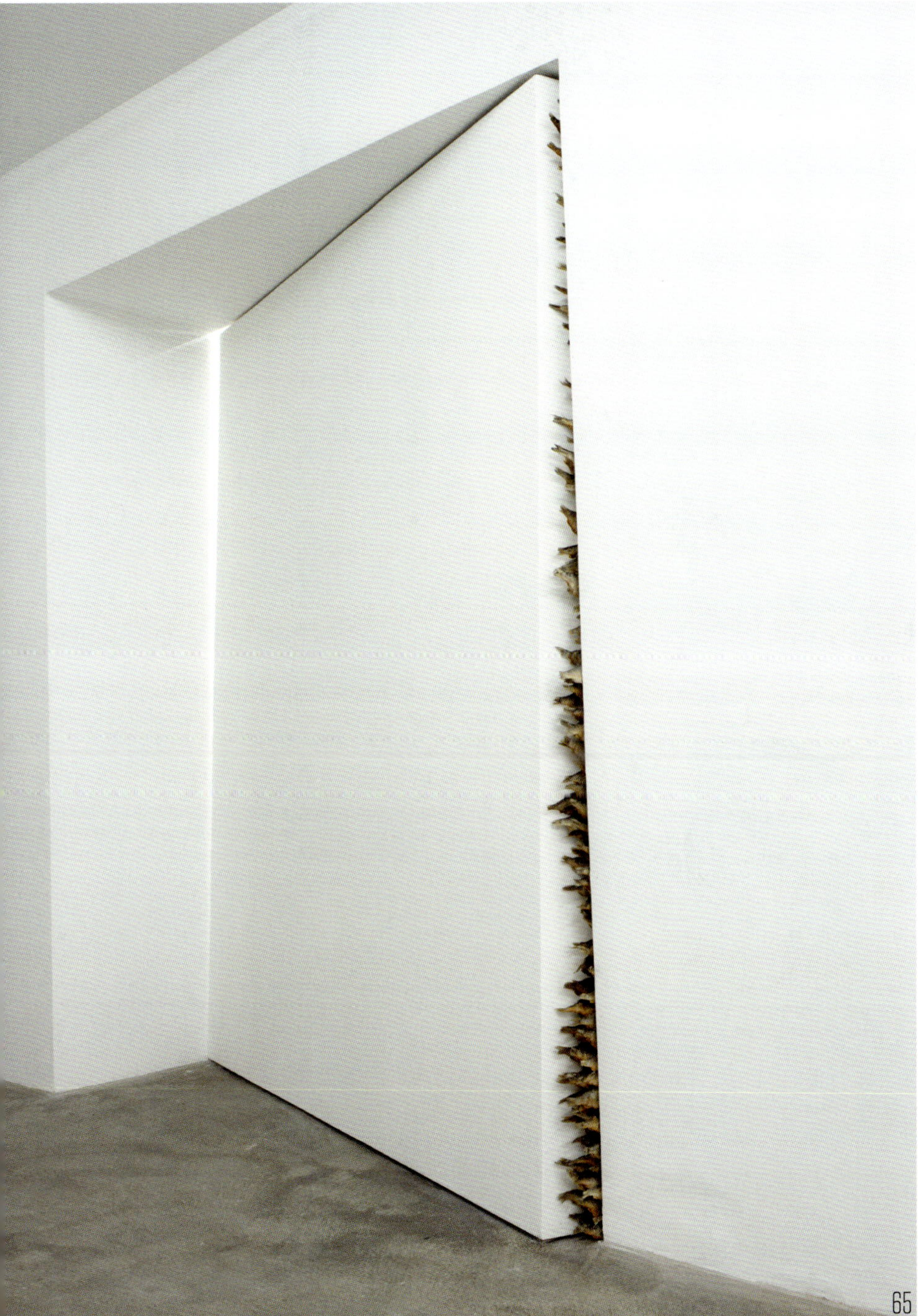

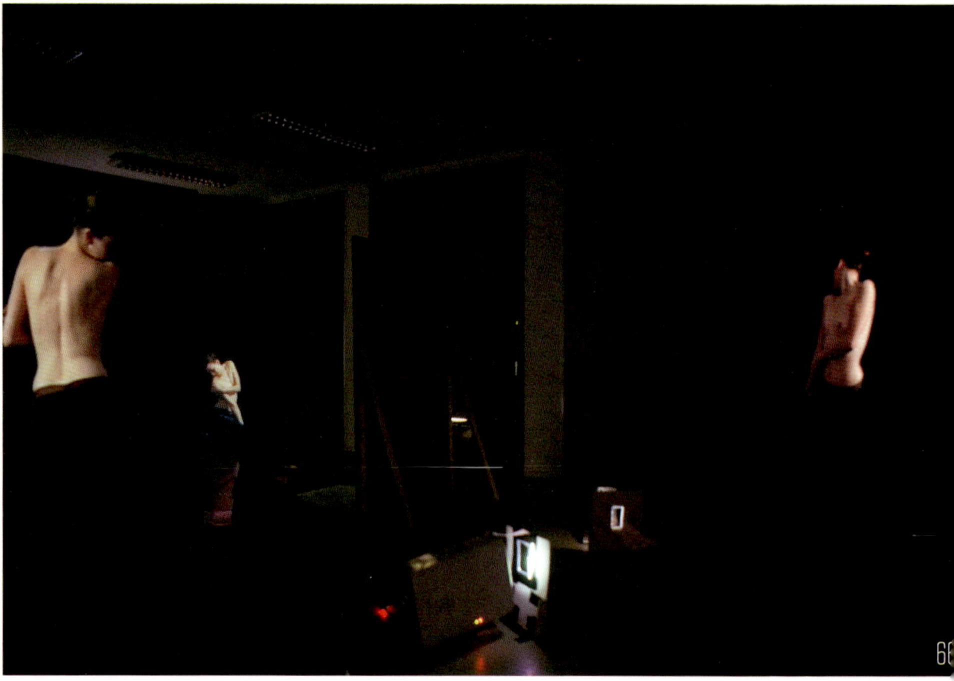
66

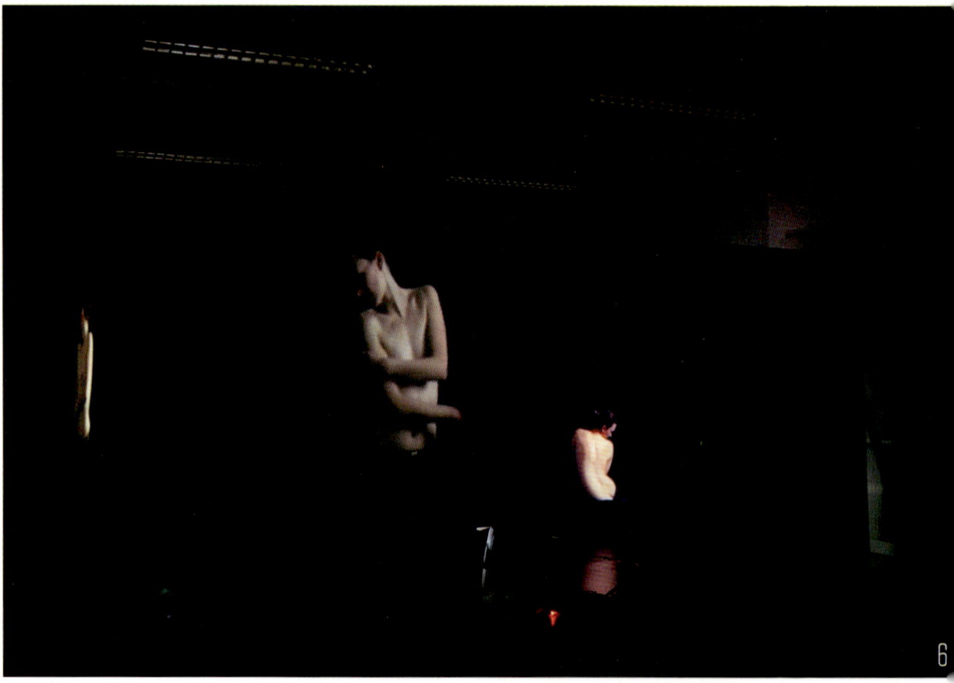
6

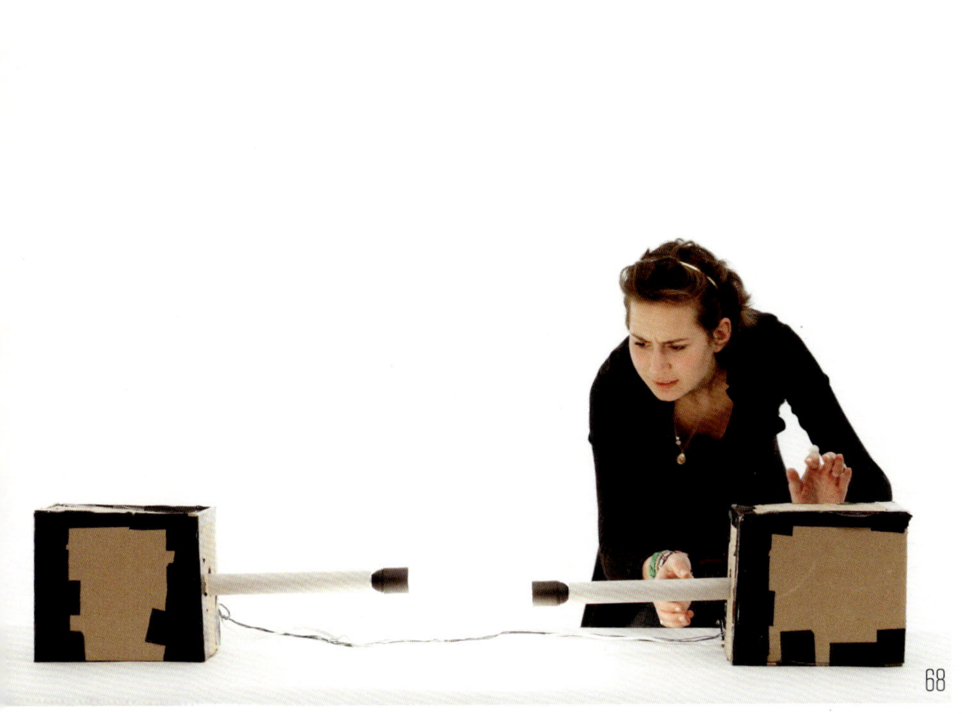

68

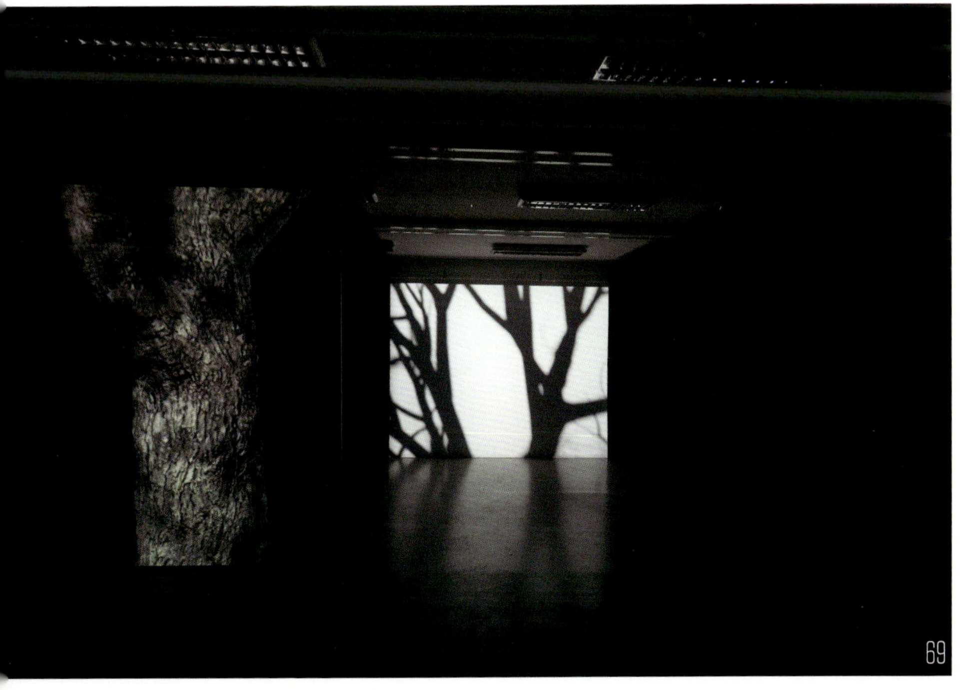

69

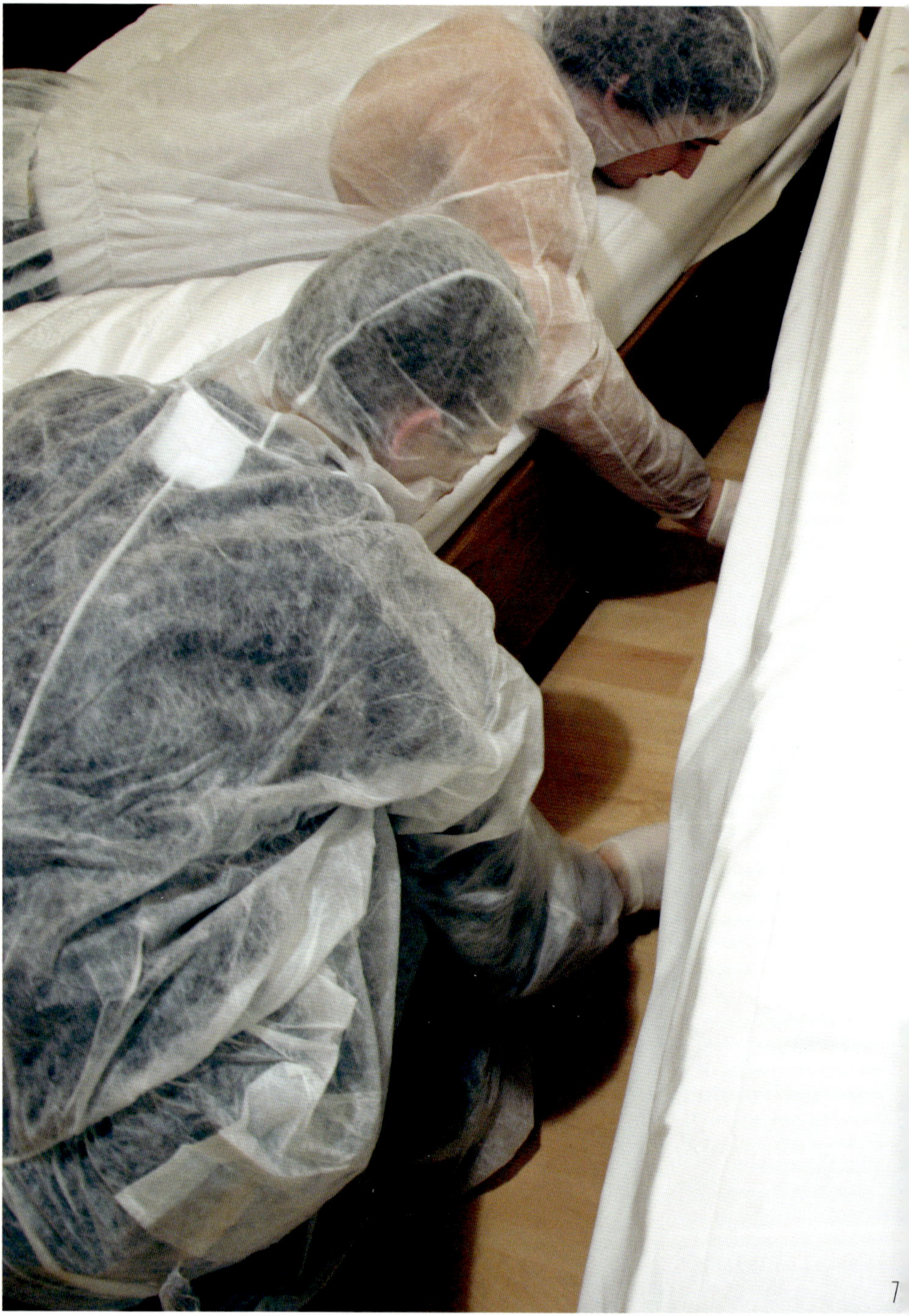

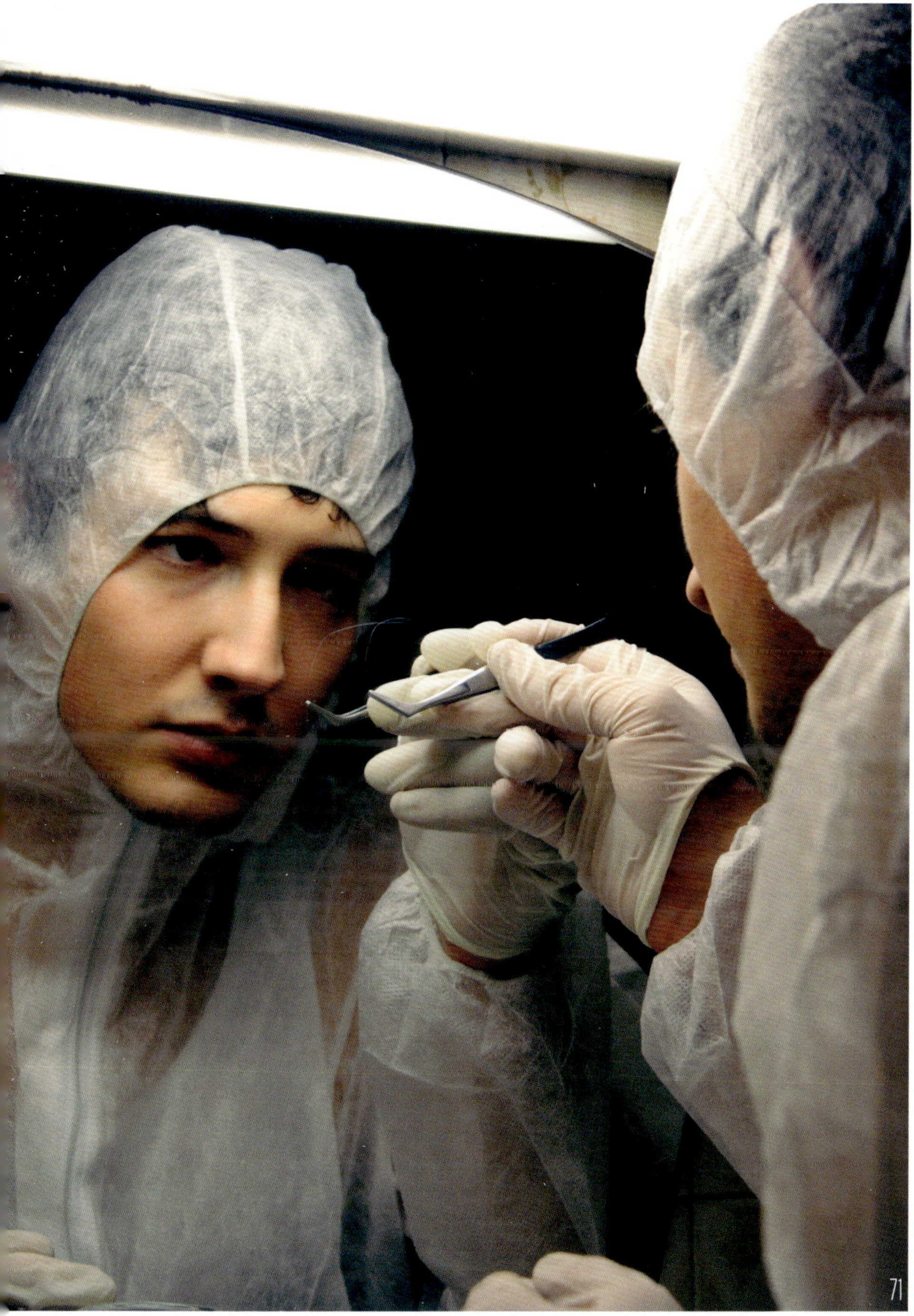

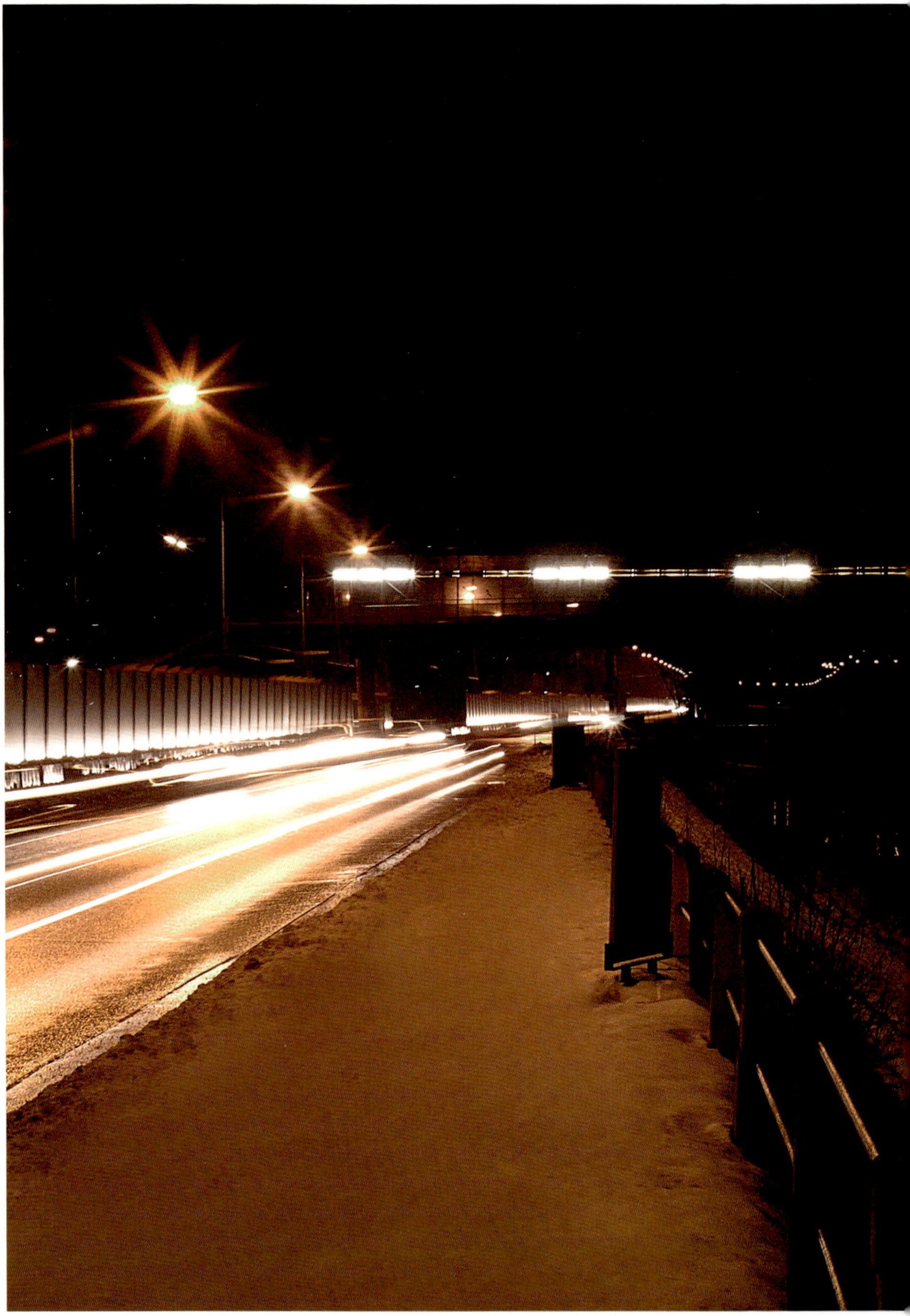

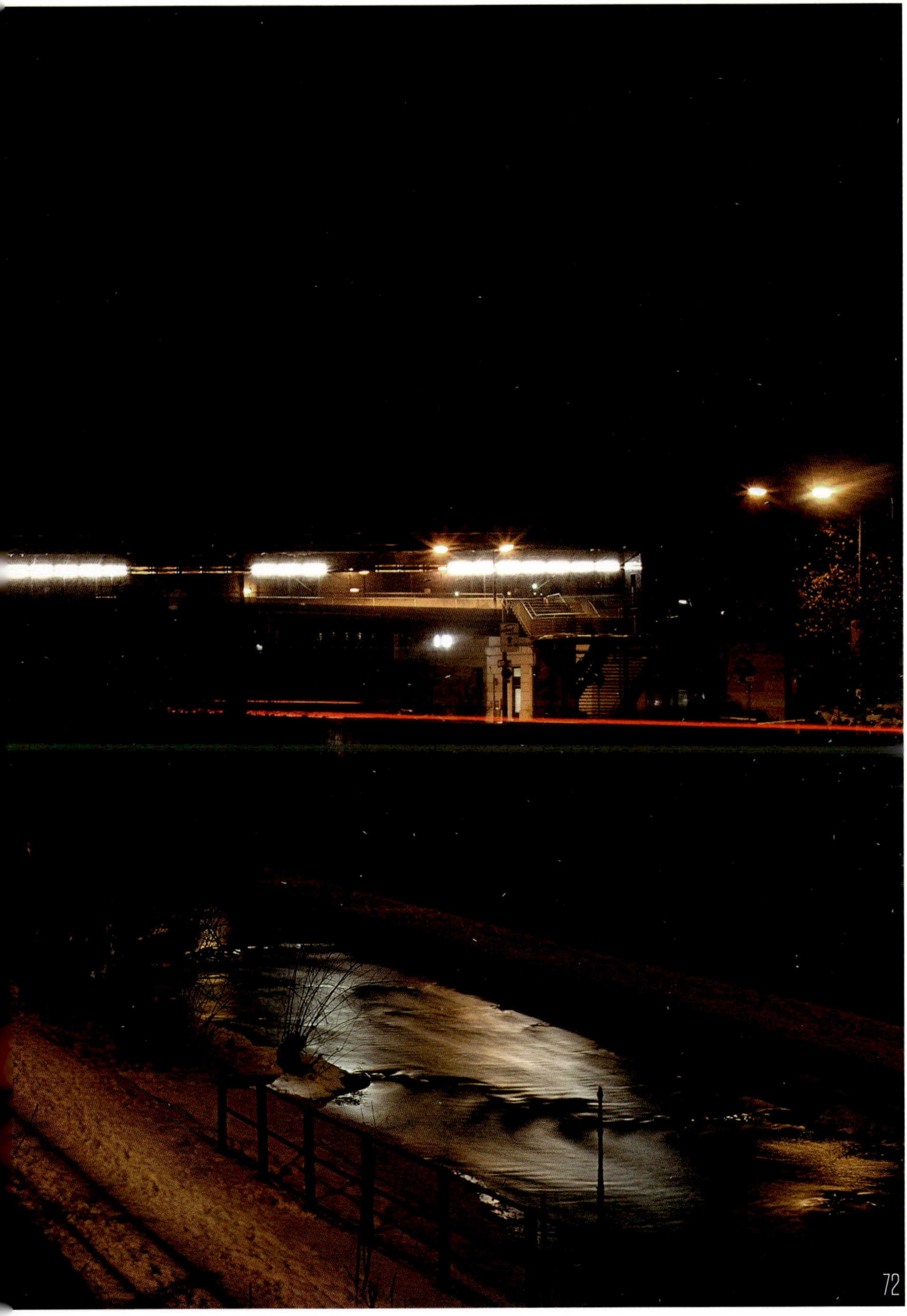

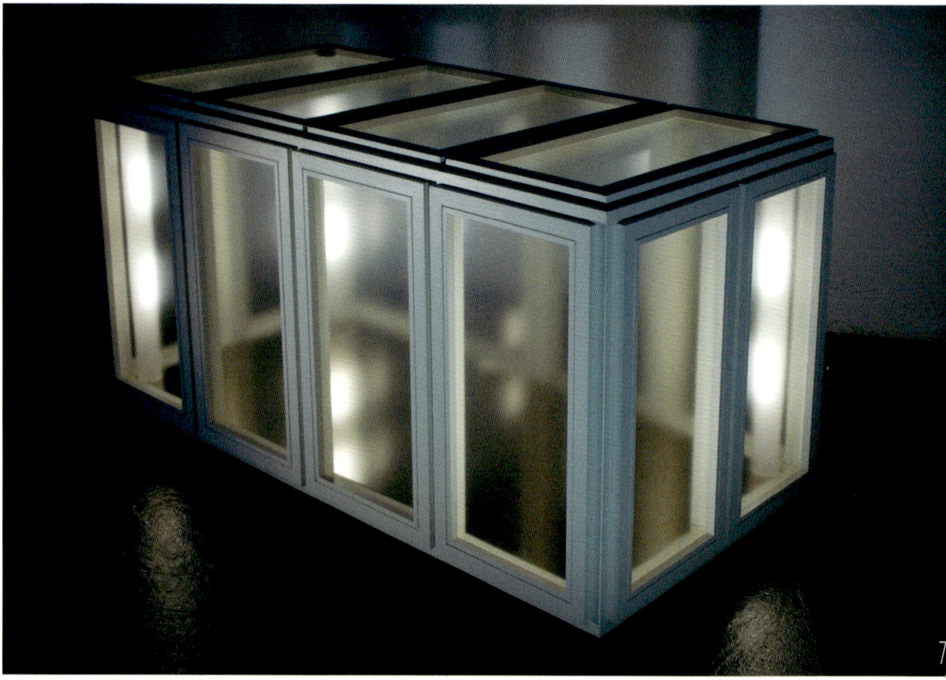

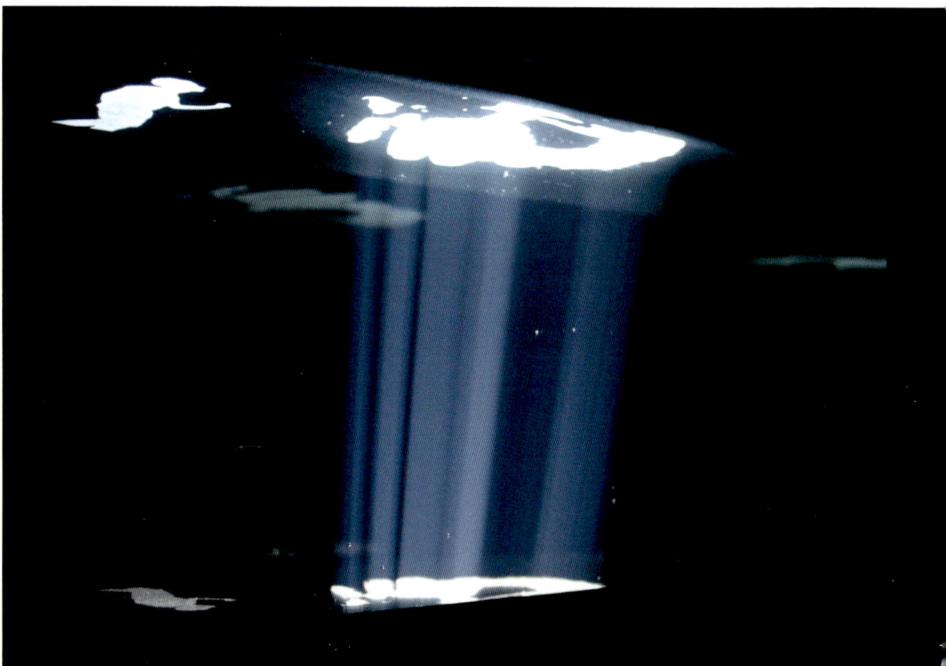

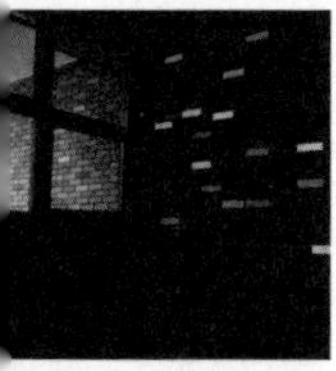

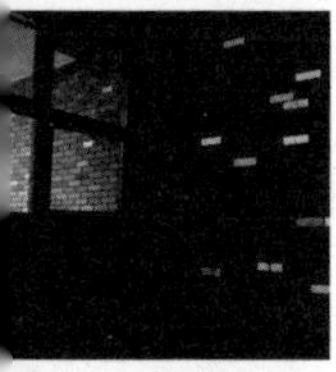

54/55 **Peter Paulhart** Another brick in the wall 2012

2 video projections, stereo-audio loop, 3:06 min.

The two projections, one inside and one otside the room and separated by a window, are mapped. By positioning the beamers exactly, coordinating the animation with the projection surface and using special software, an illusion is created as if individual bricks were lighting up. In combination with sound recordings of car indicators 36 pairs of blinkers are reproduced separately and together in a composition.

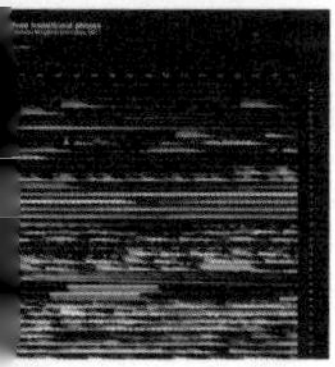

56 **Thomas Wagensommerer** Three Transitional Phases 2011

Auditive installation for three loudspeakers

Based on the organisation of seemingly indivisible acoustic events in a strictly structured score, this organisation becomes the blueprint of a dynamic body, which actuates itself in a forcedly elegant fashion. Like choreography without a subject, the crossing of three phases (of three layers) on non-geometric paths through time and space is to be taken to an absurd level.

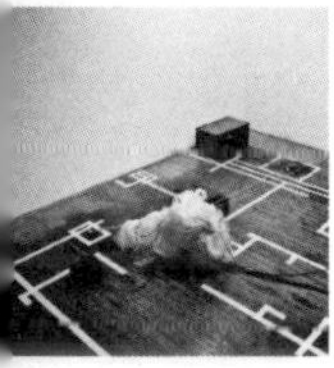

57 **Thomas Wagensommerer** Radically Generic Backdrops 2012

Real-time installation

How can air hammer? How can air chisel? How can air carve? How does air become a sculptress?

Noise, sound, tone – the obvious answer to these questions is acoustics. But to be able to hear we need sound and the air set into motion by it. Consequently it is perhaps more interesting to focus on auditivity after acoustics, for this discipline can be seen rather as a thinking through than an investigation, as the adaptation of acoustic events after they have been processed. It goes without saying that this is just as unique as the human being itself. It too can never be reproduced again. Moving air is not only the transmitter of sound but in fact produces it. It is therefore also medium and information, while the surrounding environment is the bearer of content. The object has been exposed, its dependencies shed off.

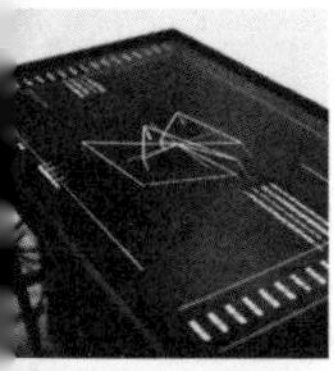

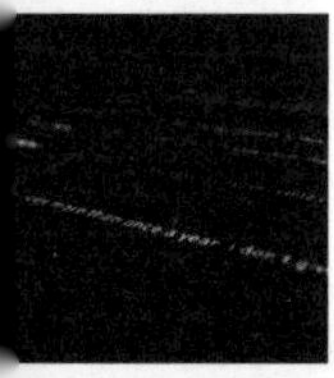

58/59 **Thomas Wagensommerer** Execute 2013

Generative real-time installation

The method of artistic production must be made visible. Should one not go a step further and demand an open access to the practice of art? But to do so the segregating system of art (as a closed market) must first be intentionally broken down and its bowels laid bare. This metaphor implies that this process though not pleasant is a necessary one. I condemn technology as a means of liberation. Consequently, dramaturgy may no longer be considered as a merely linear function but appears to be a dynamic, sculptural object. Classical dramaturgical unities are adapted here, leading to a burst of new content, whose intuitive order makes way for a new object in which classification systems and subject matter unite.

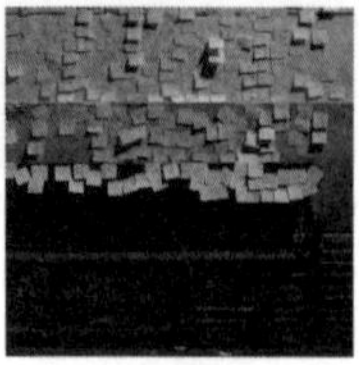

60 **Schoenberg Regl** Leave the town 200

C-print mounted on Dibond, 180 × 250 cm

E. and K., two artists inspired by the Futurist manifesto and the picture *Explosio* by George Grosz, are planning to make a bomb with the aim of creating th 'perfect picture' of an explosion. They announce the progress of their missic through Post-its affixed in public places. For the final warning before the deton tion E. and K. use a museum context – a snapshot of the Post-it dialogue is place in the exhibition room.

An extract from the dialogue:

E: Let's risk it.

K: Standing on the top of the world, we hurl our challenge once again to the star

E: We see it as a final warning.

K: I see it as a final warning.

E: To the last item on the list …

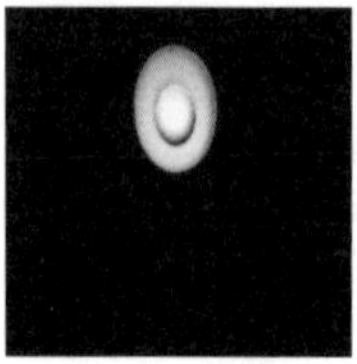

61 **Jakob Wiesmayer** Projection 1:2.8 20

Installation, mirror (96 × 40 cm), LED lighting, mounting, Reflecta 1800 AF standard lens. Size variable

A bright light source produces a cone of light that travels across the space. Wh seems like a mere reflection at first turns out to be different forms of display f the moving viewer – different stops along the beam's path. However, when th light leaves the frame the projection surface is expanded and totally free assoc ations of cause and effect result. The work has no defined beginning or end these are in a constant state of flux.

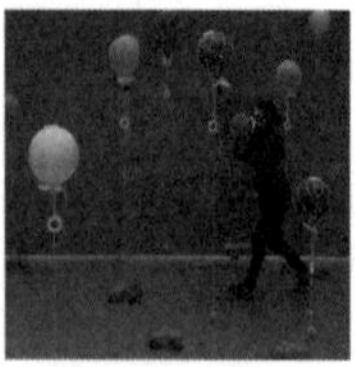

62/63 **Angelika Wischermann** Oneironaut 20

Video, 5:28 min.

A pool full of floating balloons is crossed by a woman in everyday clothing. Sh walks slowly along the bottom while taking one balloon after another to breat its air as she moves.

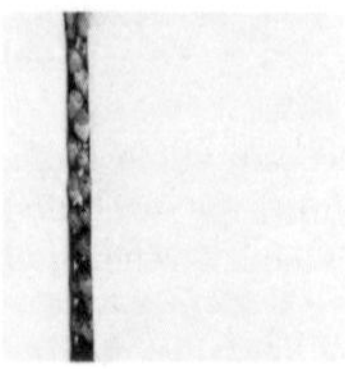

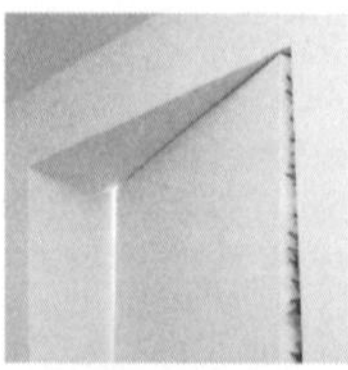

64/65 **Eugen Wist** Untitled 20

Plywood, wood, dry fish, 300 × 256 × 25 cm

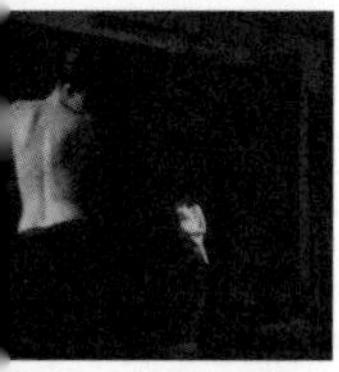

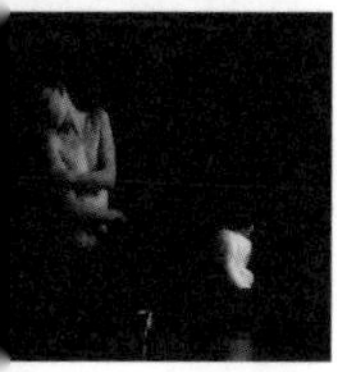

66/67 **Angelika Wischermann** Untitled 2012

Multi-part video installation

This video shows beamer projections of a woman on six black screens, her head twisting and turning as she attempts to see a point on her back (which cannot be seen without an aid). The projections offer different views of the woman (from the front, back and sides, and sitting).

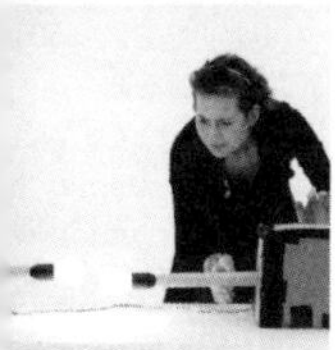

68 **Nicoleta Auersperg-Breunner** Retraction 2011

A performative sculpture

Geared motors, rail, drive belt, microswitch, tension spring, PVC, tubes, light bulbs, rubber band, MDF

Two light bulbs approach each other. Just before they collide one springs back. The sequence continues endlessly. *Retraction* is ambiguous and open to interpretation. Does it represent an awkward search, endless venturing, coming together or a warning about safety issues as a concomitant of progress? Whatever it is – an action, a feeling or a thought – it is set here in a technological context.

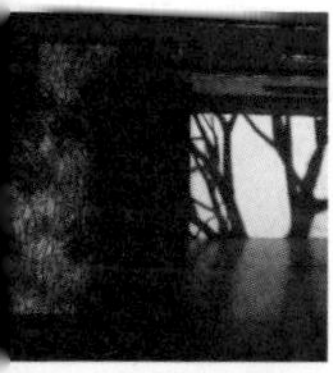

69 **Benjamin Gaier** The shadow does not fall far from the tree 2011

Video installation, 3:15 min. Photo: Birgit and Peter Kainz

The video installation *The shadow does not fall far from the tree* shows a tree modelled in 3D graphics. On a surface placed in a room the trunk is projected in portrait format with the simulated shadows of the branches to the side on the wall behind. The bark structures are scanned in circular movements and the branch structures backlit.

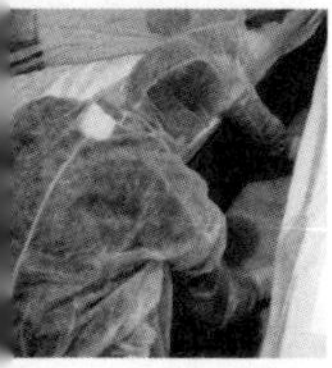

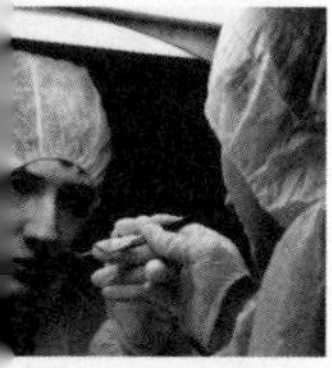

70/71 **Christian Kaufmann** Fragments of an Anonymous Person 2010

One Night II – Hotel Jarolim / Brixen (Italy), Video installation with video loop, 36 min. No sound

The video shows a search for trace evidence executed by the artist in a hotel room. The room was subsequently cleaned up by the hotel staff. During the exhibition held in the hotel itself, the video loop was played without sound on the hotel room's TV facing the bed so that visitors could sit on it to watch the film.

72 **Jakob Wiesmayer** End of traffic 201

Photo documentation, Hackinger Steg, 1140 Vienna
51 fluorescent tubes (TLD 36W), baking paper, adhesive tape, 5000 × 10 cm

Hackinger Steg is a pedestrian path next to a busy road in the 14th district c Vienna. Fifty-one fluorescent tubes light the path over a distance of around 10 metres. This horizontal line at the interface between familiar defective lightin and intended arrangement is in competition with the highly legible advertisin posters and illuminated signs in the vicinity. A lit-up area was created by darker ing the 51 lights. The unique but perceptible change (as combination or manipu lation) is contrasted with the visual impression of a dynamically changing ar flowing traffic situation. The display-like effect is visible not by adding a sourc of light; by reducing the light, changing the arrangement, a clear signal can b seen: end of traffic.

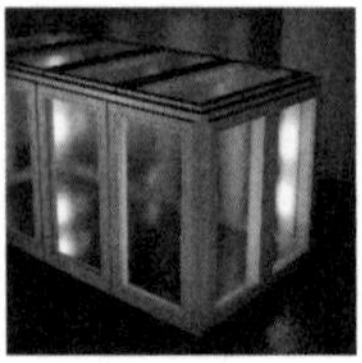

73 **Matthias Krenn** Isohunt 20

Slide projection. Dimensions variable

A constructed casing.
Opening and closing windows.
Loneliness.
The theme of room and ambiance at the point of perception.
Extremes of in/out, realistic/unrealistic, visible/invisible.
What's real, what's unreal?

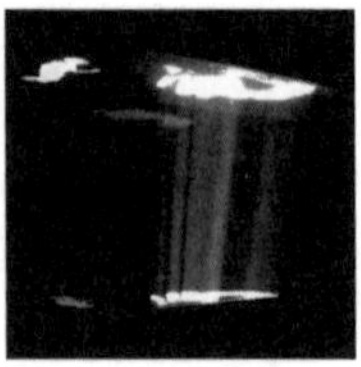

74 **Sebastian Kraner** Periagoge 20

Wood, water, aquarium, mixed media, approx. 195 × 100 × 40 cm

An aquarium stands on a high plinth in a dark room. The lower edge of th aquarium is at eye level of the viewer. A video projector, placed inside the plint projects a film from below into the water, becoming visible on the 'underside' the water. The effect of the light moving in the water resembles a dusty beam an upward directed projection in a cinema hall.

continued from page 79

on disciplinarity'.[5] 'Exploring and bursting of boundaries, disciplinarity and interdisciplinarity are essentially very closely linked'[6], Dombois states, a diagnosis, which does not suggest a merging of adjacent disciplines but, on the contrary, a 'situation of intensified juxtapositions'. Despite the great amount of talk about eroding boundaries between subjects and disciplinary containment, very little is gained in this way in terms of 'knowledge production', especially with regard to a researching art. Simply disregarding the inherent logic and disciplinary specifics – whether this is ethnography, architecture, or documentary film – and picking and choosing suitable fragments from these fields to be compiled in a production can hardly pass for a transdisciplinary process. It is only after the 'props' taken from each different field are considered from the point of view of their *inner*disciplinary status and *incorporated* in a new, common and expanded knowledge base, addressing similar agendas in their own field, only then can a production within this transdisciplinary framework take its course and truly be worthy of this name.

Yet it is precisely here that the fundamental problem truly rears its head. 'Artistic research' is on everyone's lips, enjoys increasing institutional backing, and yet there is still a palpable sense of unease as to where this opening of art to all sorts of disciplines might lead. Will the artist who explores nanotechnology become a 'nanotechnology-artist' due to this research? Someone who again only imports 'foreign material' onto home turf, despite the fact that this is undeniably becoming more porous? Someone who essentially only advances the 'compartmentalization' of the art world as has always happened when niches such as Computer Art, Sound Art or Internet Art are established? Or does this linking to another field indicate a genuine blurring of boundaries in such a way that it cannot be clearly distinguished whether this is art, a monodisciplinary study, or a combination of the two? The latter can surely only be evaluated more clearly from case to case. Here reference is only made to the fact that the efficacy of the transdisciplinary basis of contemporary art production can surely only truly unfurl when (metaphorically speaking) this also questions the notorious hyphen that accumulates disciplines like threading beads onto a necklace. It can only develop when the artist-ethnographer, artist-DJ or artist-politician makes way for a more comprehensive model of contemporary production that is not concerned with all at once validating something different, something 'foreign' as art. A utopian vision of this model would be to create new kinds of assemblages by coupling individual disciplines, assem-

---

DAVID MALJKOVIC Artist, Zagreb

DECEMBER 2011

Linear Oscillations

Lecture and Studio Visits

blages which still retain well-founded competencies from those very disciplines but which are connected in a way that is not just simply importing or adding on (as usually indicated by the hyphen).

Only by transforming a transdisciplinary approach into a guiding principle (and not a theory or method), so that the relationships between disciplines can gradually begin to change, can we ensure that the expansion, the breaking down and crossing of boundaries will not just serve a single field and be geared to its own advantage. Only when transdisciplinarity is regarded as a working principle (even though it has yet to be firmly established and formalized), subject to a new enquiring perspective, can a cross-disciplinary subject be created that does not cater to the logic of profit but eventually 'belongs to nobody'[7]. It is only if hyphenated art is prepared to omit the hyphen that a *transdisciplinary* art can slowly take shape in a way that is worthy of this name.

1 Cf. for example the collective publication Ruth Reiche et al. (ed.), *Transformationen in den Künsten. Grenzen und Entgrenzung in bildender Kunst, Film, Theater und Musik* (Bielefeld, 2011).

2 Here I would like to recall, by way of example, two relevant collective volumes that prove this theory: Ulrike Groos & Markus Müller (eds.), *Make It Funky. Crossover zwischen Musik, Pop, Avantgarde und Kunst* (Cologne, 1998) and Diedrich Diederichsen et al., eds., *Golden Years. Materialien und Positionen zu queerer Subkultur und Avantgarde zwischen 1959 und 1974* (Graz, 2006).

3 Jürgen Mittelstraß, 'Methodische Transdisziplinarität', Technikfolgenabschätzung, 14/2 (June 2005), 18–23, <http://www.itas.fzk.de/tatup/052/mitt05a.htm/>; cf. also Jürgen Mittelstraß, *Transdisziplinarität – wissenschaftliche Zukunft und institutionelle Wirklichkeit* (Constance, 2003).

4 Mittelstraß, 'Methodische Transdisziplinarität', op. cit.

5 Hans Rudolf Reust and Florian Dombois, 'Die verschärfte Nachbarschaft der Künste und ihre Unbekannte Y', *Kunst-Bulletin*, 3/2004, 22–27, <http://www.kunstbulletin.ch/router.cfm?a=20040212-142803-180-3/>

6 Ibid.

7 Roland Barthes' (wishful) statement about 'Young Researchers' (1972), cited in Tom Holert, 'Künstlerische Forschung: Anatomie einer Konjunktur', *Texte zur Kunst*, 82 (June 2011), 57.

EDGAR LISSEL Artist, Vienna

MARCH 2012

The Threshold of the Visible Lecture

Nature as Image Workshop

FRANZ SCHUH

HOW DO NEW THINGS COME ABOUT?

An essay on 'creativity'

'Principle of art: inventing more than is lost'

Elias Canetti

A raging river

Sine ira et studio, as far as I am able to, I deal in lectures and seminars with theories of artistic productivity. Why does something exist and not nothing? This is an old philosophical question and probably linked to another question: why do people think of something and not of nothing?

Not everyone who is productive wants their productivity to be accompanied by reflection: reflection can be an obstacle in practice. But just as a viewer can switch off the television if he doesn't like the programme, the artist can filter out perhaps not the reflection itself but at least the theories elaborated about artistic productivity.

I collect statements by people from the artistic field in which they position themselves, whether voluntarily or not, in

---

the theoretical debate. When Peter Turrini was asked once how much of his writing was craft and how much inspiration, he answered promptly: 'I don't believe in inspiration. This "kiss of the gods and muses" is a stupid bourgeois concept. I am intensely irritated by all this talk by artists and observers of art about meaning. I believe only in hard work. There is no need to talk about talent, as it is the prerequisite for this profession in the first place. All the writers I admire have always been dissatisfied with their work. Only pedestrian writers beam with pleasure as they read their own sentences ... The longer I remain in this business, the less satisfied I am with the results and the more difficult my work becomes. The gods don't help me in the slightest – nor the literature prizes and praise.'

This statement might also be read as a confirmation of something that is not readily admitted: behind the unspoken talent requirement and the plea for hard work (which we do speak of) is the familiar truth that the creative process is a bit of a drama that potentially challenges all artists and in reality does indeed continuously task and overextend quite a few of them. I like the encroachment of the work ethic on artistic productivity. That work is judged by the craftsmanship also has to do possibly with the desire to be master of one's trade. 'Inspiration', however distorted, ideological or bourgeois, is also the fascinating aspect for me of this subject, namely the

---

LIDDY SCHEFFKNECHT Artist, Vienna

APRIL 2012

seven minutes thirteen seconds

Lecture

(relative) unavailability of artistic production. It is unlikely, as Luhmann claims, that a work of art comes of its own accord. When a cobbler works, it is very probable that the end result will be a shoe – fortunately. By contrast, it is most unjust that a work-shy slacker or drunkard can produce a work of art, while many a hardworking artist produces nothing more than 'good work'. Life is not fair.

The indiscretion of theoretical curiosity that asks about prerequisites (including the prerequisites for talent, about which those who have it rightly remain silent) is unavoidable. I use the term 'creative' in the following fragments – against my better judgement – undogmatically. Günther Anders has placed 'creative' and 'creativity' on a black list of words that he would never say, let alone write. These words mean for him: 'presumptuous adoption of a divine attribute for the purpose of covering up the reification of the person'. I am shocked to note that there is more truth in this statement than the polemic allows: 'creativity' has to do with the strenuous attempts to escape reification. But the polemic also contains a truth: 'creativity' is one of those modern catchphrases with which society drives its sheep. Everyone has to demonstrate it – woe betide if they don't! It is as a slogan that 'creativity' really contributes to reification.

The emphasis in my considerations is on artistic produc-

ZILVINAS KEMPINAS Artist, New York **MAY 2012**

Slideshow Lecture

Physics and Metaphysics of Visual Art

Workshop and Studio Visits

tivity, but I have the feeling that the various ways and disciplines by which new things are brought into the world have distinctive but also common properties. Take the Mekong, for example. It is the 'raging river' – and in China there are too few bridges crossing it. So ropes were spanned over the river and each of these ropes has a pulley. A person wishing to cross the river is suspended in a carrier. The pulley has to be oiled – but if it is too well oiled it is not possible to brake the movement, and if it has too little oil, it won't make it across. 'Creativity' has to do with problems like this.

Creative industries

A good reason to investigate 'creativity', in other words how new things come into the world, is the old question: 'What is man?' After all, it is inventive people who are cited as models for 'humanity' in general. Not all inventions are 'creative', but 'mankind' has demonstrated over time that it does not simply accept the conditions it finds (particularly what comes 'from nature'). It often has ideas.

People transcend the conditions of their existence and live, whether happily or not, in an artificial world: they lighten the night and do not live outdoors but in specially constructed buildings. The following is so improbable that I wonder whether my memory is playing tricks on me, and yet I seem to remember that among Peter Handke's early texts there is also one in which the author praises the remoteness from nature of a shopping centre made of concrete. It was no doubt a strand of that enduring contemporary era known as 'the Modernist period: the substitution of nature by art or at least the products of technology. Nature is often depicted as the limit of our sovereignty. Why should we allow such a limitation – only enemies of civilization, make it responsible for something like the sinking of the *Titanic*, Karl Kraus, for example, who noted that God – unlike the designers of unsinkable luxury liners – had not studied shipbuilding. Of course, only idiots believe in things like 'unsinkability', and yet in Wagner's *Ring* Erda says specifically to Wotan: 'Listen! Listen! Listen! / Everything that is ends.' The designers were not stupid either, they just didn't have a scenario for the sinking of the *Titanic*. Euphoria about the technology did the rest and, if we overlook its end, the *Titanic* was indeed an enormous technical achievement.

Hans Blumenberg offers a good description in an essay of mankind's intermediate position in creation: it sees how a bird flies and wants to do the same. But if it simply imitates the bird's flight it will fall to the earth. In order to fly, it must first invent the motor – and that has little to do with the flying lessons given to it by birds. By taking a creative approach to

---

MANFRED WIPLINGER Gallery Director, Curator, Vienna

JUNE 2012

SITUAKTION

Workshop and Exhibition

creation, mankind effectively create itself as a kind of anti-nature, for which it is often accused – and by no means in all humility – as suffering from hubris.

Accepting the existing state and transcending it creatively forms/provides the basis for various constellations in different cultures: letting be, serenity and nervousness but also exhilarating and liberating change are variously emphasized. But it can nevertheless be claimed that creativity, the bringing forth of something new, is perhaps **the** decisive possibility offered to mankind. In artistic activity and inactivity, which in our societies are often advocated as the epitome of creativeness, two conflicting and yet complementary components can be discerned: first, the unavailability of creativity. For all of Odo Marquard's 'communism of genius', according to which everyone is an artist, in reality not everyone is one.

This has lumped artists (those who are successful) with the social privileges of an elite and with ideologies like the cult of genius, which politicians once jealously salivated over and tried to benefit from. This does nothing to change the fact that the specific creativity called art is unfortunately not distributed democratically. Worse still, even those who rightly consider themselves artists and are also considered so by

continued on page 134

FOLKE KÖBBERLING Artist, Berlin

OCTOBER 2012

Intervention Models Lecture

TIME Workshop

A network of artists, scientists and other players in the art system, holding alternating lectures and workshops, replace single persons as heads of classes.

ALMUT RINK Artist, Vienna

OCTOBER 2012

SolidGrowth

Lecture

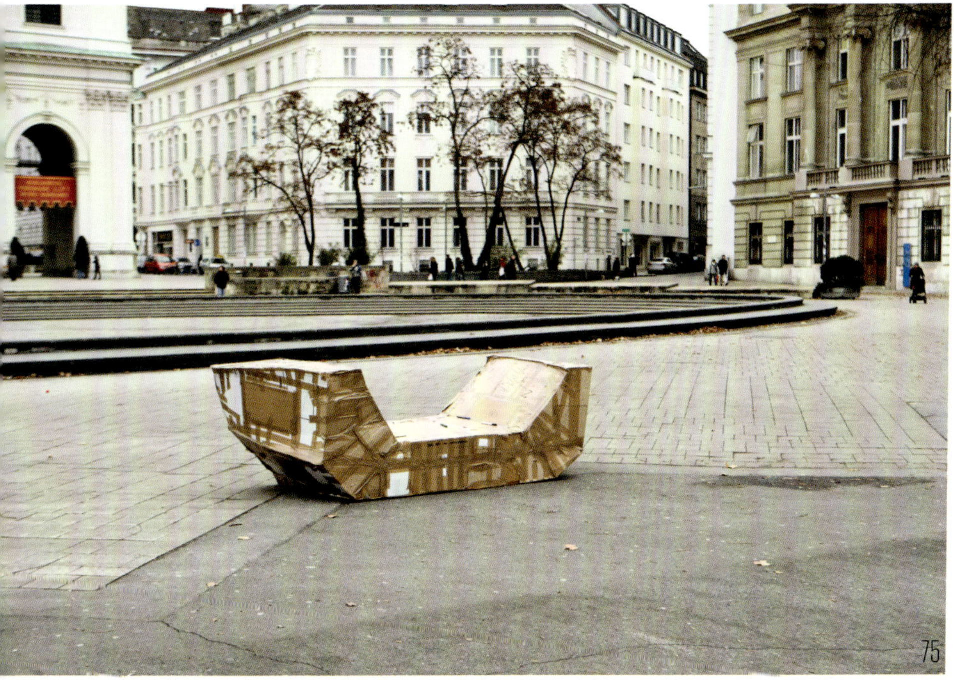
75

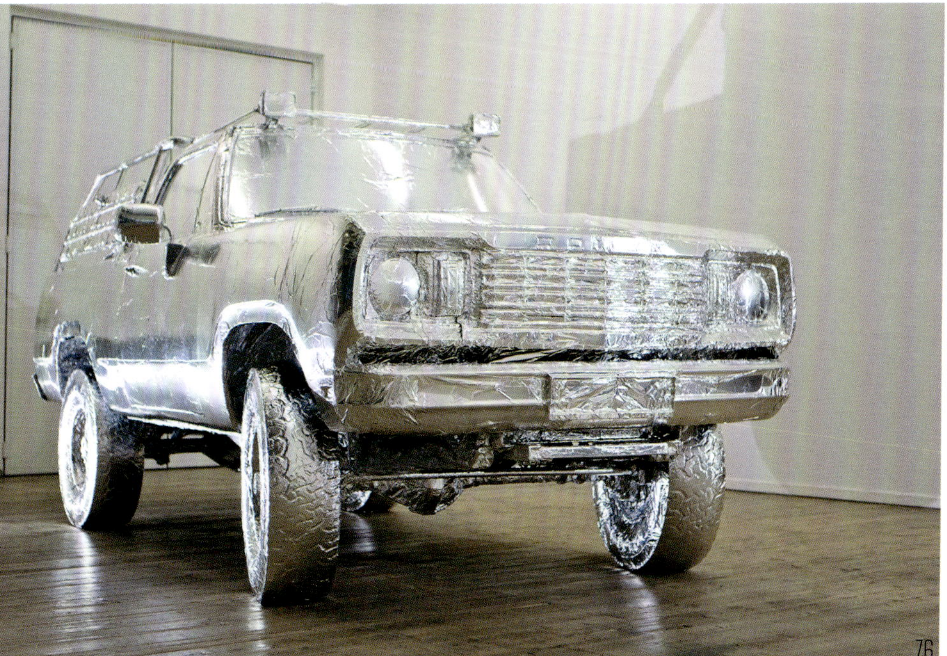
76

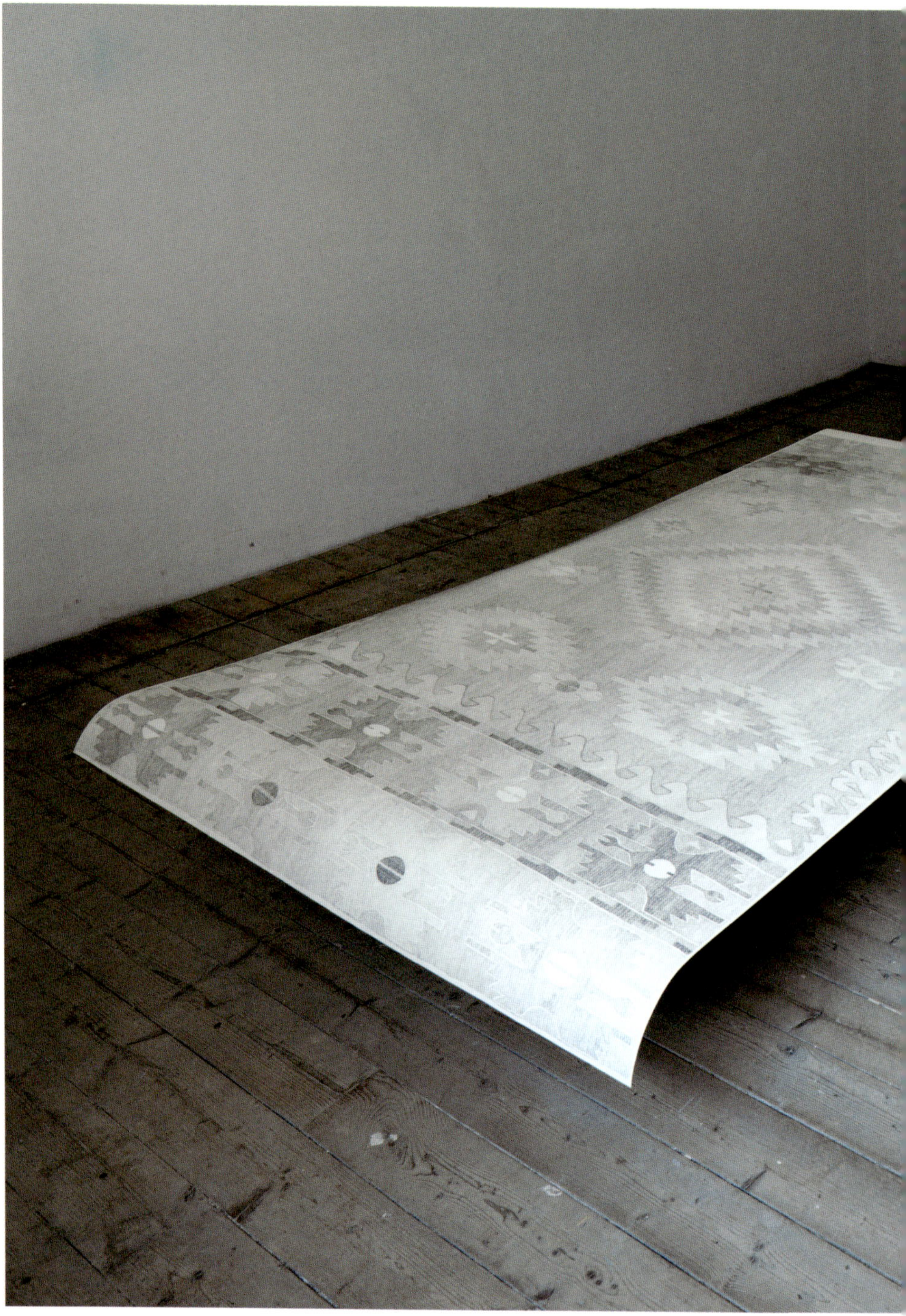

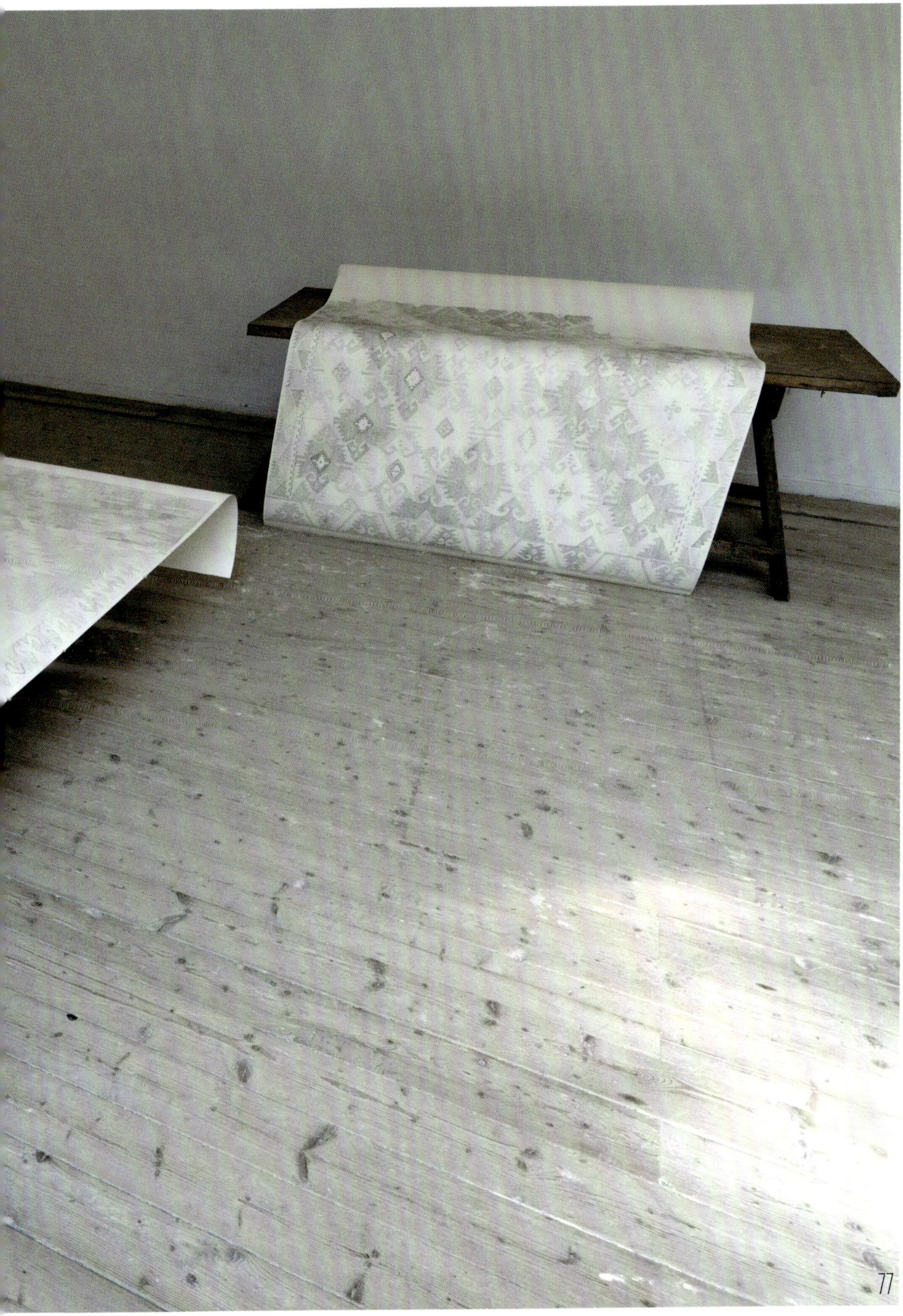

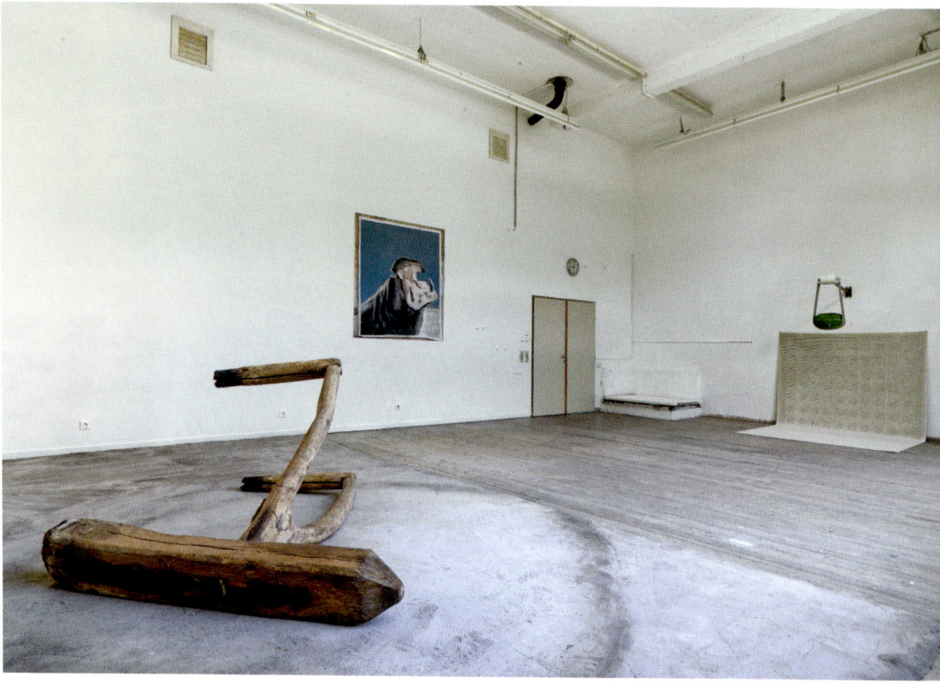

7

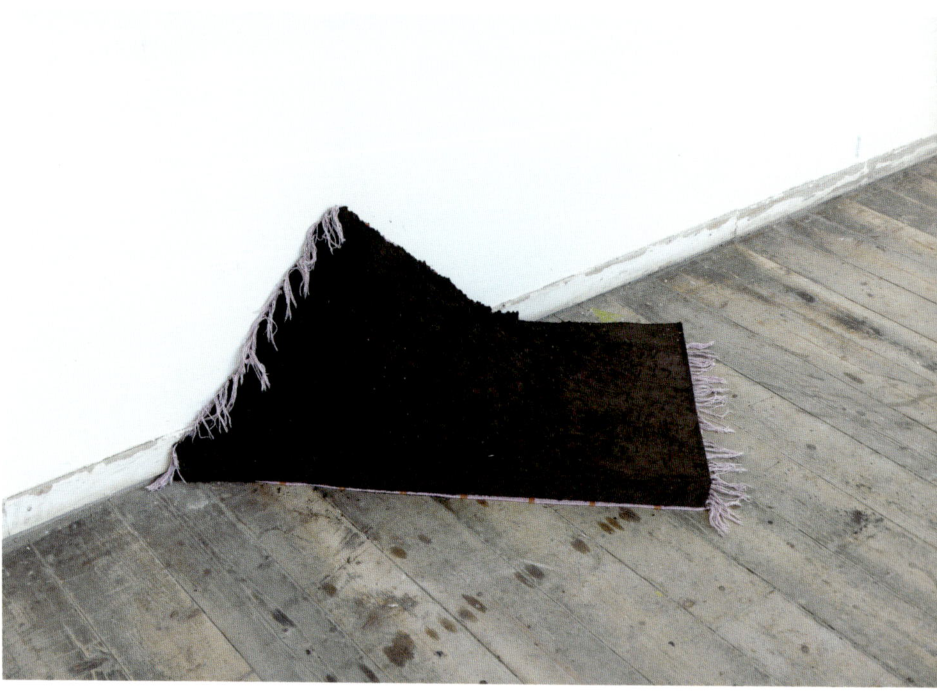

7

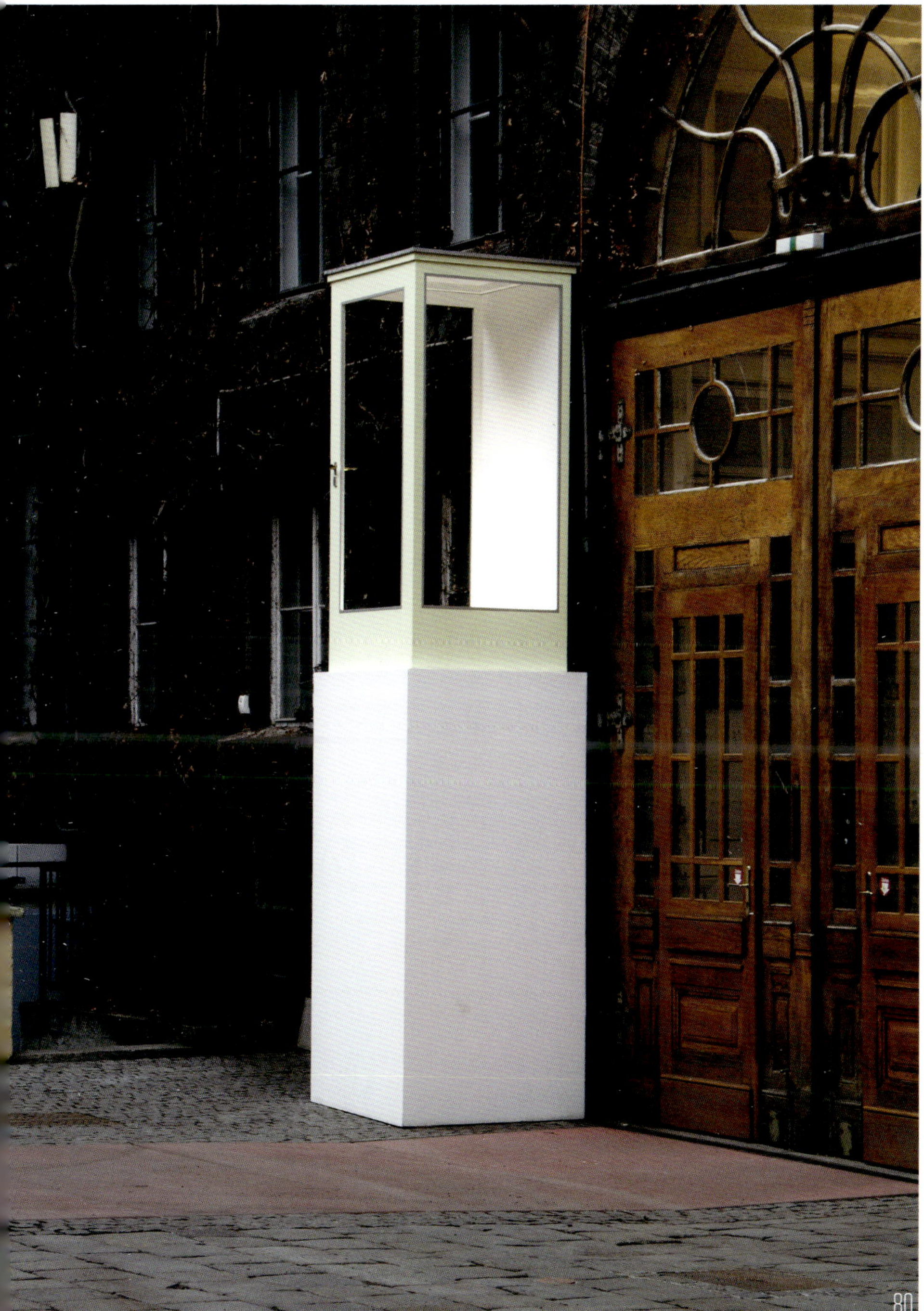

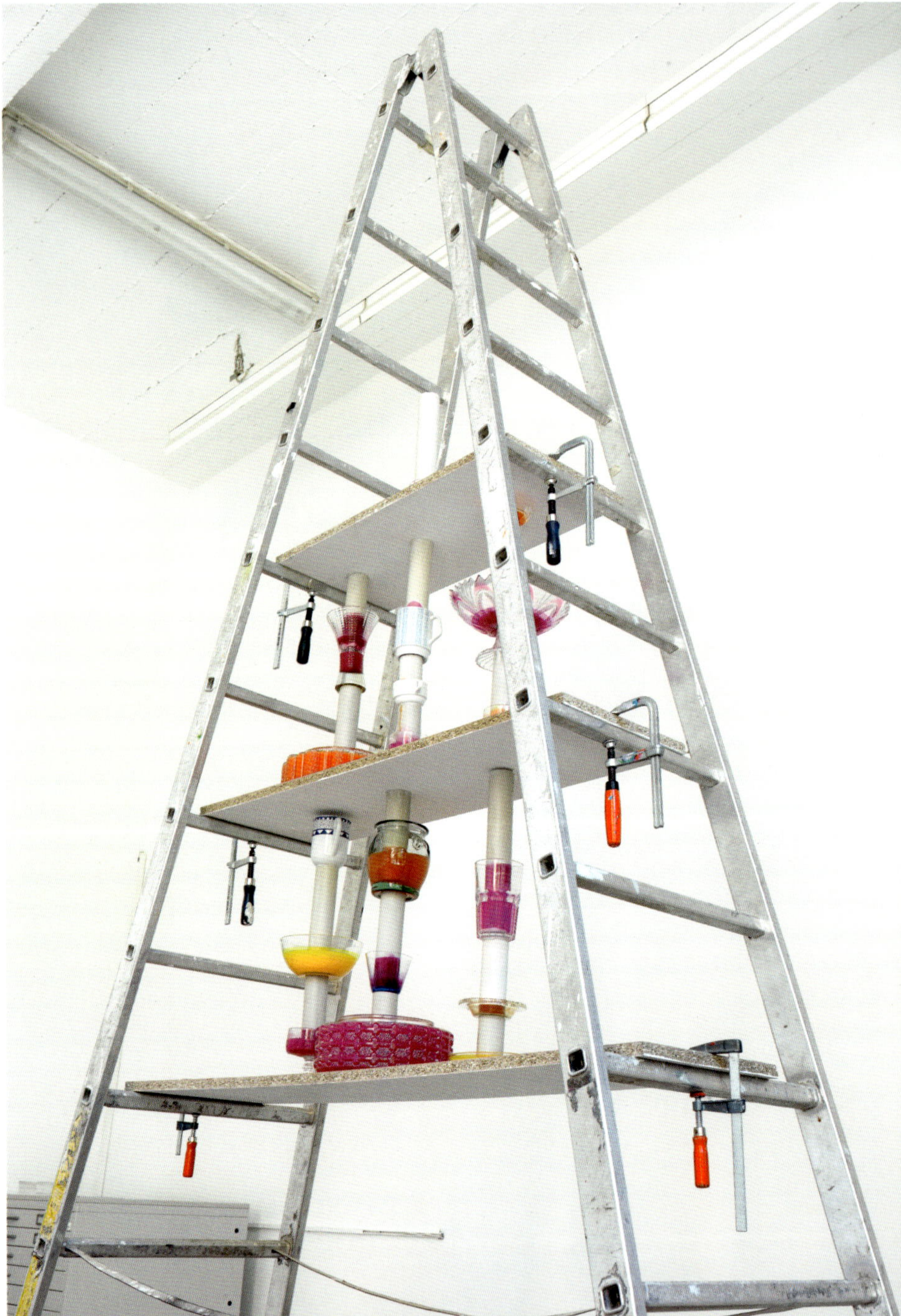

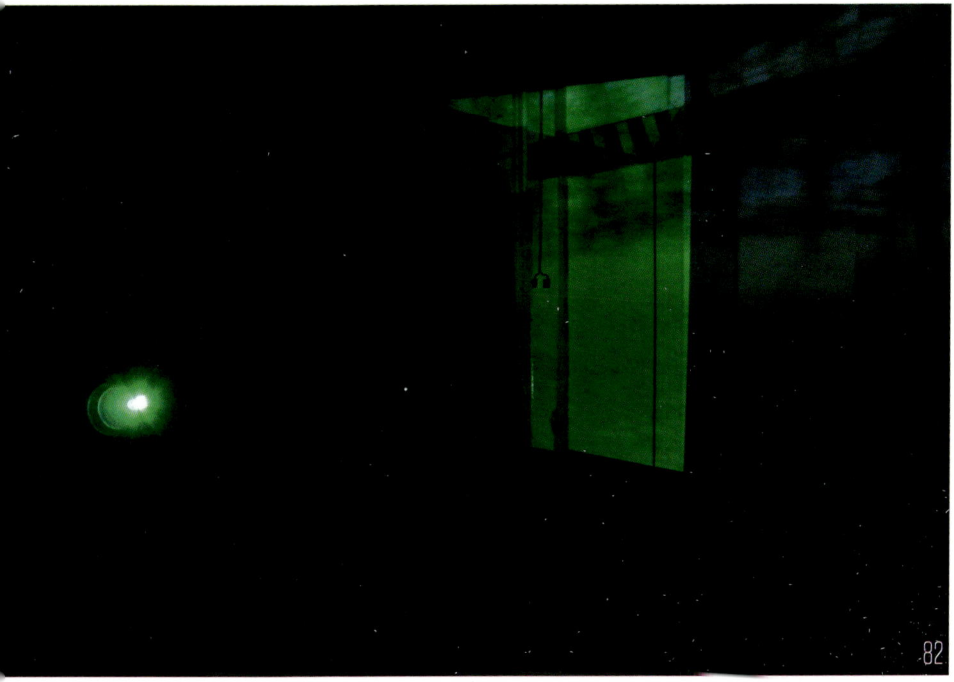

82

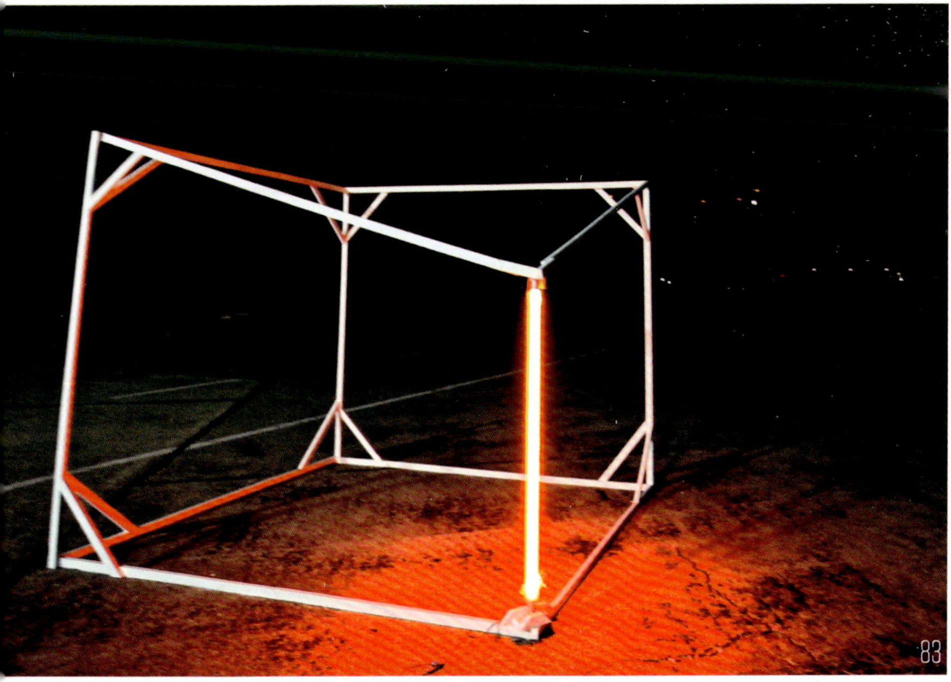

83

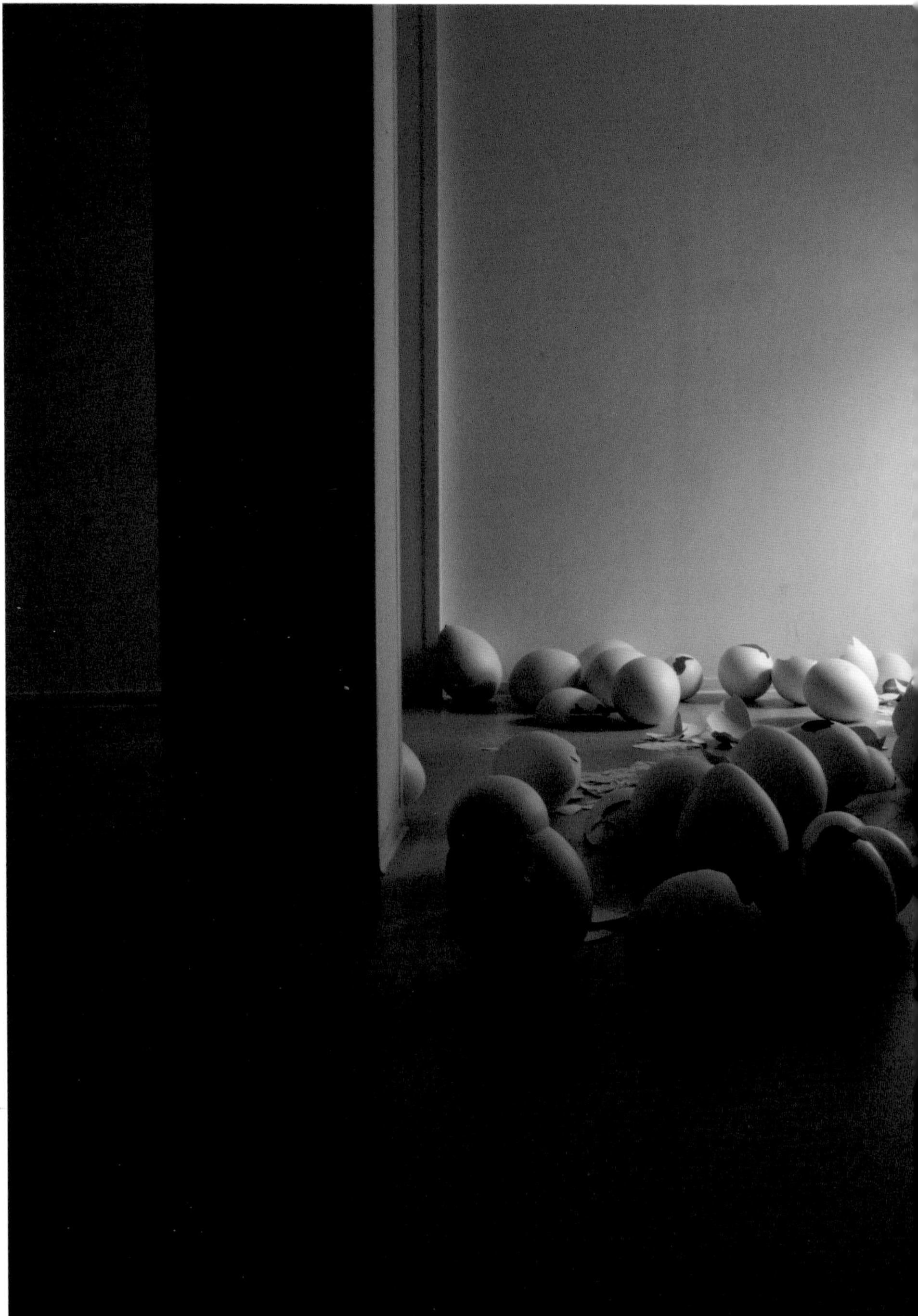

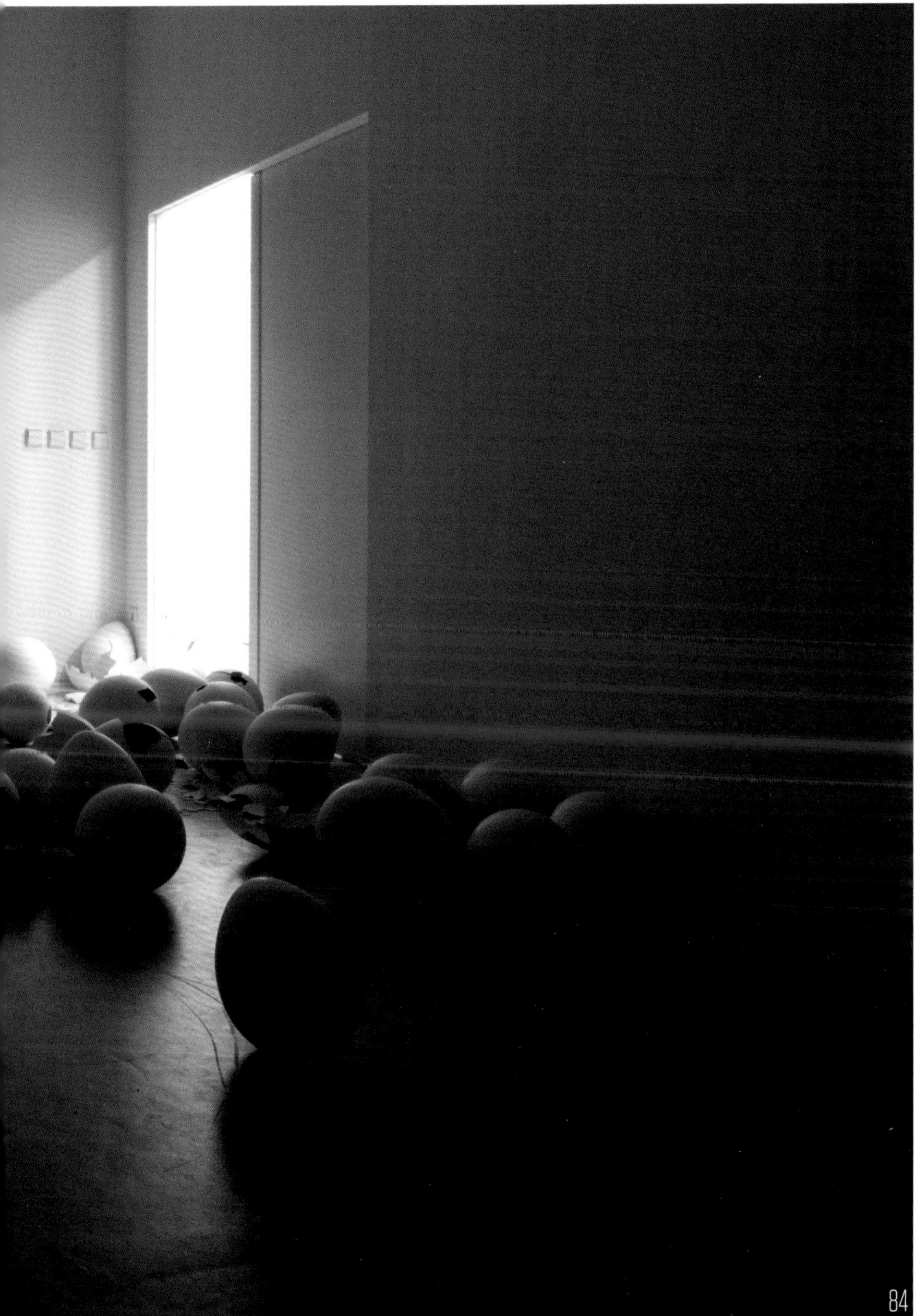

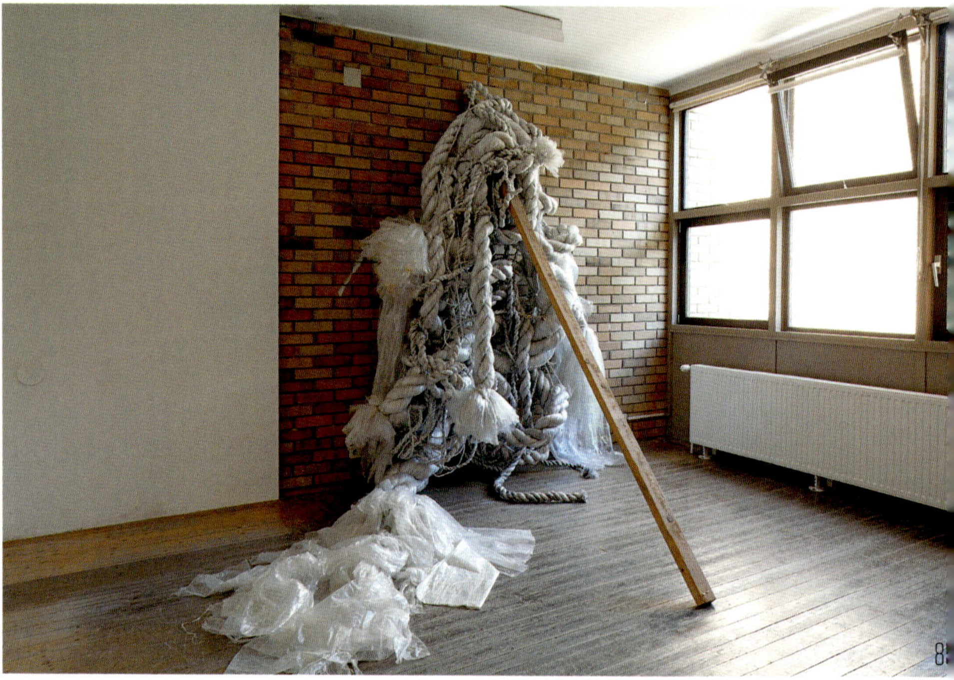

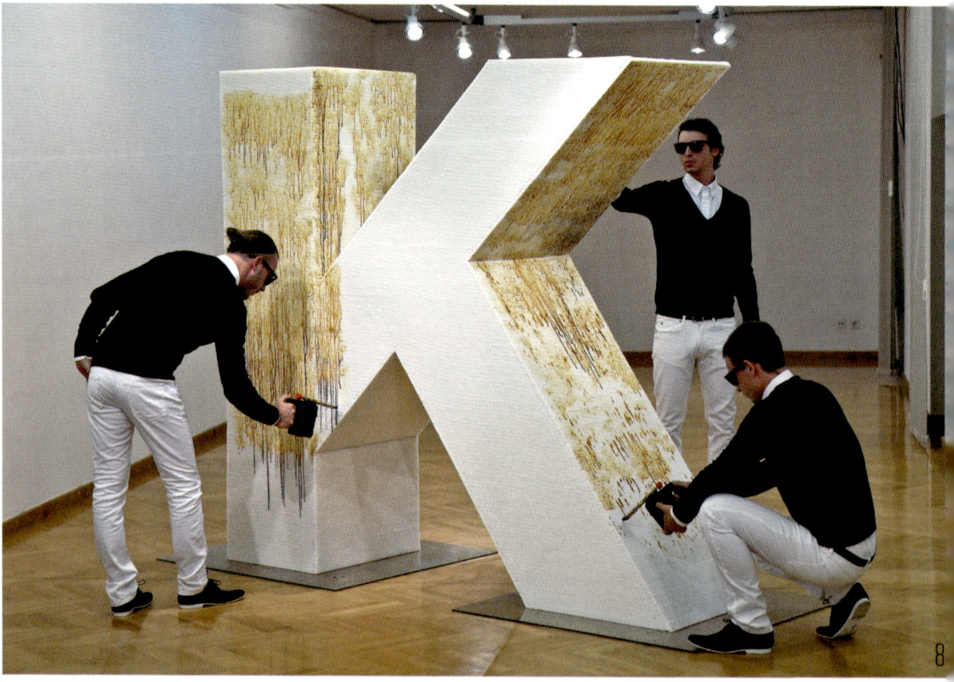

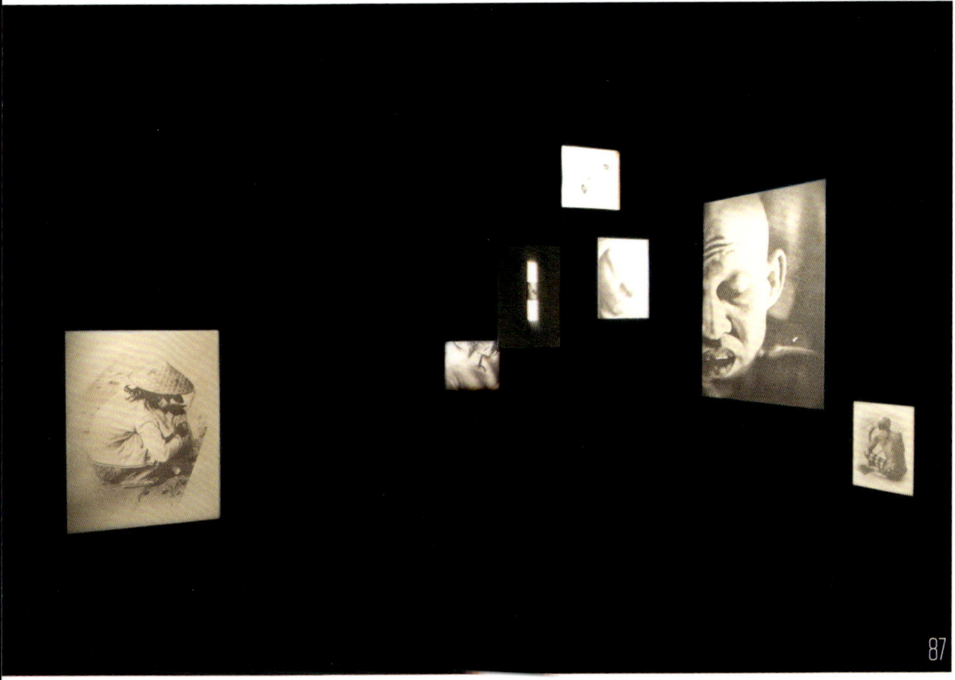

87

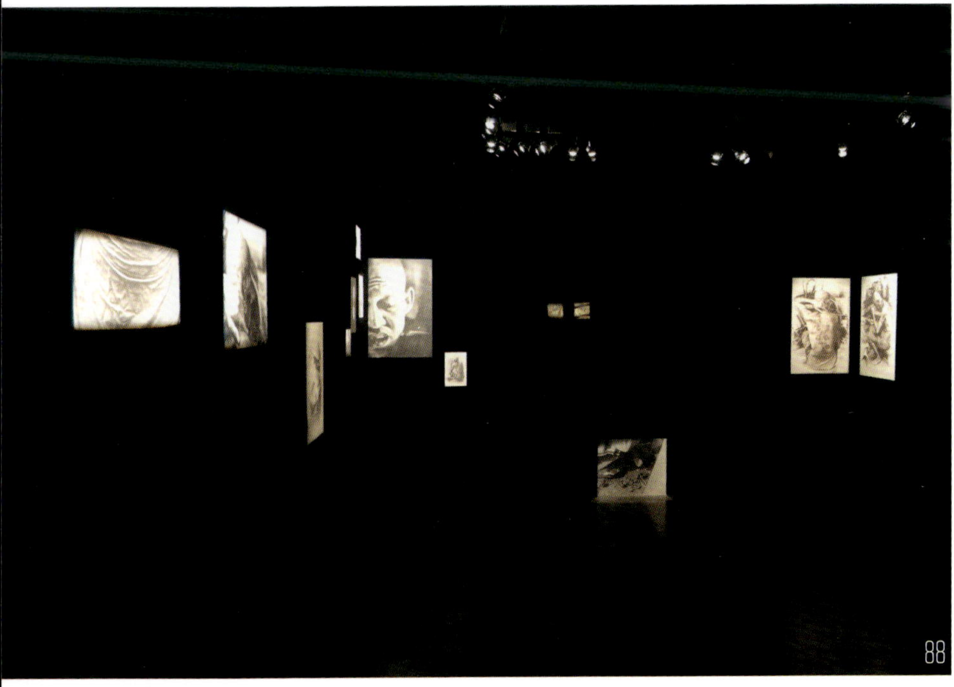

88

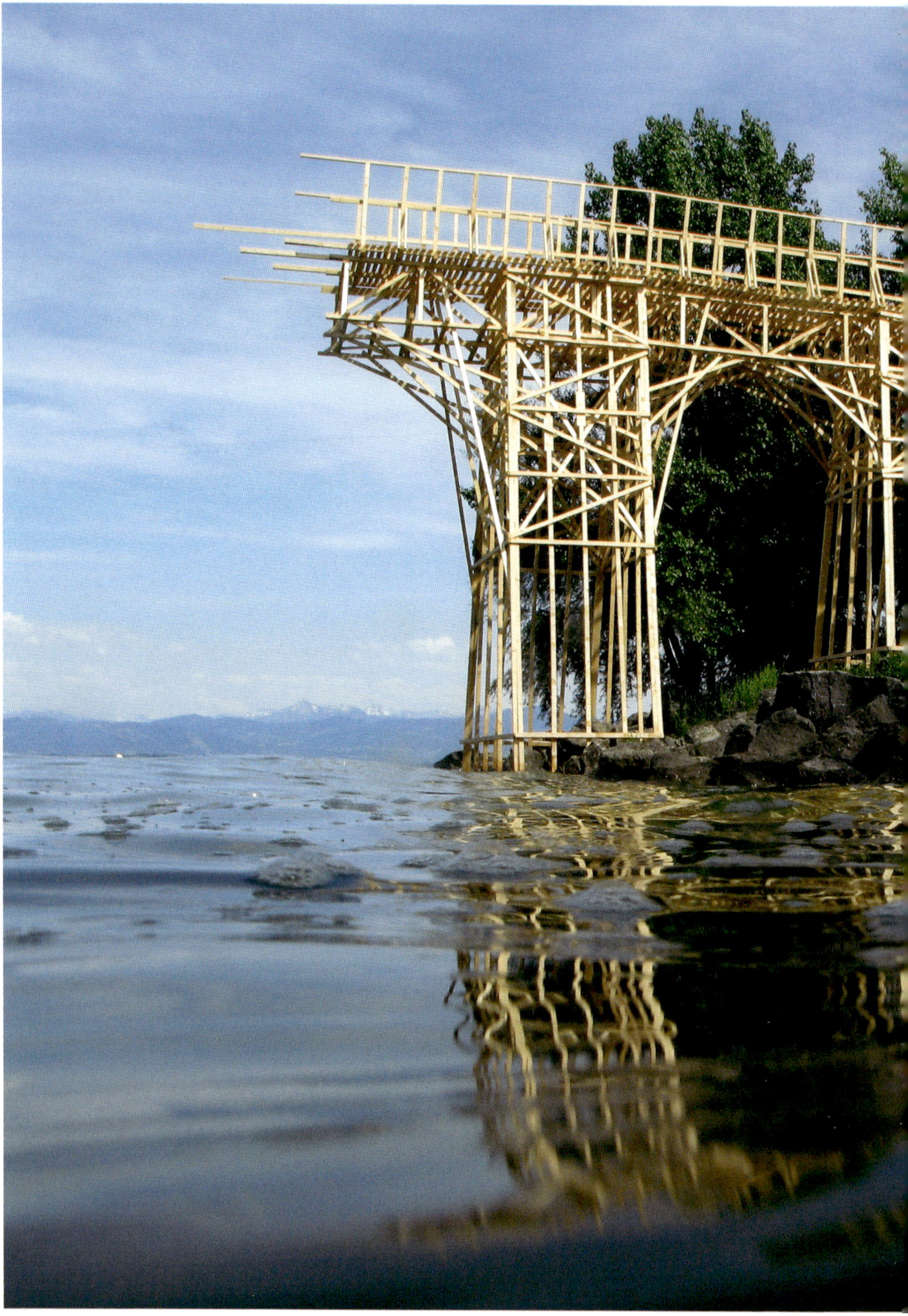

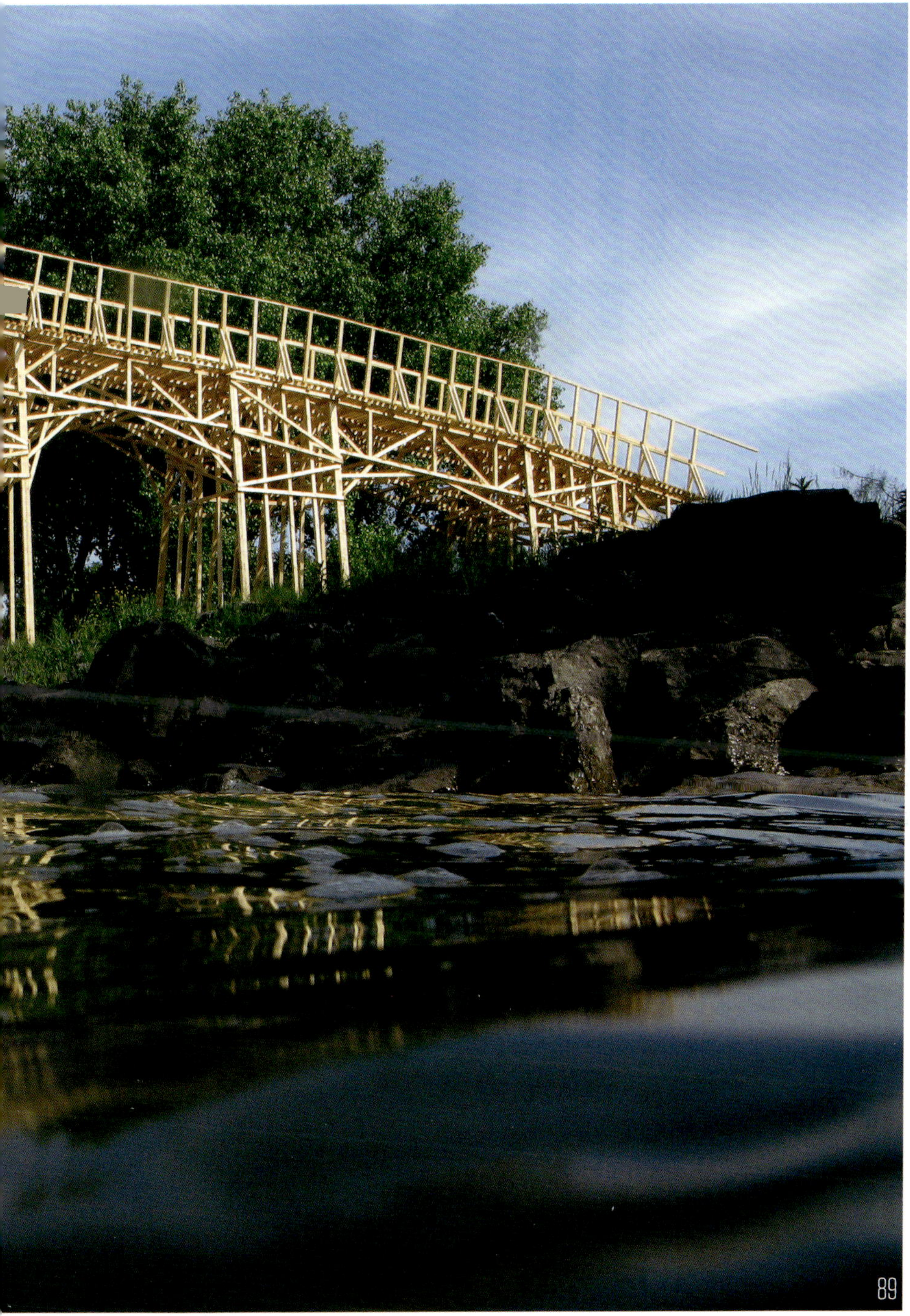

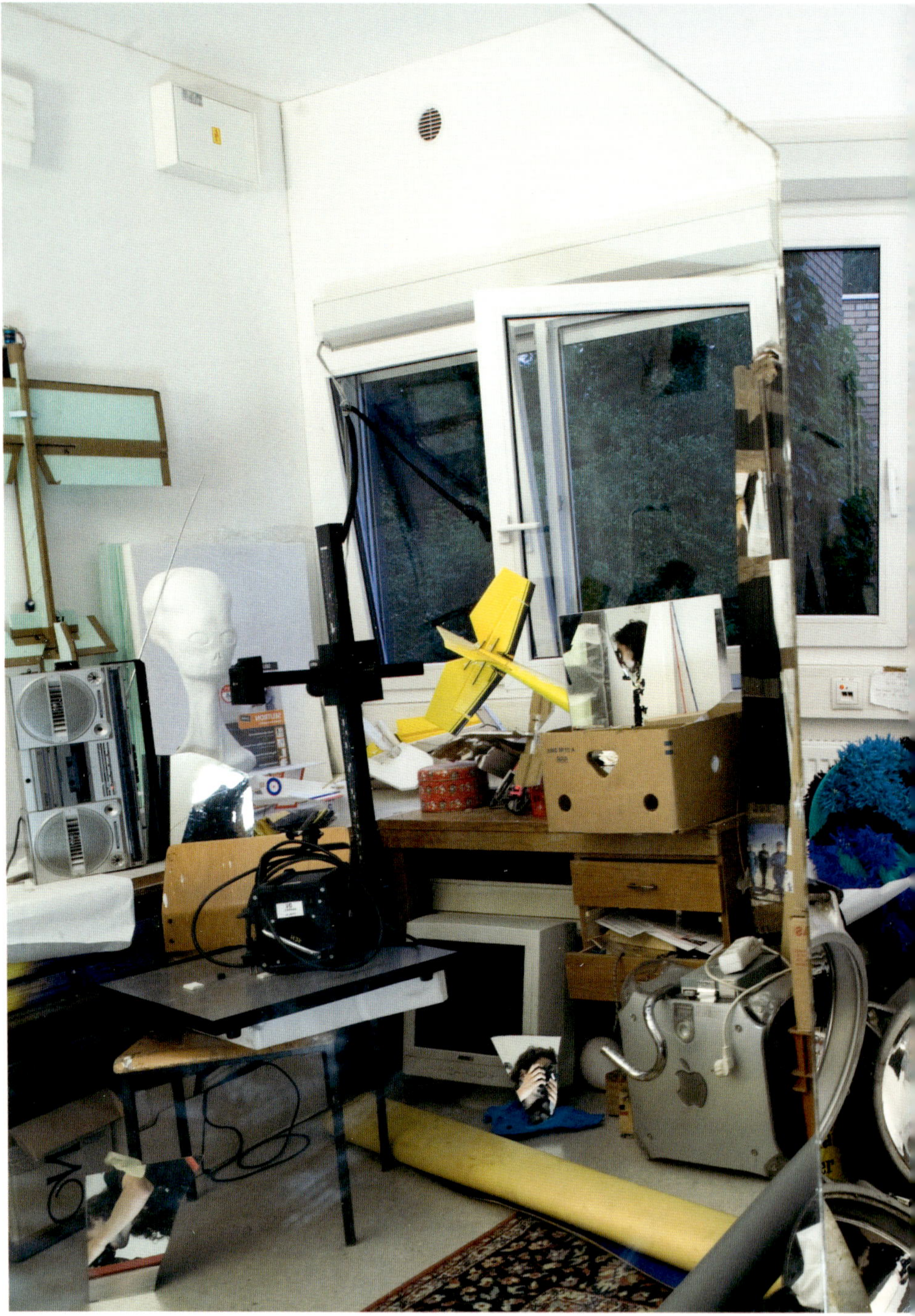

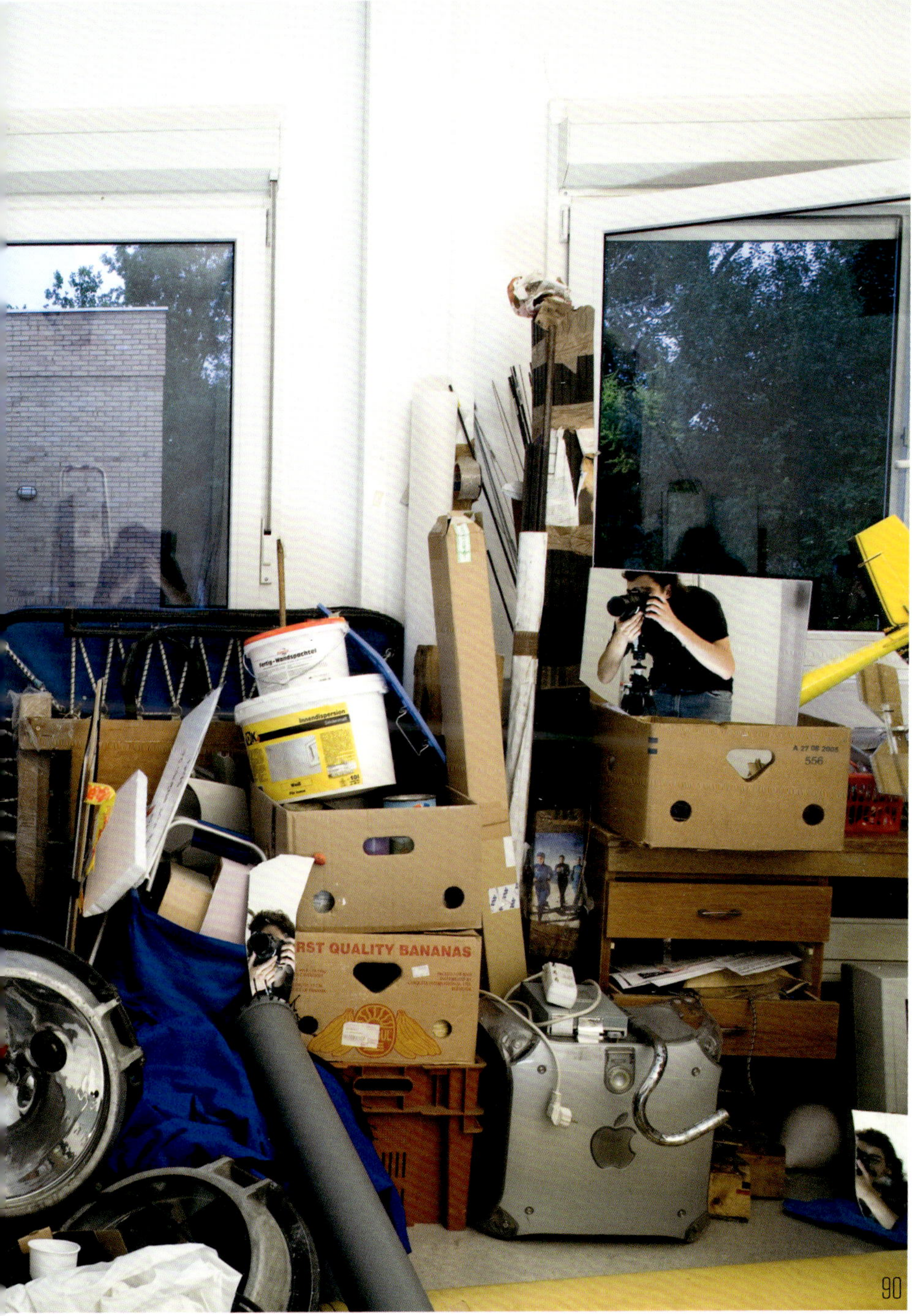
RST QUALITY BANANAS
556

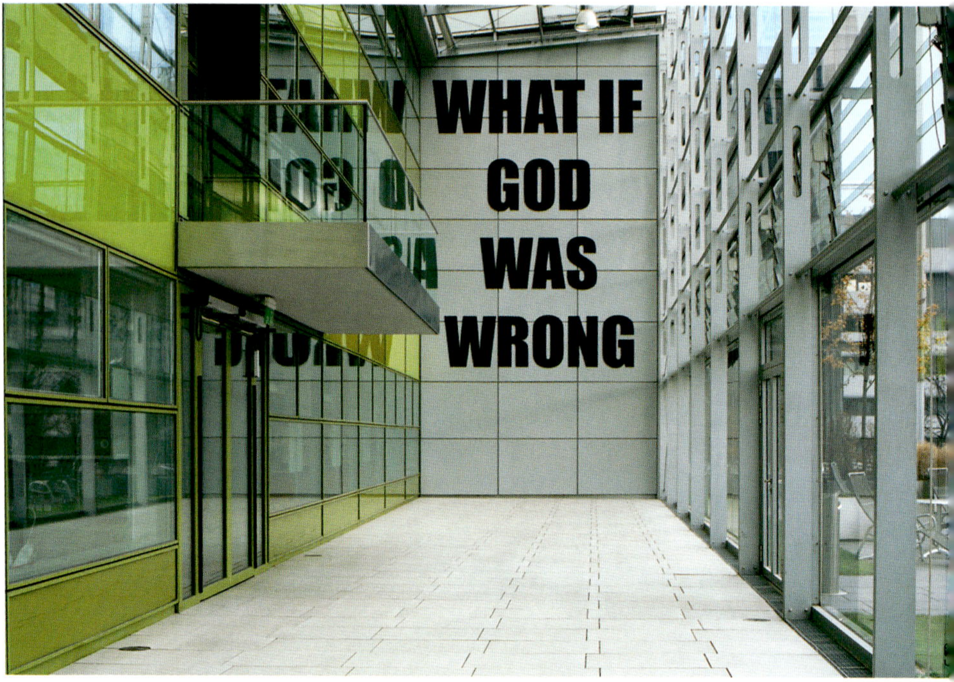
WHAT IF
GOD
WAS
WRONG

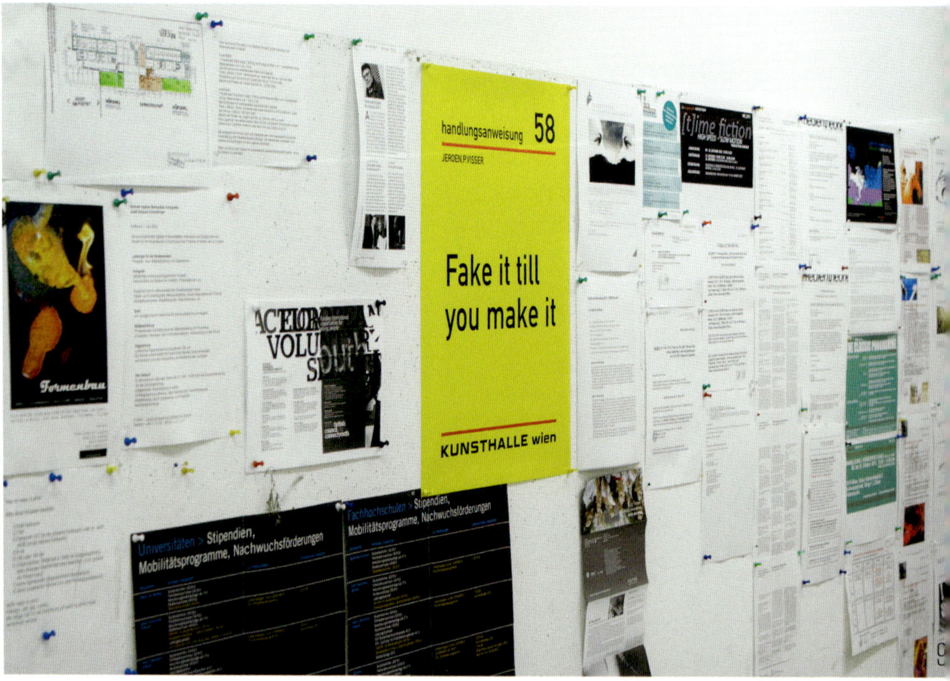
handlungsanweisung 58
Fake it till
you make it
KUNSTHALLE wien
[t]ime fiction
Formenbau
Universitäten > Stipendien,
Mobilitätsprogramme, Nachwuchsförderungen
Fachhochschulen > Stipendien,
Mobilitätsprogramme, Nachwuchsförderungen

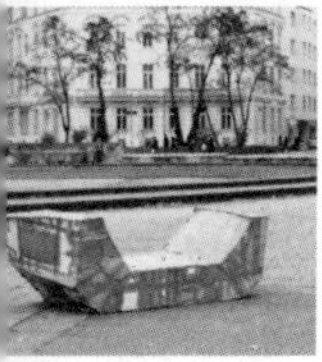

75 **Pawel Szostak** This ain't MQ, motherfucker! 2012

Cardboard, approx. 80 × 300 × 150 cm

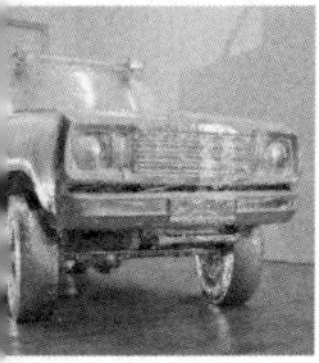

76 **Lukas Troberg** Charger 2011

Pick-up, aluminium foil, 200 × 420 × 240 cm. Photo: Matthias Bildstein

Charger – a huge pick-up wrapped in aluminium foil. This metaphor is a game that makes me feel melancholic, because cars have become part of families, so to speak. Wrapping a car in household aluminium foil is an appropriate and at all events symbolic action. It is a fact of society that individuals and people in general will never manage to find a reasonable approach to machines, preferring either to trivialize or diabolize them, a fact that art can and should emphasize both ironically and in all seriousness. And so the huge vehicle is there, wrapped in foil, waiting to be picked up.

Text: Franz Schuh

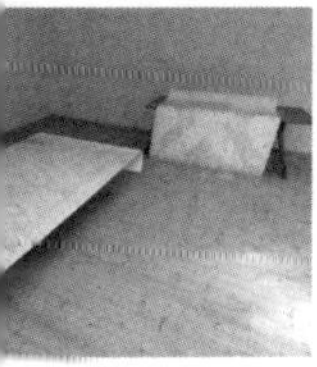

77 **Charlotte Schnabl** Monument 2012

Installation, Photo: Birgit and Peter Kainz

Monumental in size, fragile in its nature, the large-scale drawing as symbol of questioning and transience. The fascinating aspect of the drawing is in the recreation by hand of the real motif in its original size. Its strength lies in the meditative action in contrast to the daily stress and distractions, by which a large-format picture is created. A photographic reproduction could be made more rapidly and accurately, but here the charm of a questionable relationship between effort and result also plays a role. Because a drawing cannot be made with a click and corrected at the touch of a button, the real-size reproduction is like a declaration of love of the imperfect.

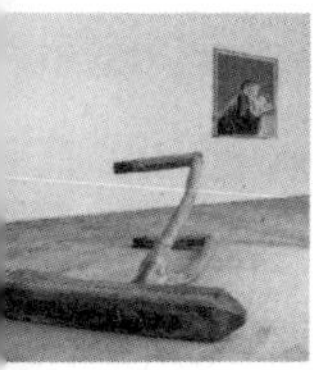

78 **Laura Wagner** MINDSTUCKPALACE 2012

Installation view. Photo: Peter and Birgit Kainz

In this work Laura Wagner investigates various materials and forms by playing with their possible meanings. The household objects used appear curious, although they are or were part of our everyday life. The artist draws attention to the unusual features of functional form and gives the observer an idea of the confusion that daily life as constructed by human beings leaves behind.

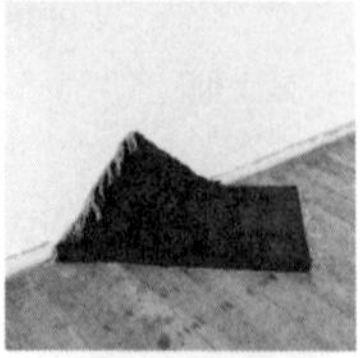

79 **Angelika Loderer** Pink Snow (detail) 20

Quartz sand (pressed), carpet, 80 × 60 × 30 cm. Photo: Birgit and Peter Kainz

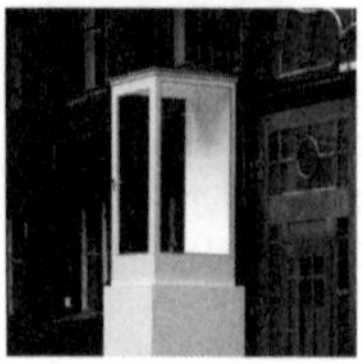

80 **Sebastian Gärtner** Kenotaph 20

440 × 96 × 96 cm. Site-specific installation

Turned into a pedestal and put on a pedestal. With the intention to make t exhibition space itself the theme of his project, Sebastian Gärtner encas DieKunstzelle (The Art Booth) at WUK in Vienna with wooden boards, turni the alternative space into a plinth on which he presented a 1:1 model of t KunstZelle itself. The sheer size of the over four-meters-high object, conjur associations to a monument – or a cenotaph.

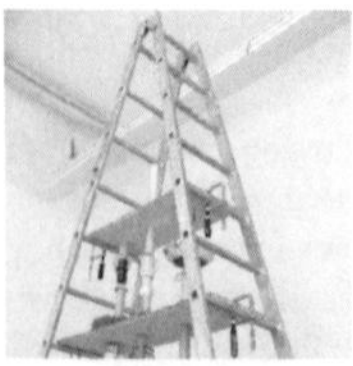

81 **Angelika Loderer** Pink Snow (detail) 2

Plaster rods, vessels, fruit juices, ladder, 300 × 150 × 40 cm. Photo: Birgit and Peter Kainz

Reductive objects made of plaster and sand are placed in the room. Like spong they absorb fluids from containers, an altered state of passivity. Casting moul are rearranged. Resistance, fragility and transience correlate. These process-bas artworks result in unpredictable experiments with the banality of the comm place.

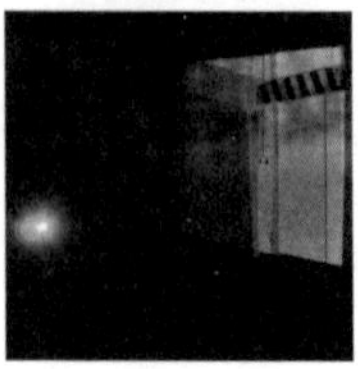

82 **Jana Rinchenbachová** Whirling 20

2 panes of reflective glass, 200 × 320 cm, silicon, projection

Viewers are invited to enter the installation, become part of it and allow the selves to become disoriented by the multiple projections and their own reflectio in the glass. I was looking for a situation in which I would become so much p of an action that I would be unable to stop because if I did I would fall down i mediately. Holding a camera in my hand I started to spin around until I reach the point when I was not turning by will but by the momentum of the moveme itself, like the Sufi Dervish dancers who enter a state of trance by whirling hours in search of their inner centre and silence.

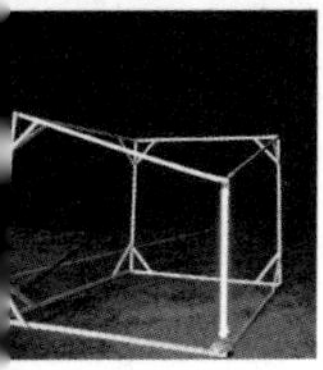

83 **Anna Mai** der narr auf wolke 12 2011

Installation, 11 cubes made of laths, 1 cube painted white with fluorescent lamp, approx. 300 x 300 x 300 cm

Falling out of line (breaking ranks/marching to a different drummer).
The chaos zone of a system contributes to liveliness and the development of peculiarity – character and personality.
Chaos (instability/highest level of sensitivity) is the birthplace of ideas and innovation, not linear, not always rational, often foolish and therefore enriching and manifold.
The installation was set up amongst 11 other equally shaped cubes, built by members of the Aspern public who invited artists to reflect on the Aspern Urban Lakeside, a part of Vienna which is being planned and will be developed over the next five to ten years.

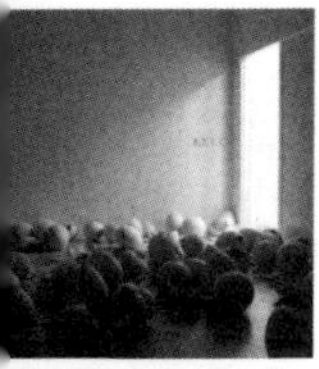

84 **Perihan Keles** Egg Shells 2012

Plaster, approx. 50 pieces, partially in tact, partially fragmented, Ø 20–50 cm

The production process of this installation continues in the exhibition space. The effort of pouring plaster into rubber balloons, shaking and coaxing it into a thin shell results in a very fragile and easily destroyable product. The way the shells are placed in the room makes their destruction inevitable. I thus involve the viewer into the process of installation and subsequently of the work itself.

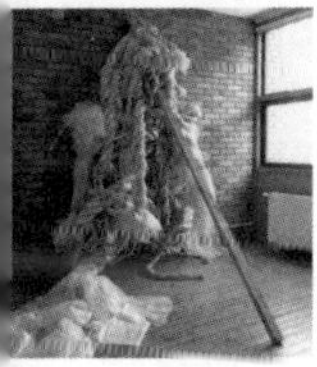

85 **Sophie Hirsch** Untitled 2011

Sculpture, Dimensions variable

Sophie Hirsch twists used sheets of plastic packaging into strings and ropes. After a long and strenuous process she exposes the transparent resource material that once covered merchandise to extreme tension in order to force it into another form. The intertwined sculpture assumes a physically experienceable dynamic that triggers a succession of associations.

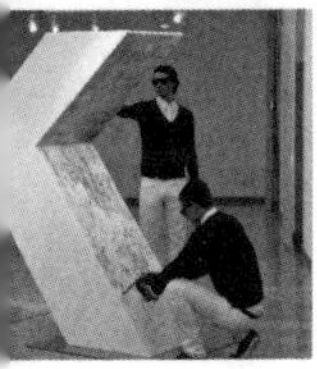

86 **Perfekt World** Sugar K 2011

Performance

PERFEKT WORLD is a pool of creatives from the art and design sector mainly consisting of 5 people. In our early days we all worked in different fields such as advertising, art, web development, social media. We approach the businessworld with an innovative idea that brings together the strongest parts from art and commercial creativity. Our offer is to create art, advertisements, marketing concepts and design on the cutting point of art and creative research with the focus on artistical expression and commercial sustainability. A very important field of activity is research & development. So that we can always be state of the art and push things forward.

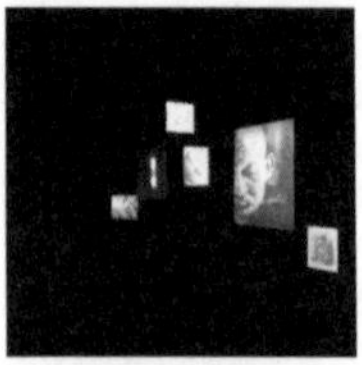

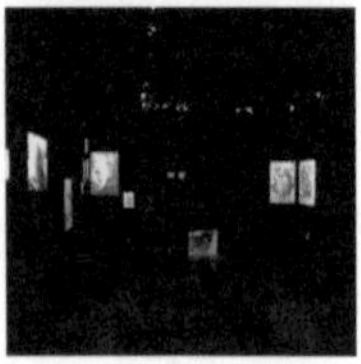

87/88 **Fabian-Benjamin Rainer** The Aorist 2

Installation view. Photo: Birgit und Peter Kainz

The Aorist investigates the reading process, the study of a photograph for pictor
information and method of development. Using my own black and white phot
graphs it looks at how the way a photograph is printed changes the relationsh
to the information in the picture. The linking of reality with the past in photog
phy and its immobility underlies the analysis, like a patina as witness of its tin
The real objects in the here and now play on the contrast between being and il
sion as a possibility for deception and thus for investigating selective perceptic
The experimentation with different types of development not only changes t
surface of the paper but also, by virtue of the physical and chemical proce
makes the image unique – a dynamic and irreproducible aspect of photograph
development.

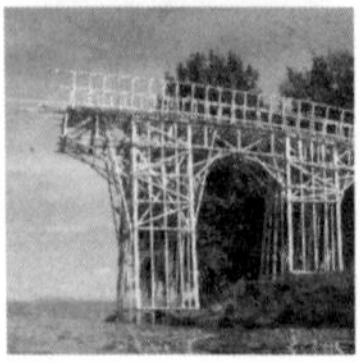

89 **Bildstein | Glatz** As long as the budget lasts 20

Wood, screws, 900 × 2800 × 500 cm, Courtesy of Kunsthalle Arbon, Switzerland

This object is about art, play and the imagination and within this triumvira
forms a construction of the absurd. Everything looks right: the height of the ti
bers, their thickness and number, the distance from the ground to the horizon
walkway, the substructure, the railings. But what is it? A bridge to the other si
to the German bank? A springboard so as to be able to swim across? In trying
pursue the idea through to a logical end, the viewer inevitably lands on the ha
ground of reality – or belly flops into the water. This bridge fragment entitled
long as the budget lasts satirizes the utopia of an imagined world with cultu
tolerance, resources and equal opportunity.

Text: Brigitte Schmid-Gug

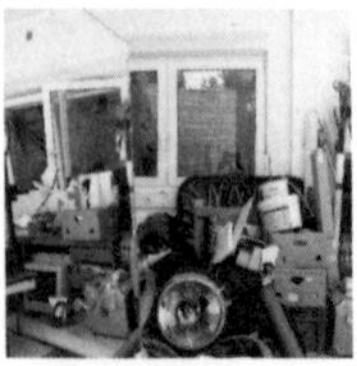

90 **Leander Schönweger** Where's Wally? 2

Inkjet print, 89 × 59 cm

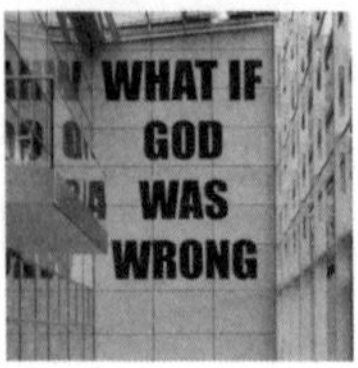

91 **Lukas Troberg** WHAT IF GOD WAS WRONG 2

Laser-cut PVC adhesive letters , 1200 × 550 cm. Photo: IMBA/karlmayr.com

The Institute of Molecular Biology in Vienna sees itself as a pioneering resear
centre for genetic engineering. The fact that genetic engineering not only mak
crucial contributions to the developments in medicine but also targeted interv
tions in the DNA of living creatures possible is fascinating yet questionab
Lukas Troberg plays on precisely these controversies in his work at the IMBA
The approximately 12 meter high and five-meter-wide sentence WHAT IF GC
WAS WRONG can be read in the partially glazed conservatory of the IME
Whether it is to be understood as a question or a statement is left open as in
cated by the omission of the punctuation mark.

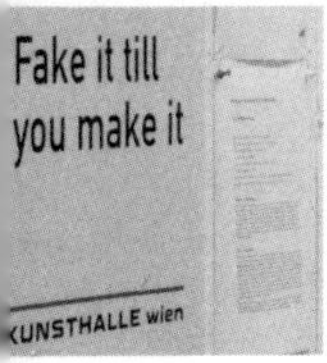

92 **Jeroen Visser** Fake it till you make it 2013

Poster (off-set print), 42 × 29.7 cm

'Fake it till you make it' is a common catchphrase that means to imitate confidence. The same principle can be applied to artistic practice. Pretend you're already a successful artist and success might just follow.

I decided to do an intervention in public space in Vienna by using a familiar form that is commonly associated with renowned art institutions representing established artists. The *Instructions* project realized by the Kunsthalle Wien in 2004 was perfect for my purpose.

Resselpark was originally chosen as the park forms the core of Karlsplatz and is home to a number of important historic cultural institutions: the Künstlerhaus and the Secession, the Vienna Museum and the Kunsthalle *Project Space*.

continued from page 111

others cannot reliably plan and make use of their creativity. It eludes all creative intentions.

Second, artists are used (trained) to making productive use of the opportunities that their creativity offers. Martin Walser spoke of 'organized spontaneity', a strategic arrangement of spontaneous forces invested into artistic activity. There are differing views and ideas as to how unavailability and organization are connected. For me, at least, it remains a puzzle. If we knew more about it, we could adapt better to it. Typically, however, there are 'individual secrets to success' but no rules to build on.

A personal definition of creativity

'Creative' means producing something that did not exist before but whose existence then does appear necessary. People – or at least many of them – cannot and do not want to do without it any more. It changes the world, or at least part of it. The world becomes different through creative achievements. 'Creative' in the emphatic sense is thus something new that is not random – although it didn't exist before – but becomes necessary and hence something old itself. In addition, there has to be a *possibility for the reception* of this achievement. Creative achievements seldom occur in isolation but most often when there is also a willingness to reflect upon and recognize them. They always prevail against resistance and gain stature and character as a result. But if the resistance was total, these achievements would have no chance.

Creation has to do with *fitness for the future*, a concept embedded in the idea of creativity. The philosopher Villem Flusser spoke of a three-way relationship, subject, object and project. It is about the efforts of the subject in the face of its objects; a proper subject cannot but make a project out of itself and its objects. And within the project the conflicts between the subject and object are temporarily abandoned.

Creativity requires obstinacy, *originality* – a production ethic, a stubborn determination not to be distracted from the project. The product of creativity is initially *surprising*. Great creative achievements are performed by individuals who are strong (at least in their own fields) but they then belong at least formally – to everyone. Provided the electricity bill is paid, electric light belongs to everyone whose way it illuminates. And Beckett is not the owner of *Endgame*. Decisive creations are continuously democratized, and yet creativity remains an *elitist* concept: creative people are those who can do more than most.

In mass societies there will not be a perfect or levelling

FRANZ SCHUH Writer, Vienna

NOVEMBER 2012

Creativity: How New Ideas are Found?

Lecture

balance, but – and this is the core of education policy – a *relationship* should be possible *between the creativity of elites and the majority*, bearing in mind as well that outside its own field every elite belongs to the majority: the utopia of a mutual permeability/inclusive understanding of the action/existence problems of the majority, which as a group – the REVOLUTION, for example – can also be creative.

Fortunately, creativity does not exist only in the emphatic sense but also in a limited form and small framework and relatively, in other words relating to individuals and their world. In some individual standards, things that in an elitist sense would be unimportant are regarded as creative. When I took my school-leaving exam, MATURA as they call it in Austria, I studied Sartre, and the examiner asked me, after the exam, which dealt with great decisions, BETRAYAL OR DEATH, whether I thought that sensitive decisions also existed in daily life. I had my answer prepared: 'Yes, of course, Sir, marriage for example.'

Abrupt conclusion or it can't go any higher

There is a time-honoured resolution to this tension between discipline and unavailability, which can be countered through a strategy of organized spontaneity: inspiration. 'Inspirare' meant originally to blow in, to be enthusiastic, then, in the

---

ELECTRIC INDIGO DJ, Composer, Musician, Vienna **NOVEMBER 2012**

Generative Transformations, Competence and Performance in Art Practice

Lecture

eighteenth century, to incite and illuminate, and so transcendence just vanished from the word. Originally the inspiration came from without, blown in on a breath (Latin: spiritus).

Why is the Holy Scripture holy? Because it is based on inspiration, because it was inspired by God. True, God's word is written, but the language of the scripture is the work of man, a translation into something comprehensible and of human proportions. Thomas Aquinus said that at the revelation the spirit of the prophet is touched, moved, by the Holy Spirit, just as an incomplete instrument *(instrumentum deficiens)* is moved by the principal agent *(principale agens)*. In other words, the communication of the holy on earth is always deficient – in contrast to the spirit, which communicates itself, which inspires. The quality and outstanding property of the Holy Scripture is its immaculateness. Where and how could mankind claim this with the help of reason?

The Holy Scripture is superior to all art because, as the church father Ambrosius said, the hagiographers, the human scribes of God's word, 'wrote what the spirit inspired them to do.'

But, in this strange constellation of incomplete instrument and God, the omnipotent, who uses this instrument, there is one abiding question, namely who speaks when we speak? Who is the author and with what authority does he speak?

WERNER REITERER Artist, Vienna **NOVEMBER 2012**

How to Hammer in Thinking into an Artwork and More or Less Fail! Lecture

100% Target Group Workshop

p. 138

Who is the originator – for example of all the unworldly sounds? Is Richard Wagner, not a great man, the producer of his music, or is there a divine element to genius, is the deity playing its own unworldly music on the incomplete instrument?

The artist is a creator – if he moves beyond the phase of imitating nature, if, like in Plato, he does not just make an ideal that would exist without any effort on his part. Paradoxically, according to Blumenberg, it was Christianity, with the idea of the Demiurge, an idea that compares the artist with the creator. This also exists in humble variants. A poet, says Nabokov, claims to be a writer of secondary literature about Creation. Full of understanding for God, for his superior, the great Vladimir Nabokov wrote in 1925 that he could understand that God was delighted when he created the world. According to him, we (the poets) are translators of God's creations, his little plagiarists and imitators who, enchanted by his stroke of genius, add something gracious to the perfect line.

I read this as an explanation of the unavailability of the artistic but also as an explanation of how one can obtain this unavailability. Even the author is amazed at the new thing he has brought into the world. Can the incomplete instrument that he is possibly have done that himself? If one has sufficient discipline, one can also ultimately rely on inspiration.

CHRISTIANE MÖBUS Artist, Hannover/Berlin **DECEMBER 2012**

Loud and Soft Pieces On the Back of Animals. Lecture

On the Back of Animals Workshop

openness

ANNA JERMOLAEWA Artist, Austria/Russia

DECEMBER 2012

... shows her work

Lecture

round tables

ROUND TABLE DECEMBER 2010

THE IMPOSSIBILITY OF REALITY - I

AUGUST RUHS Psychoanalyst, Professor at the Medical University of Vienna
PETER WEIBEL Media Theoretician, Artist, Curator, Director ZKM | Centre for Art and Media, Karlsruhe
ANTON ZEILINGER Quantum Physicist, Professor for Experimental Physics, University of Vienna
Moderation: **ROBERT PFALLER** Philosopher, Professor at the University of Applied Arts Vienna

ROUND TABLE MAY 2011

THE IMPOSSIBILITY OF REALITY - II

JOSEF PENNINGER Genetic Engineer, Scientific Director IMBA, Vienna
MARTIN WALDE Artist, Vienna
Moderation: **MARTIN HAIDINGER** Science Journalist, ORF, Vienna

---

MARKUS HANAKAM & ROSWITHA SCHULLER Artists, Vienna **APRIL 2013**

Artefacts

Lecture

ROUND TABLE **MAY 2012**

LET US DEMAND THE IMPOSSIBLE!

Realism in Art, Film Theory and Theoretical Physics

JUDITH EISLER Artist, Professor for Painting, University of Applied Arts Vienna
JENNIFER FRIEDLANDER Professor for Media Studies, Pomona College, California
HENRY KRIPS Professor for Cultural Studies, Claremont Graduate University, California
Moderation: **ROBERT PFALLER** Philosopher, Professor at the University of Applied Arts Vienna

ROUND TABLE **MAY 2013**

CLIMATE / RISK?

SYLVIA ECKERMANN Artist, Vienna
HANS PETER KAMMERER Vienna State Opera Singer, Vienna
HELGA KROMP-KOLB Meteorologist, Climate Researcher, Professor at the University of Natural Resources and Life Sciences, Vienna
FRIEDRICH STEINHÄUSLER Physicist, Risk Researcher, Professor at the University of Salzburg
Moderation: **MARTIN HAIDINGER** Science Journalist, ORF, Vienna

---

ANNA JERMOLAEWA Artist, Austria/Russia **APRIL 2013**

An Introduction to the Austrian Film Museum's Collection Lecture

Alone in an Atelier Performance for the camera. Workshop

exhibitions

EPHEMERAL
TransArts - Show # 23.–30.4.2013
Kunstraum am Schauplatz, Vienna
Curated by Amer Abbas, Roman Pfeffer and Lukas Willmann

KENOTAPH, SEBASTIAN GÄRTNER
21.3.–17.4.2013
Kunstzelle im WUK
Curated by Christine Baumann and Roman Pfeffer

LAST CALL, NEDA NIKOLIC
24.4.–25.5.2013
Kunstzelle im WUK
Curated by Christine Baumann and Roman Pfeffer

AN:ORDNUNGEN
13.1.2012
An exhibition choreographed by TransArts at the Liquid Loft Studios, Vienna
Curated by Chris Haring

AGAIN & AGAIN
Interventions in public space at Karlsplatz in cooperation with the ecm Department
21.1.2012
Presentation at the Kunsthalle Project Space, Vienna
Curated by Isabelle Blanc, Elisabeth Lacher and Roman Pfeffer

DIE KUNST DER INTERVENTION
PROJEKTE DER LICHTENBERG-STUDIOS
28.3.–27.4.2012
Galerie im Ratskeller Berlin
Curated by Uwe Jonas

VON AUSSEN NACH INNEN NACH AUSSEN
9.5.2012
Kubatur des Kabinetts, FLUC, Vienna
Curated by Nita Tandon, Ursula Maria Probst and Martin Wagner

---

CHRISTIAN HÖLLER Art Theoretician and Critic, Vienna

APRIL 2013

Cross Trans Lateral

The transdisciplinary basis of contemporary art
Lecture

SITUAKTION
22.–30.6.2012
Krinzinger Projekte, Vienna
Curated by Manfred Wiplinger

PHOTOGRAPHY FICTION
11.9.–20.10.2012
Galerie beim Engl, Luxembourg
Collaborative project with nine European universities as part of photomeetings luxembourg

0,192 M³
14.–20.1.2011
Kunstraum Praterstraße 15, Vienna
Curated by Nita Tandon

VOYEUR
THE HIDDEN PHOTOGRAPHER
6.–24.9.2011
Konschthaus beim Engl, Luxembourg
Collaborative project with nine European universities as part of photomeetings luxembourg

DON'T HAVE SEX WITH YOUR EX
26.11.–11.12.2010
Krinzinger Projekte, Vienna
Curated by Peter Nagy and the TransArts students

MAGAZINE PHOTOGRAPHY
7.–25.9.2010
Musée d'Histoire de la Ville de Luxembourg
Konschthaus beim Engl, Luxembourg
Collaborative project with nine European universities as part of photomeetings luxembourg

---

OLAF NICOLAI Artist, Berlin

MAY 2013

Ritornello Lecture
The Star on the Forehead Workshop
Grid and Poetry

MATTHIAS MICHALKA Curator for New Media, MUMOK, Vienna **MAY 2013**

Research Seminar for MA students

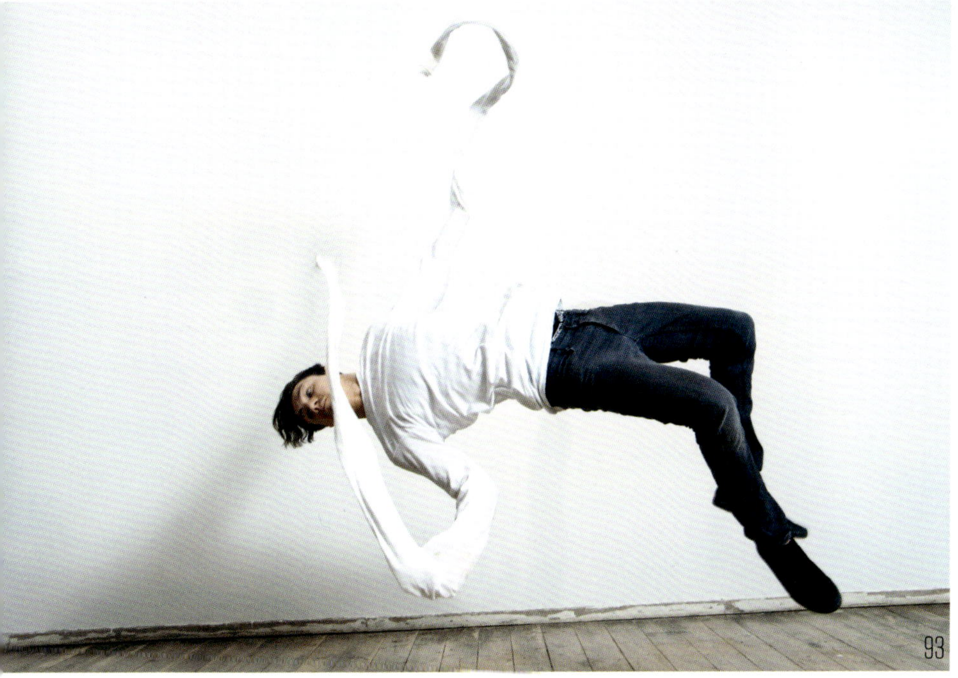

93

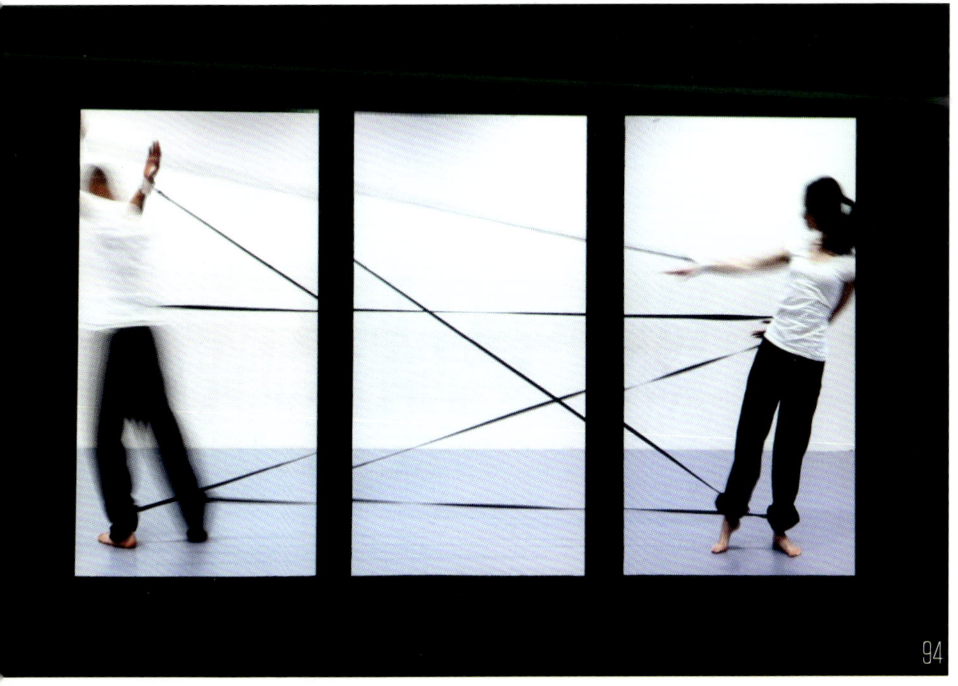

94

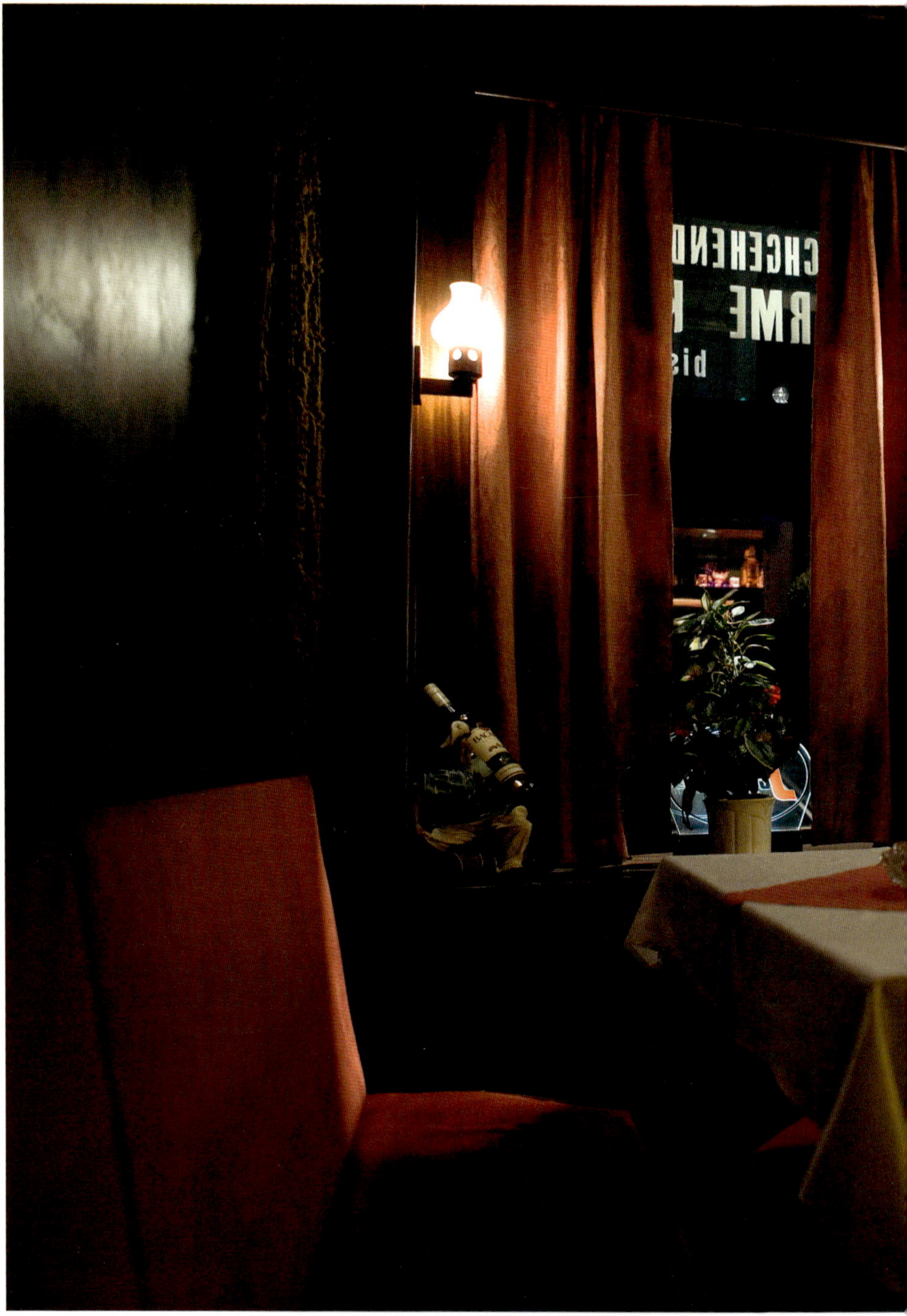

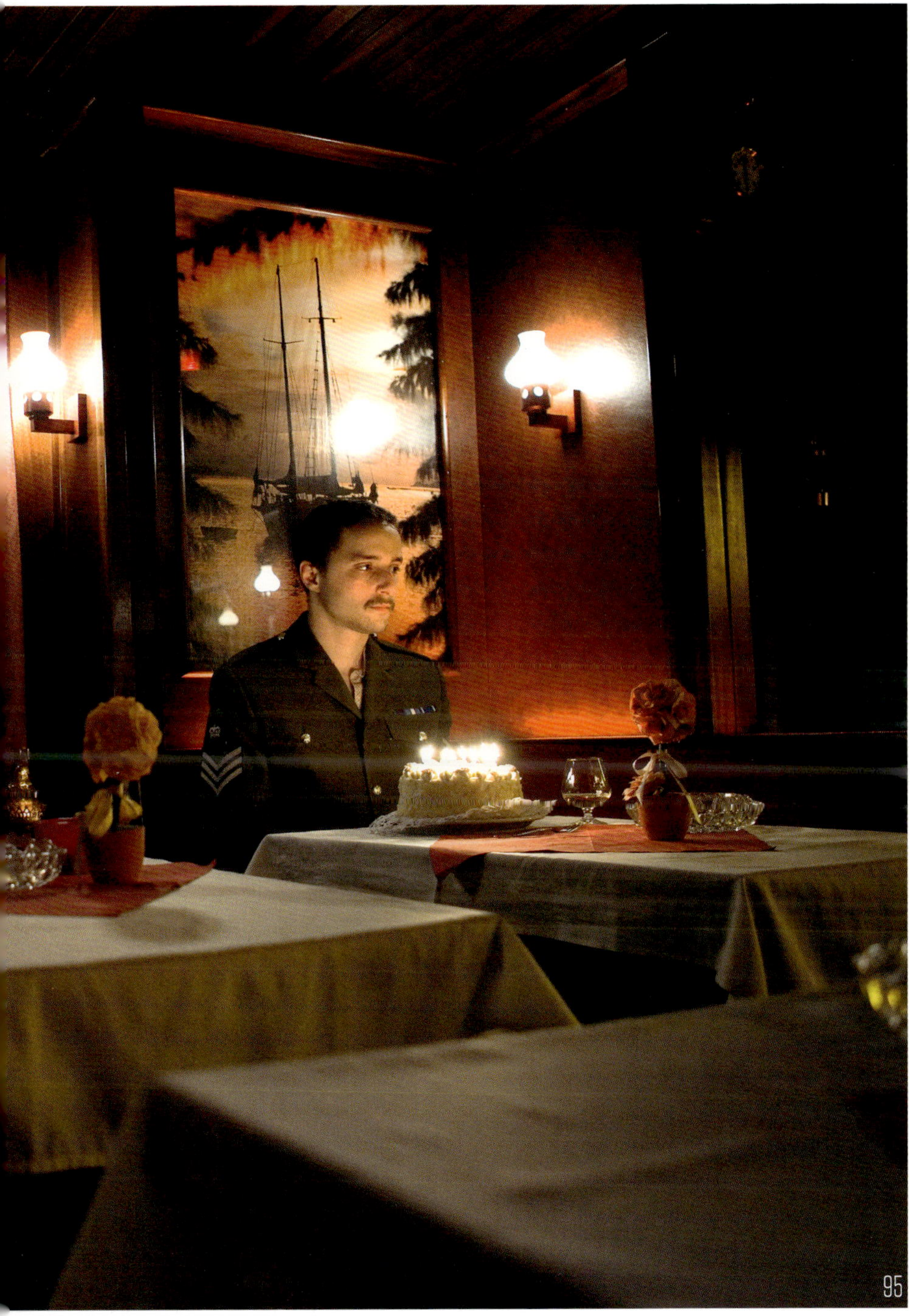

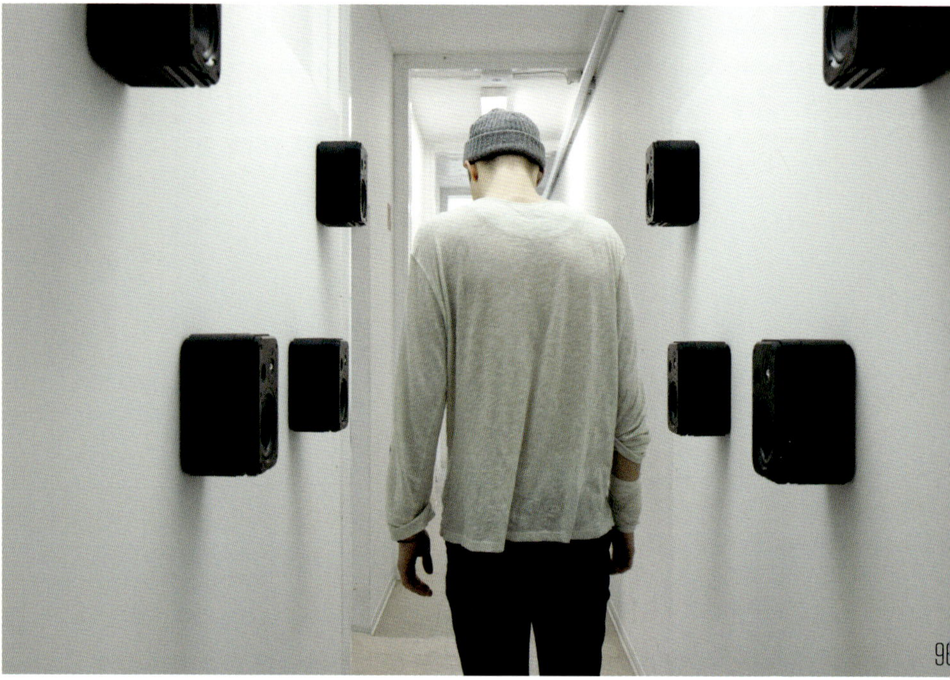

96

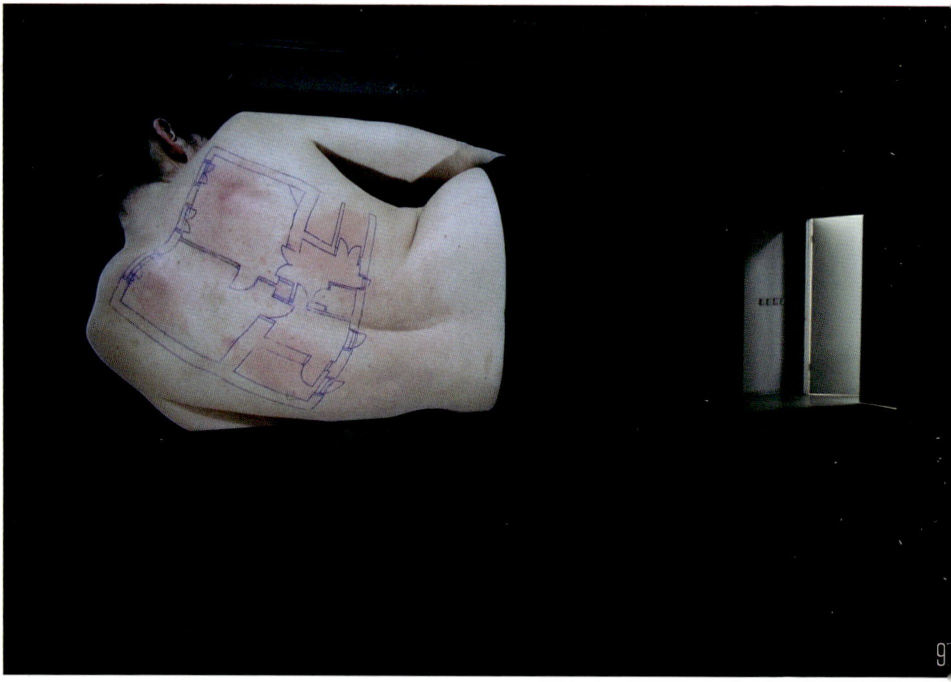

97

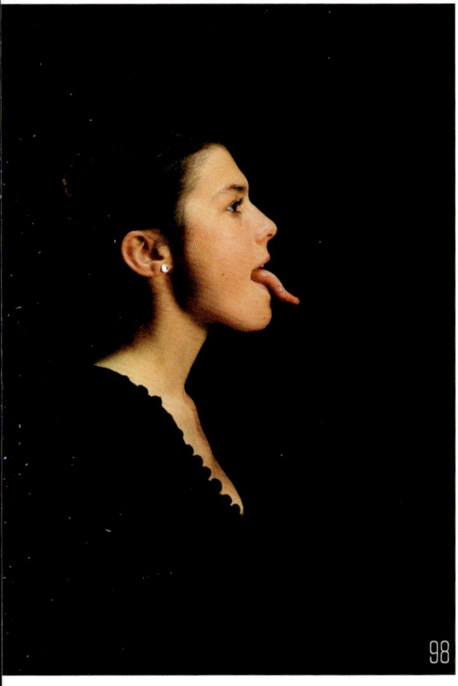

98

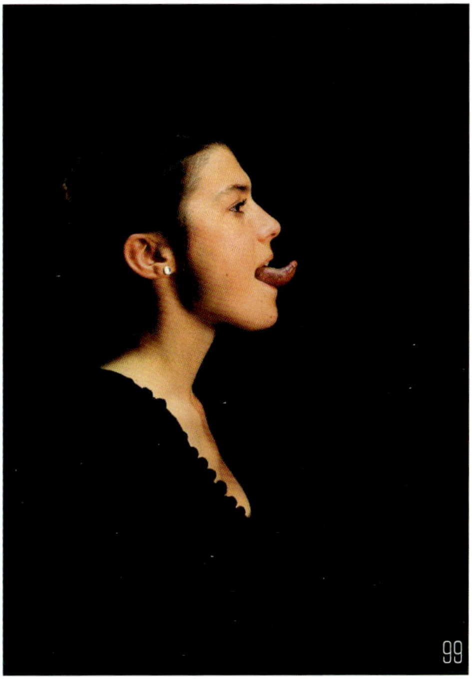

99

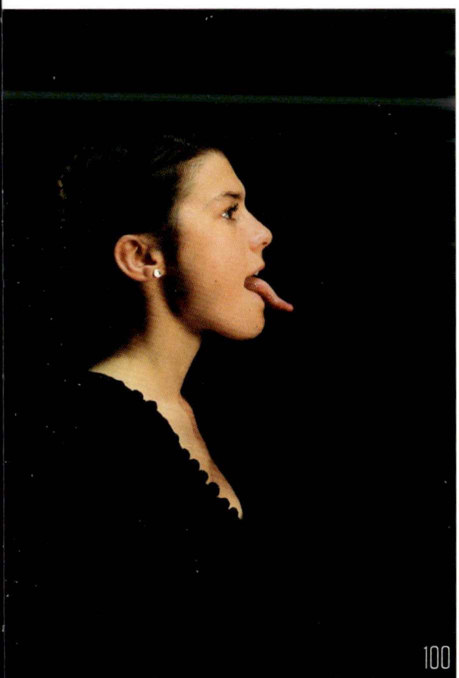

100

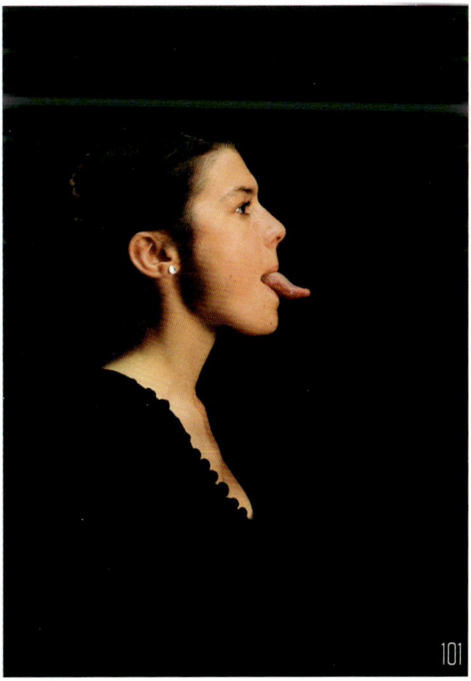

101

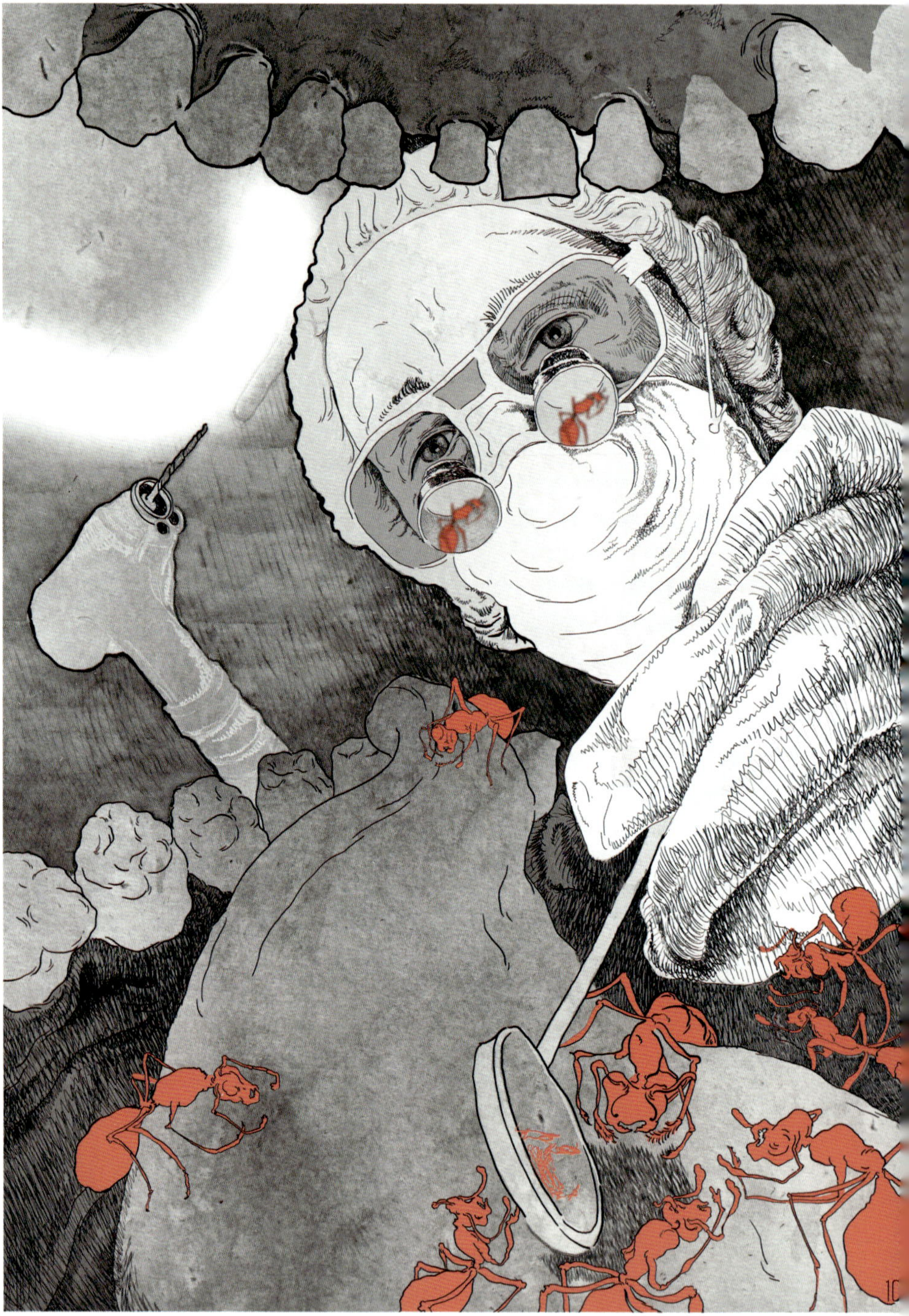

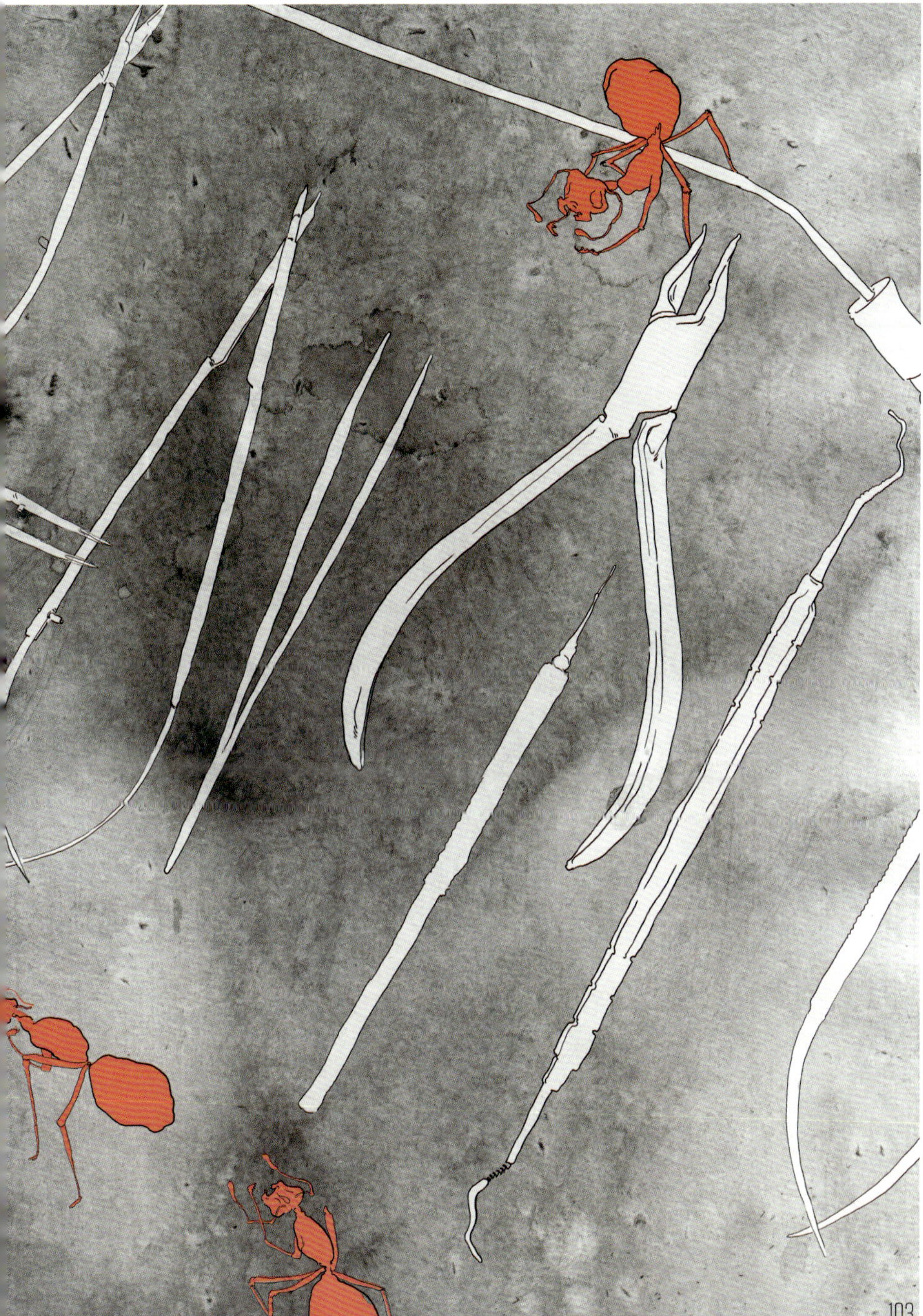

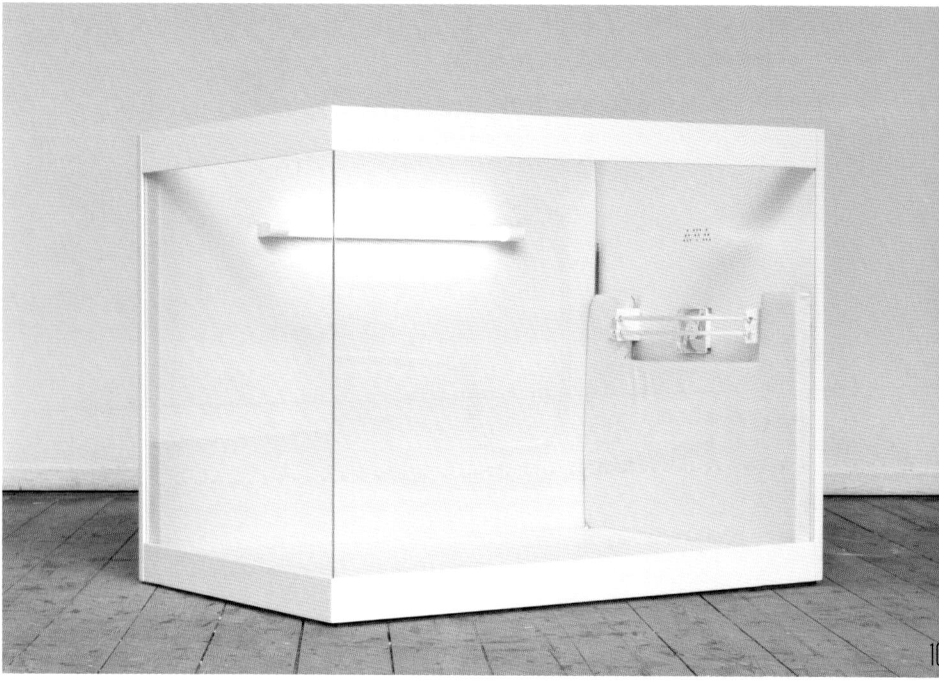

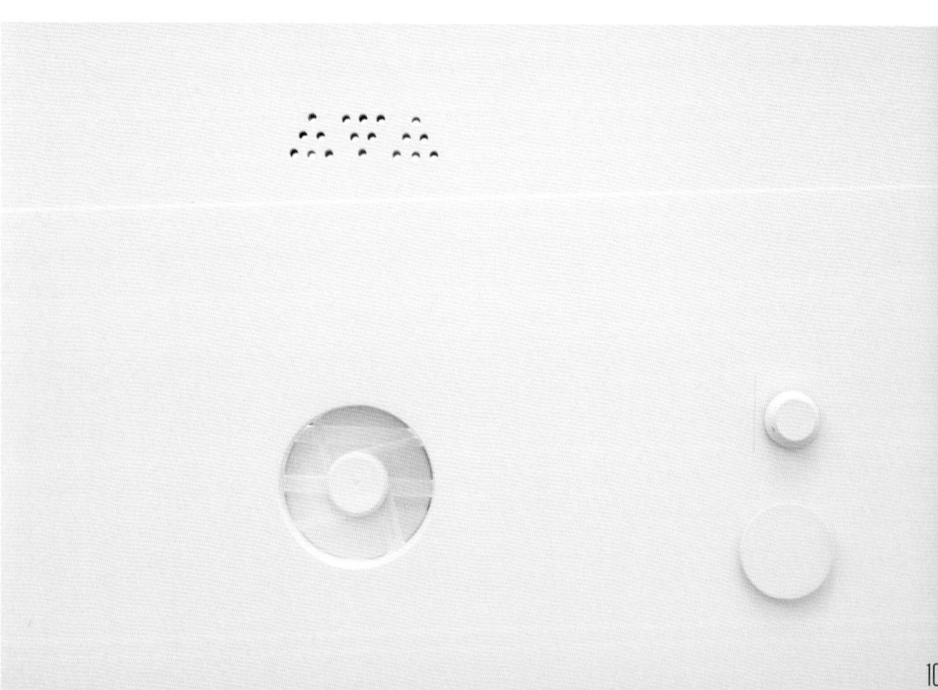

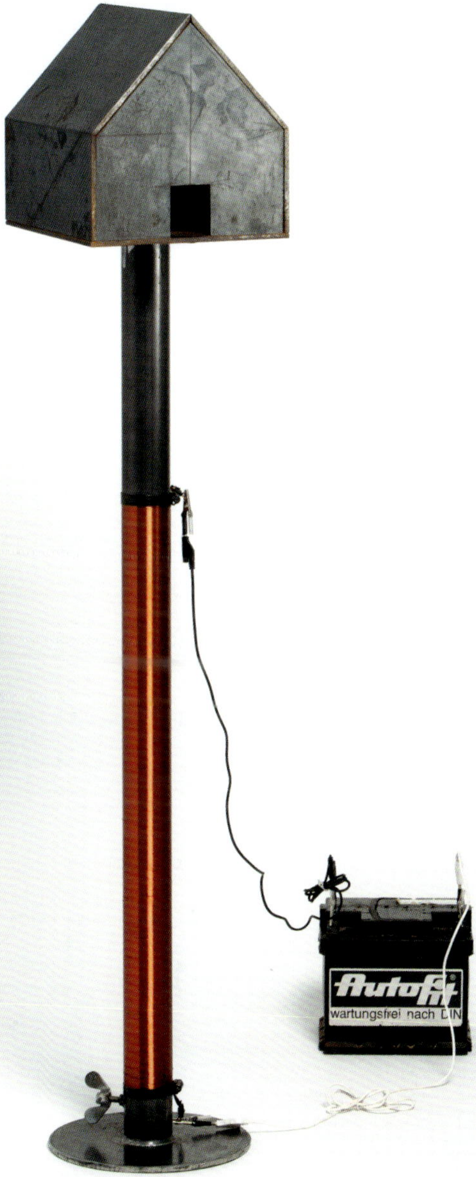
Autofit
wartungsfrei nach DIN

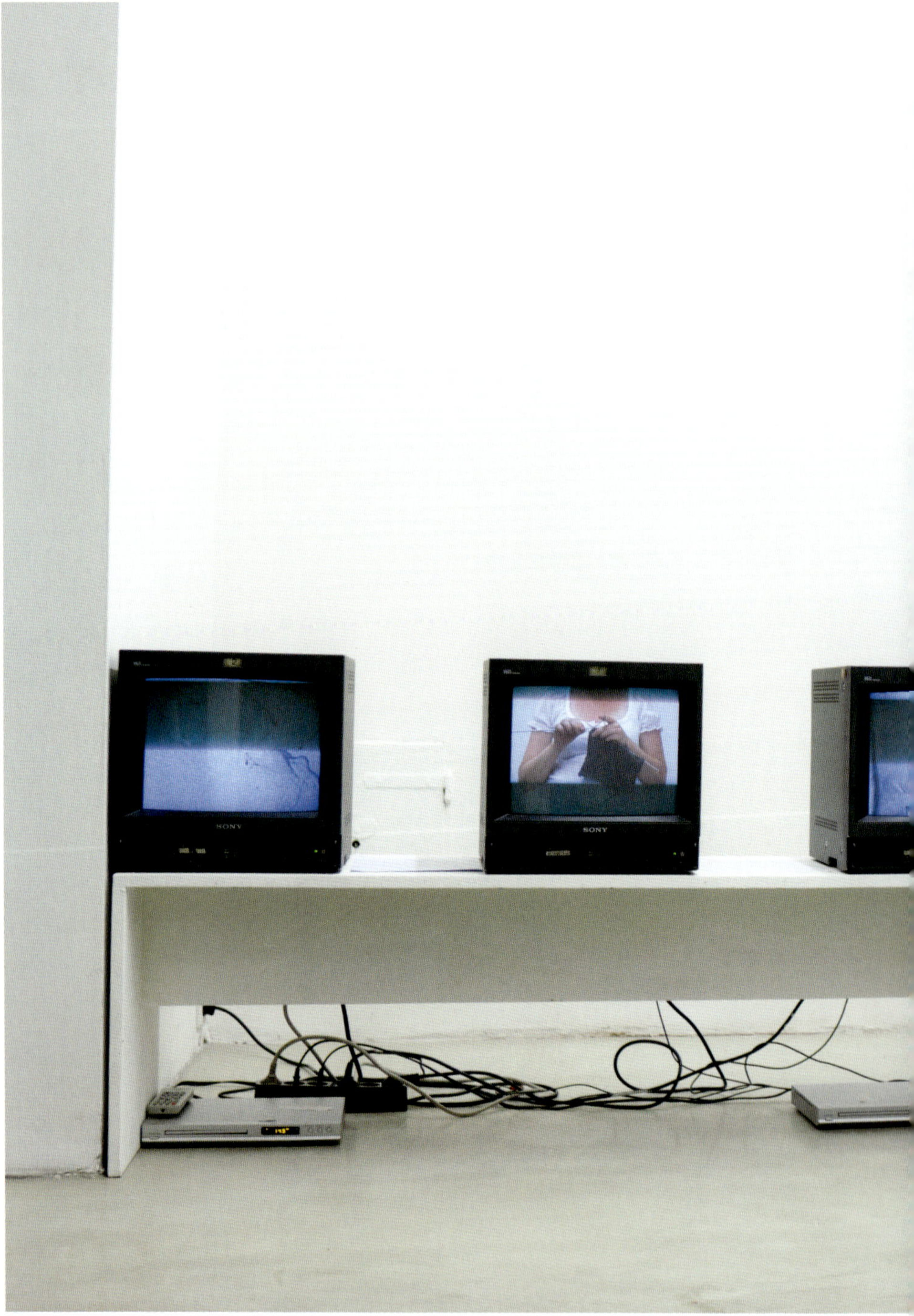
SONY
SONY

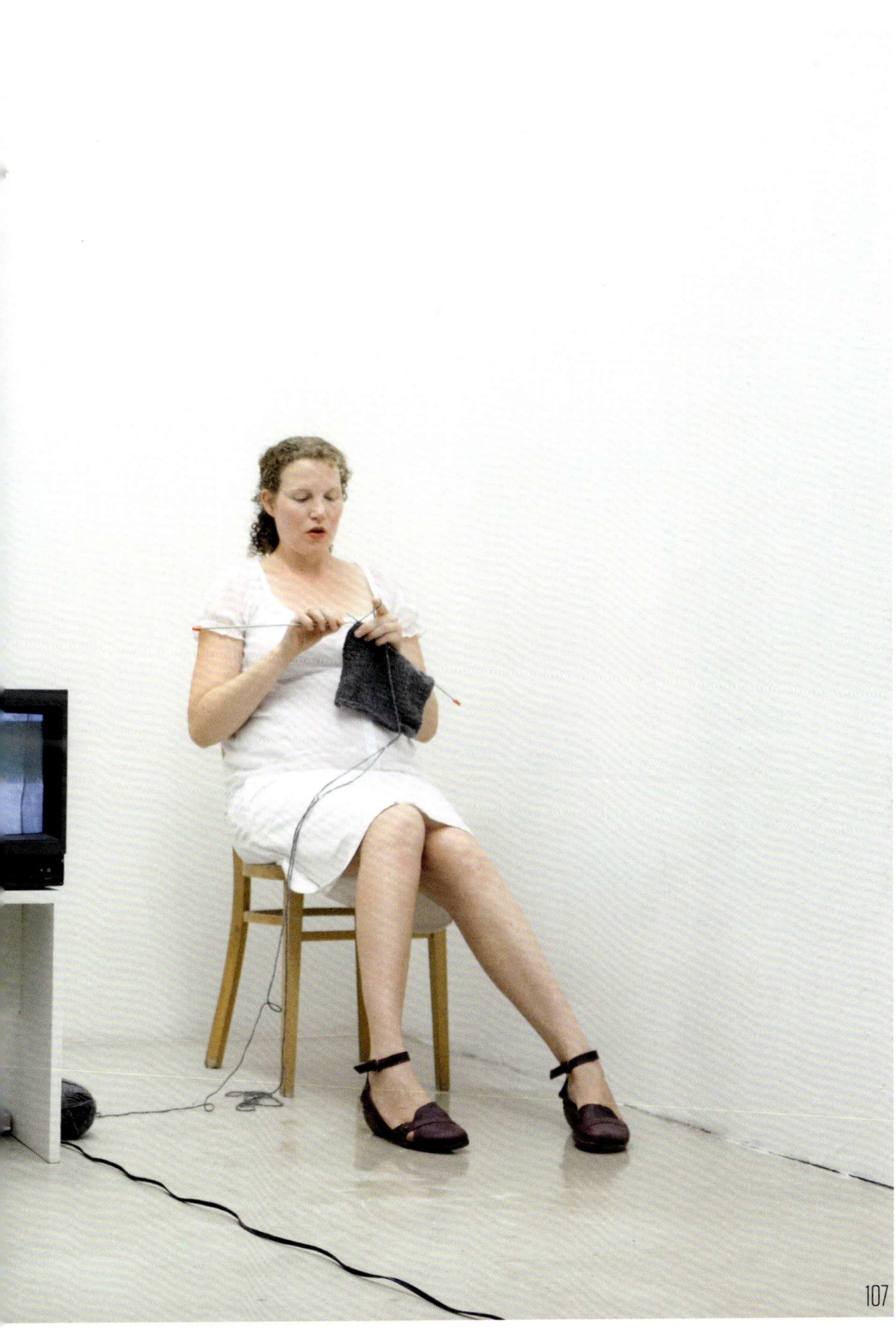

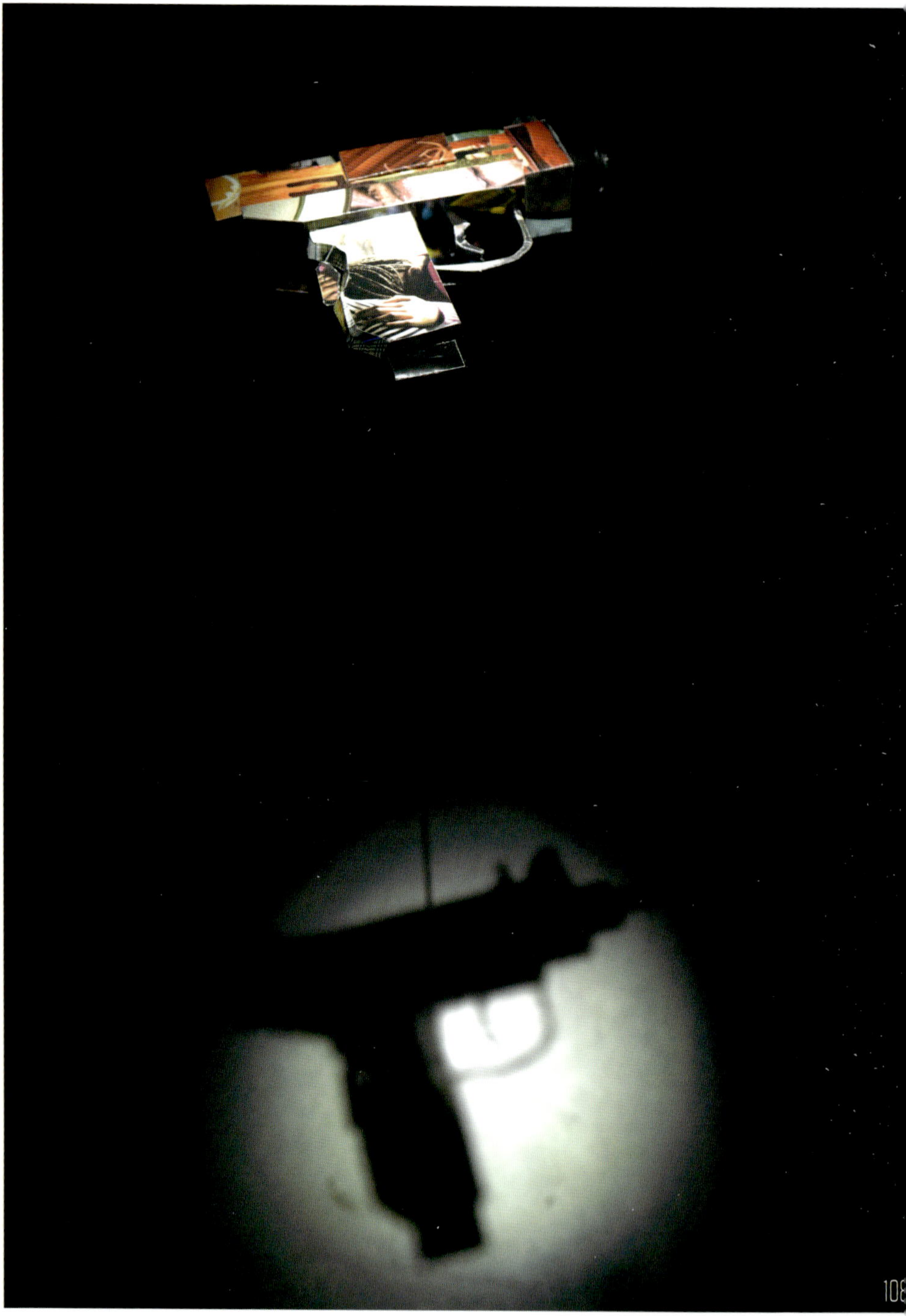

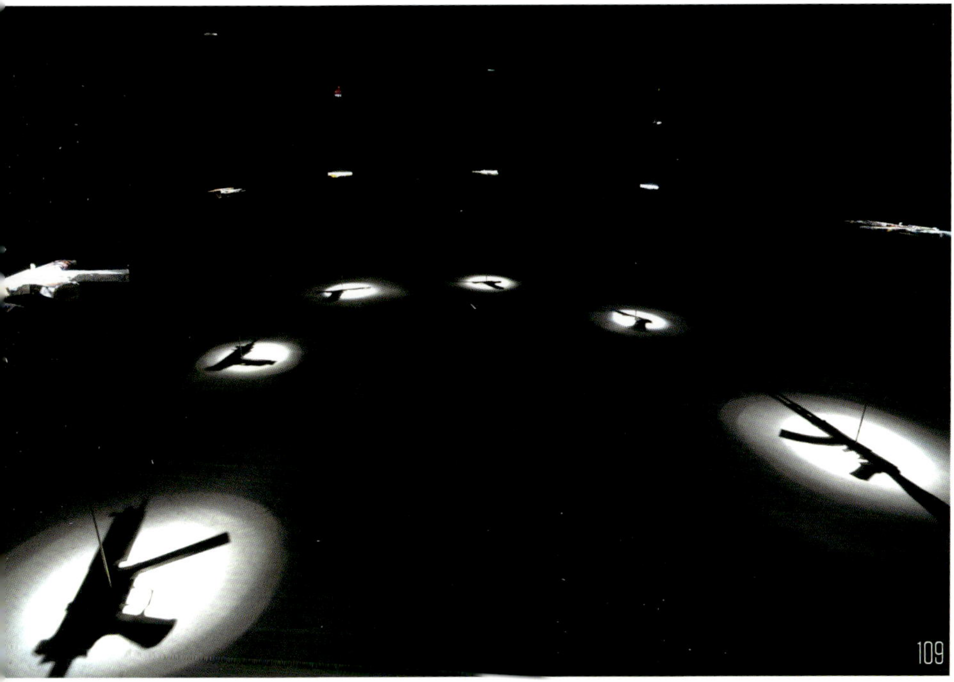

109

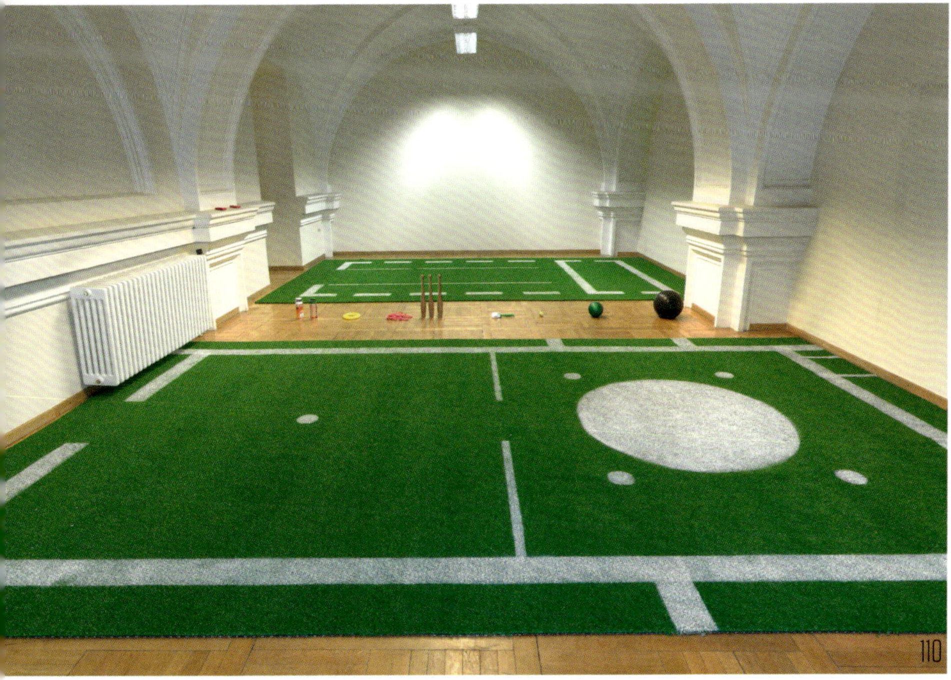

110

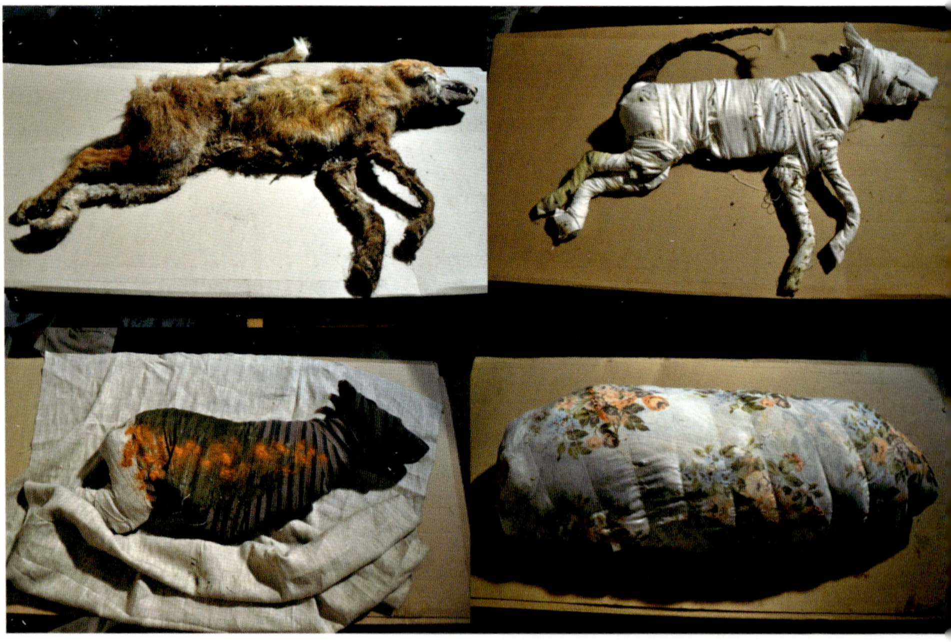

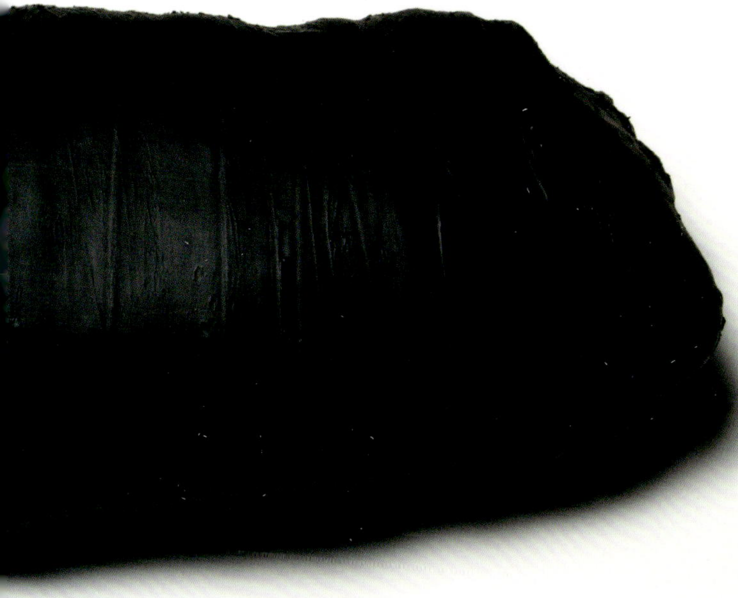

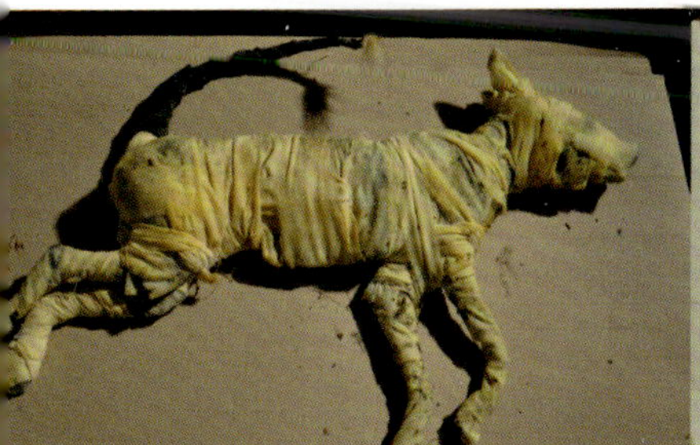

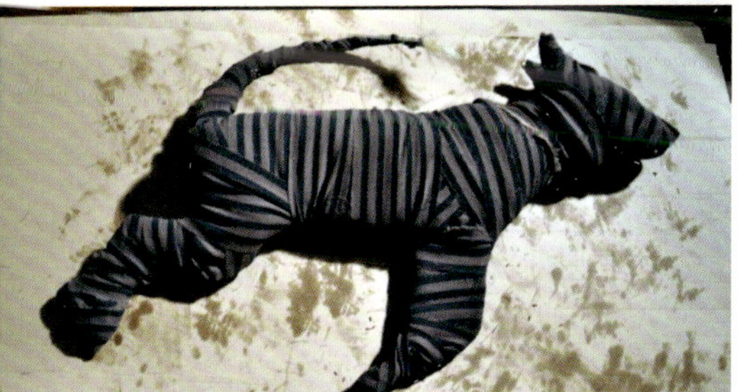

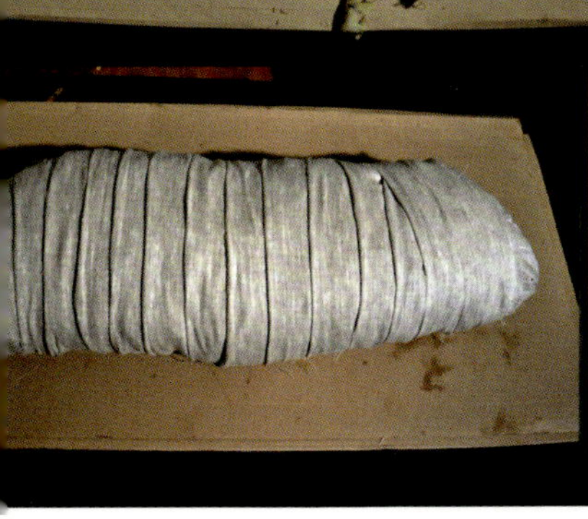

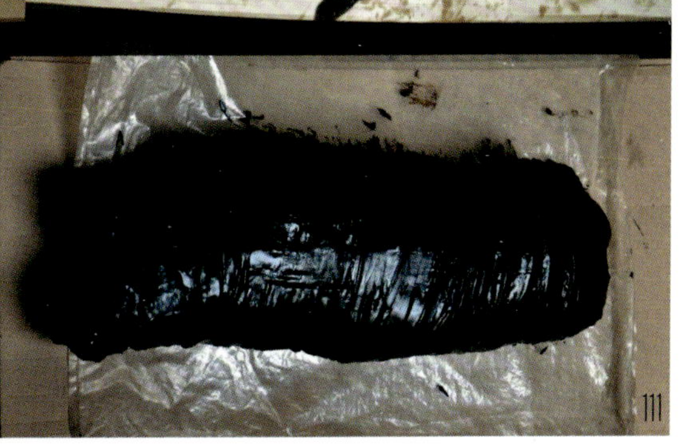

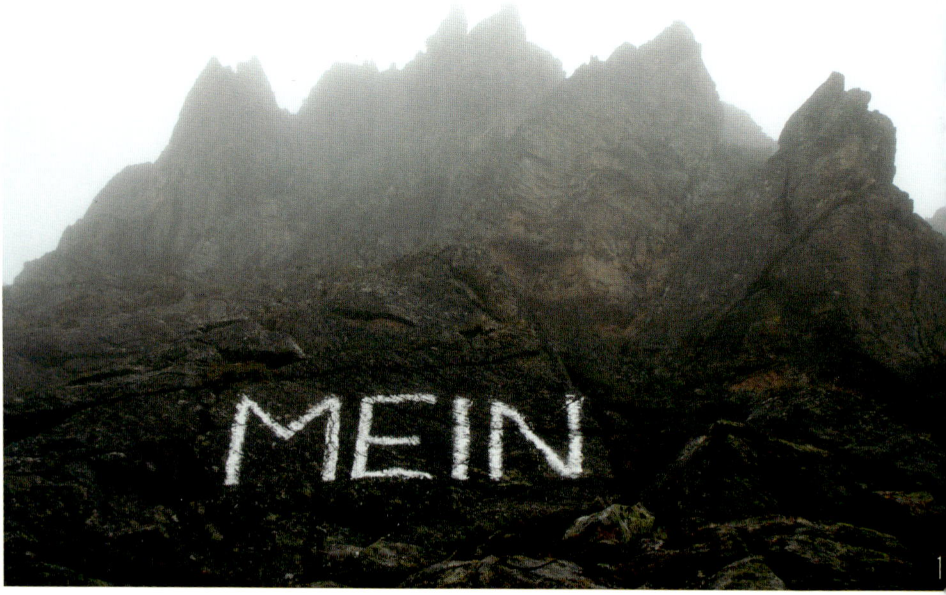

1

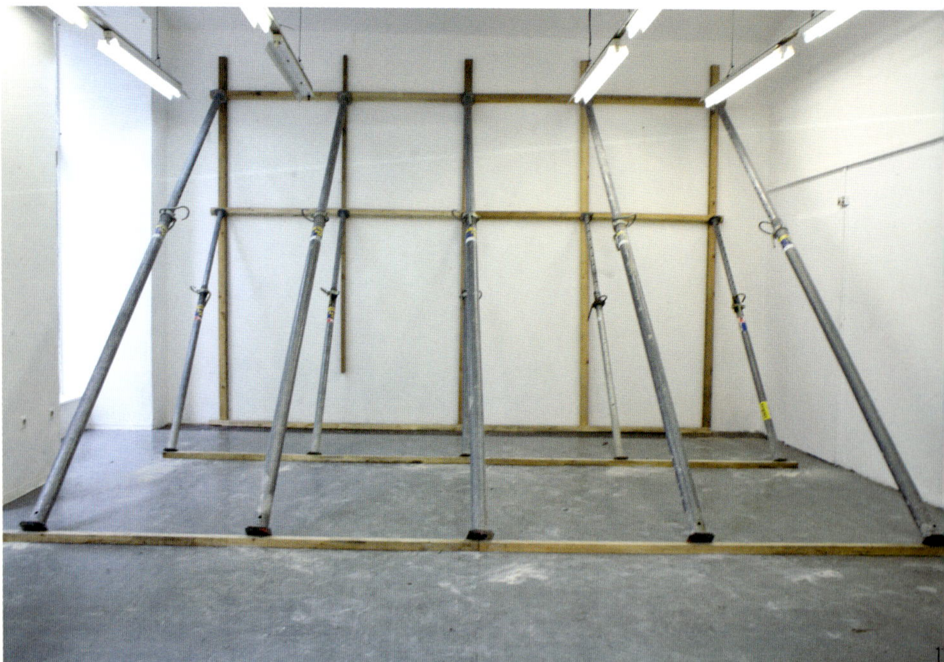

1

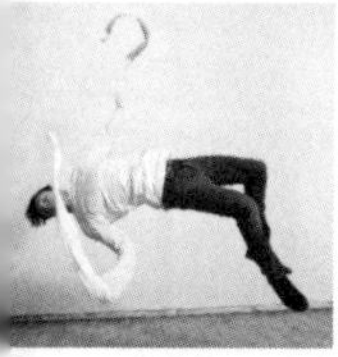

93 **Eugen Wist** Gravites 2011

Performance. Photo: Elfie Semotan

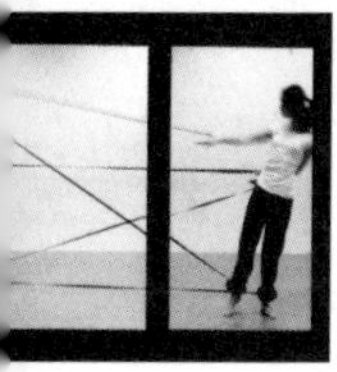

94 **Jonas Droste** Sketches of dance 2013

Video loop

Movement is action and does not refer to one as such. Dance is thus the attempt to perform a concrete action in the present. It is neither game, nor reference. This statement is valid for both the theoretical conception as well as reflection about dance. It is possible as both interaction with and through an object which could be mediator, or equal player.

The film is an overlap of three, dynamic image planes: the isolated body of each dancer moving in a specific way; the entire constellation of figures as well as the sequences of movements which result in dependencies and interrelationships ensuing from physical restrictions of the bindings; the elastic bands that produce ever-changing ephemeral drawings against the background – both as side products and as directions for the movements.

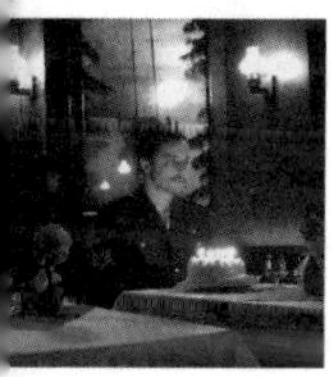

95 **Riki Werdenigg** The Major 2011

C-print on aluminium, 80 × 120 cm

Inspired by Ernst Jandl's 'blind man', this piece, like my work in general, strongly references home, man as a primitive species and his habitus.

blind man
my father spoke
of a blind man
i don't remember his words
or what he said
but i remember the cake
on which every candle was right
it was my tenth birthday
and there were definitely ten candles
which my father first counted
but i also know precisely
how he said
'poor blind man'
and repeated it
'poor blind man,
poor blind man'
(Ernst Jandl – der gelbe hund, 1980, Luchterhand Verlag)

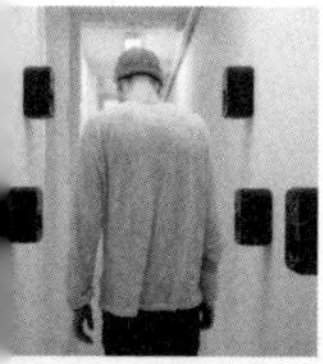

96 **Miriam Hamann** Pendulum 2013

8-channel sound installation

Pendulum deals with the act and sound of swinging. Referring to the rocking motion a binaural recorded sound moves from speaker to speaker in a U-shaped installation. Thus it passes the recipient and creates a sense of movement despite the static spatial situation.

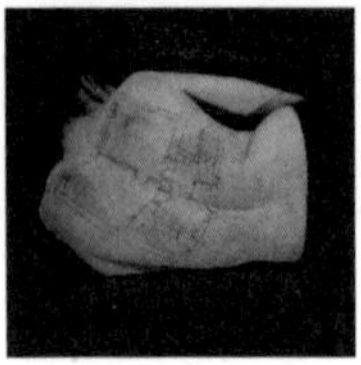

97 **Hannah Luegmeyer** fern-geschehen 201

Video installation

In the work *fern-geschehen* I transferred the ground plan of an apartment on m back. The plan begins to distort due to the movements of my body. As a revers conclusion and intentional error, the movements of the body rearrange th choreography of the rooms. Would the rooms go along with this dynamic the walls would collapse. The representation of these movements is used as the bas for a 3D model and is graphed.

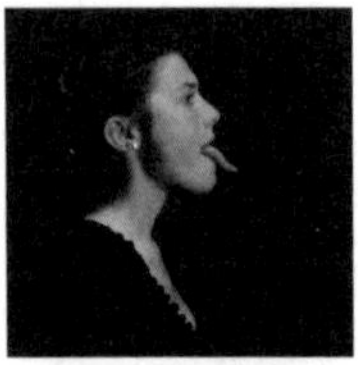

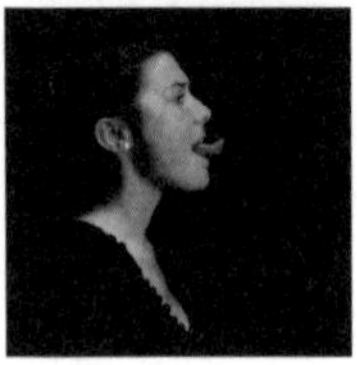

98–101 **Laura Wagner** Self-portrait with Tongue 20

HD video 16:9, loop, 2:04 min.

The video *Self-portrait with Tongue* is the logical continuation of LW's work wi photographic self-portraits. The historical context is to be found not only in th image itself. The major references to classical portrait painting – whose aesthet is adopted even today in photography – are reinterpreted in this video by focusin on the one hand on the need to remain still and, on the other hand, on bringin life to the portrait and creating a symbiotic link by means of the moving tongu In contrast to portrait painting, however, the artist does not attempt to commun cate any subjective values about herself, but shows merely a form of externalize materiality that can be understood through the medial process itself and man fests itself through the sticking out of the tongue. The clip also references a element of the classical diptych, whose male counterpart appears to be missin The video as single image thus emphasizes not only the inherent life of the tongu but, also and above all, the self-referencing aspect of the work.

Text: Andreas Müll

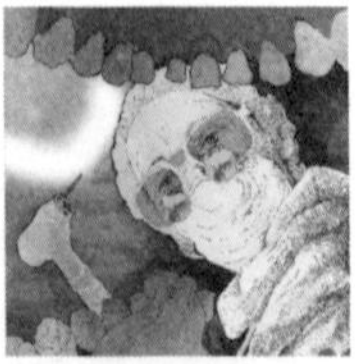

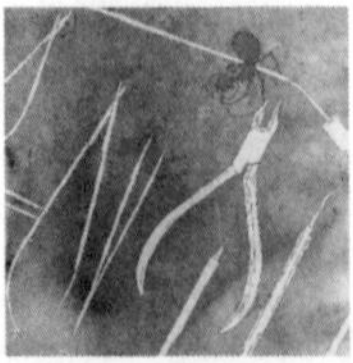

102/103 **Dimiter Ovtcharov** The Dentist 20

Watercolour, computer processing

They use high technology but their tools look like medieval instruments of to ture. People are afraid of them. Dentists. The mere mention of the word creat an irrational fear. Dentists are masters of pain. But ants are stronger than the are. One day every dentist will be food for ants and his technology will disappe with him. Nothing is for ever – not survival nor progress, only fear.

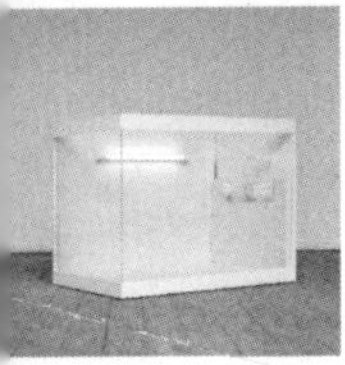

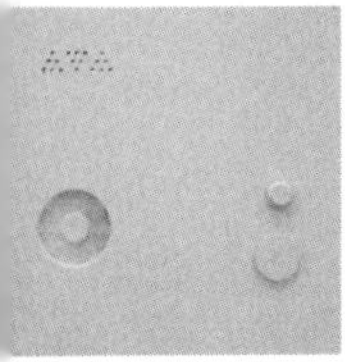

104/105 **Céline Struger** Environment 2012

MDF, acrylic glass, foam, synthetic leather, fluorescent tube, air filter, 86 × 115 × 75 cm

This work is a hermetically sealed space whose climate is controlled from the outside. Three of the inner sides are padded and covered with washable white synthetic leather. The other three surfaces are made of transparent glass. The box is opened by removing the lid. The heating rod inside can be controlled by a thermostat and the hot air distributed evenly by means of a fan. The fluorescent tube gives neutral light (5000k), which can be dimmed or intensified from outside. The switch elements are recessed in plates on the outside and have scales.

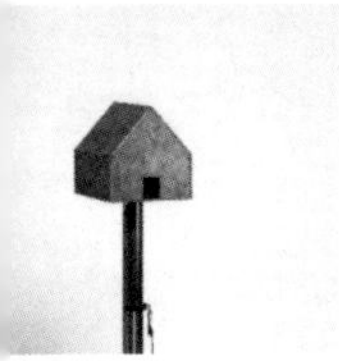

106 **Céline Struger** Birdhouse 2011

Steel, copper wire, car battery, 145 × 25 × 30 cm

Migratory birds find their way by using the earth's magnetic field to fly south from their original nesting places. They fly without seeing the earth's surface. The fluctuations in the intensity of the magnetic lines alter certain molecules in the animals' retina during flight so that they have a flight map in their inner eye, so to speak. The object is made of 6 mm steel plates slotted rather than screwed together. The copper coil wound round the iron post and the battery form an electromagnet. A magnetic field is created when the cable is attached and a 0.5 AMP. current runs through it.

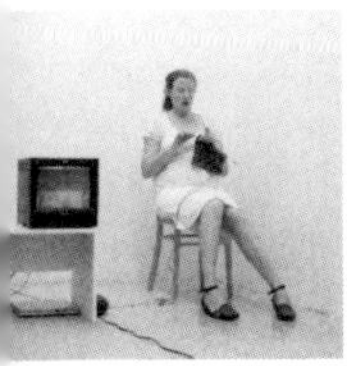

107 **Dorothea Trappel** A new pullover for Brus 2012

Performance. Photo: Steffi Schöne

Of all the films of Günter Brus – *Osmose, Pullover, Inhaling-Exhaling – Pullover* (part of this work), which shows his wife Anni knitting, was filmed from an angle that makes it difficult to see that Anni is eight months pregnant. The sketch and flyer printed by Brus for this work show a different angle. The performance *A new pullover for Brus* deals with this 'mistake'. By moving the camera a little and using a real pregnant woman knitting, the picture is corrected so that in the centre, as in Brus's sketch, is the pregnant woman. This puts the focus on the theme of birth and life. The work deals with aspects of the original idea that were not shown in the film.

Thanks to Günter Brus, the Museum moderner Kunst Stifung Ludwig Vienna and Eva Badura-Triska.

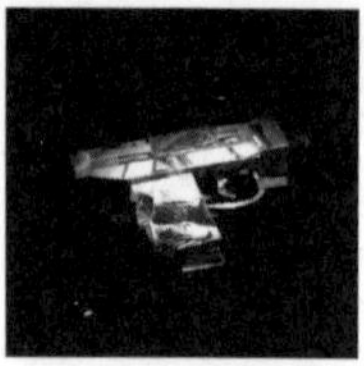

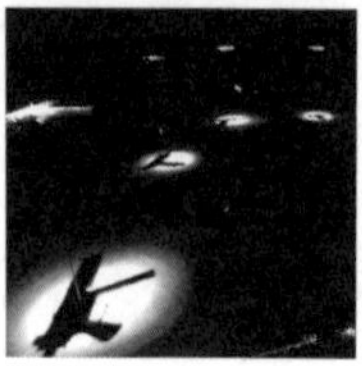

108/109 **Uli Kühn** Parabellum

Paper, glue, metal, LEDs, Room installation 350 × 350 cm, Photo: Birgit and Peter Kainz

```
                                          _
 |^\                         ___________ ´  `__/\_
|~~~|------------~~~~~~~~~~~~~~~~~~~~~~~`~~´~~~~~~\
|___|-----------==|___|~~~~~|_____------,;'//     ||
                      ||~~~||   |~~~~~~~~~~~~~  //   //
                       \(_(=)~~ ,-~-\          \ __/
                        ~~~~~~\[  \  \       \/
                              |   |  ()       \\
                               \___  \\        \\
                                     \\       \\
                                      \\       \\
                                       \         ||
                                        \         ||
                                         |\_( )_||/
                                         \_/( )\_/
```

The secret is committed to paper, which my heirs will publish.

Friedrich Schiller, *The Robber*

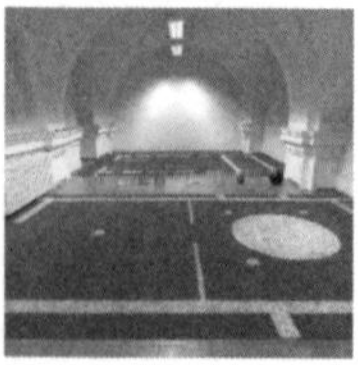

110 **Monika Palka** Battlefields 20

Installation made of artificial grass. Photo: Birgit and Peter Kainz

At a time when transculturality is seen more and more as a threat, the work draw attention to the 'alien' in us. Two artificial grass carpets have the outline of a basi ica and a mosque drawn on them with white lines. The stadium aesthetic was cho sen for several reasons – not least because sport is one of the greatest provider of images today. The work attempts to make the transition between a rigid syster and a moving narrative form.

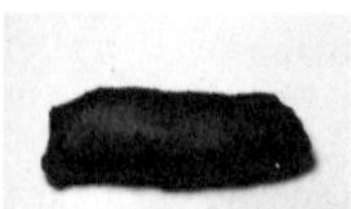

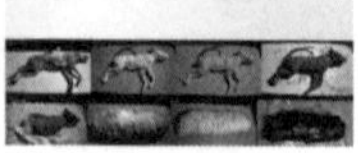

111 **Céline Struger** Untitled 20

Fox, bitumen, resin, fabric, 20 × 110 × 40 cm

The object consists of the mummified corpse of a fox, which has been disembow elled, dehydrated and preserved by means of formaldehyde injections. It has bee stuffed with material soaked in linseed oil and glued in layers with resin. Th carcass was sealed with bitumen.

112 **Matthias Krinzinger** MEIN (Mine) written on a rock in the Tyrolean Alps 2010

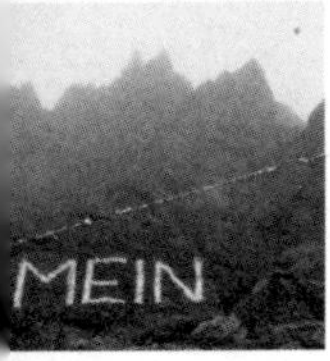

Traffic marking paint, 2 to 4 meters. Photo: Clemens Ascher

This photograph is the documentation of a documentation.
MEIN (Mine) is a possessive pronoun written on a rock in the Alps, the biggest uninhabited landscape of Europe. Someone surely owns it, although it is a public space, used mostly for recreational activities like hiking and skiing.
The viewer on the mountain is – as in the case of graffiti – somehow forced to see the writing. The documentation as a photograph, shown in art-related spaces, the viewer chooses what he/she wants to see in it.
While the word MEIN is profoundly present on the mountain, it is nearly hidden on the photograph. Here ambiguity and inoperability become function; they shape art into an instrument with which to challenge human thinking and perception. Stereotyped thinking blurs, dissolves and recurs again in different stereotypes.

113 **Lisa Langeder** Untitled 2010

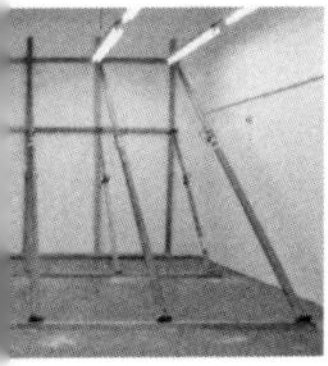

Wood, ceiling supports, 350 × 400 × 350 cm

The idea for this work came from a photograph of a dilapidated house that I took in Cairo in 2009. I reconstructed the support structure with the standard building elements here, liberating them at the same time from their original support function.

THE AUTHORS

Gerald Bast

Rector of the University of Applied Arts Vienna

Christian Höller

Christian Höller is editor of *springerin – Hefte für Gegenwartskunst* (www.springerin.at) and has written extensively on art and cultural theory. Between 2002 and 2007, he was Visiting Professor at the École supérieure des beaux-arts in Geneva. He was curator of the special programmes *Pop Unlimited?* (2000), and *No Wave. New York 1976–84* (2010) at the International Short Film Festival Oberhausen (the latter was also shown at the Austrian Film Museum Vienna in 2010, and at HAU – Hebbel am Ufer Berlin in 2011). In 2011, he co-curated the exhibition *Hauntings – Ghost Box Media* (Medienturm Graz) as well as the accompanying concert series *Sonic Spectres* for steirischer herbst 2011.

In 2001, he edited the anthology *Pop Unlimited?* (Turia + Kant, Vienna); in 2005, the volume *Techno-Visionen* (Folio, Vienna/Bolzano; co-editor) as well as the catalogue *Hans Weigand* (Walther König, Cologne). His volume of interviews *Time Action Vision: Conversations in Cultural Studies, Theory, and Activism* was published by JRP Ringier, Zürich/Les presses du réel, Dijon, in 2010.

Franz Schuh

Dr. Franz Schuh, a renowned writer, critic and lecturer, lives in Vienna. He studied philosophy and German philology and acquired a PhD on 'Hegel and the logic of practice'. He has lectured extensively at the universities of Vienna and Klagenfurt, Austria, and is currently lecturer at the University of Applied Arts Vienna, the Mozarteum, Salzburg, and the Reinhardt Seminar, Vienna. As freelancer he contributes regularly to the German weekly newspaper *ZEIT*.

He has published numerous books and received several awards, among them the Austrian State Award for Culture Journalism (1985), the Jean Amery Prize (2000) and the Essayism Prize of the Leipzig Book Fair (2006).

THE TEAM

Directorial Team	Stephan Hilge (Artist) Roman Pfeffer (Artist) Nita Tandon (Artist)
Teaching Staff	Amer Abbas (Gallerist, Curator) Richard Hilbert (Scientific Staff Member) Gerald Matt (Curator) Roland Reiter (Sculptor) Franz Schuh (Writer, Culture Philosopher, Essayist) Marcelo Slama (Photographer) Johannes Steurer (Scientific Staff Member) Rainer Wölzl (Artist)
Tutors	Sebastian Kraner Florian Regl Lukas Troberg Thomas Wagensommerer
Office	Ulrike Holper

IMPRINT

Editors Stephan Hilge, TransArts, University of Applied Arts Vienna
Roman Pfeffer, TransArts, University of Applied Arts Vienna
Nita Tandon, TransArts, University of Applied Arts Vienna

AMBRA |V is part of Medecco Holding GmbH, Vienna
Printed in Austria

Printed on acid-free and chlorine-free bleached paper
With 165 coloured figures

Photographs © the artists, if not indicated otherwise and:
Beatrix Bakondy, Matthias Bildstein, Emanuel Ehgartner, Sebastian Kraner, Angelika Loderer, Detlef Löffler, Steffi Schöne
Graphic Design Rainer Dempf, Fiona Fleck
Image Editing Florian Regl
Translation Rebecca Law, Nick Somers, Nita Tandon
Copy-editing Nita Tandon
Printing Rema-Print-Littera, Vienna

Thanks to Gerald Bast, Rector of the University of Applied Arts Vienna

ISSN1866-248X
ISBN 978-3-99043-577-9

di:'Angewandte
Universität für angewandte Kunst Wien
University of Applied Arts Vienna